William Norton

A Translation, in English daily Used, of the Peshito-Syriac Text

And of the received Greek Text, of Hebrews, James, 1 Peter, and 1 John

William Norton

A Translation, in English daily Used, of the Peshito-Syriac Text
And of the received Greek Text, of Hebrews, James, 1 Peter, and 1 John

ISBN/EAN: 9783337243814

Printed in Europe, USA, Canada, Australia, Japan

Cover: Foto ©Lupo / pixelio.de

More available books at **www.hansebooks.com**

A TRANSLATION,

IN ENGLISH DAILY USED,

OF THE

PESHITO - SYRIAC TEXT,

AND OF THE

RECEIVED GREEK TEXT.

OF

HEBREWS, JAMES, 1 PETER, AND 1 JOHN.

WITH AN INTRODUCTION, ON THE PESHITO-SYRIAC TEXT, AND THE REVISED GREEK TEXT OF 1881.

BY WILLIAM NORTON,

Of North Devon.

London :

W. K. BLOOM, 22A, FURNIVAL STREET, HOLBORN.

1889

Contents of the Introduction.

Introduction.

I.—The many countries in which Syriac was spoken.

Syriac is a very ancient language. It belongs to the same family of languages as the ancient Hebrew. In the time of the Redeemer it was spoken, in slightly different dialects, in many countries.

Syriac became the language of Palestine.—Dr. Frederic Delitzsch, Professor of Assyriology, in the University of Leipzic, in a work on " The Hebrew Language viewed in the light of Assyrian Research, 1883," p. 2, says, " The transportation of the ten tribes from Palestine to Mesopotamia and Media, and the close intercourse of those left behind with people of different nations, as the Elamites, Babylonians, and Arabs, who supplied the places of the exiled Israelites, struck a deadly blow at the ancient language of the kingdom of Israel. Nor was it destined to flourish much longer in the kingdom of Judah......The termination of the Babylonian exile marks the beginning of that process," that is, as to Judah, " by which Hebrew gradually disappeared from among living languages. It is true that a small portion of the nation, those who availed themselves of the permission to return to the holy land, still wrote and spoke Hebrew ; but the Aramaic [the Syriac] dialect, which had been favoured by the Persian kings, and was almost regarded as the official language of the western portion of the Persian empire, had already begun to bring its deteriorating influence to bear upon it ; and, rapidly advancing, was conquering one portion of Palestine after another. This process continued under the dominion of the Greeks.........At the time of the Maccabees, Hebrew had already ceased to be a spoken language. ....The learned among the Jews, during the last two centuries before Christ, even preferred to *write* in Aramaic ; and at the time of Christ, Aramaic reigned supreme as the adopted language of the country."

Those of the ten tribes who were " carried away into Assyria," (2 Kings xvii. 6,) adopted the Syriac language also, as well as those of them who remained in Palestine. We have proof in holy Scripture that Aramaic, now called Syriac, was spoken by some of the Assyrians, when the king of Assyria sent Rabshakeh against Jerusalem. For the elders of the Jews asked him to speak to them in Aramaic, that the rest of the Jews might not know what

A2

he said. (2 Kings xviii. 26; Isa. xxxvi. 11.) The language then called Aramaic, and now called Syriac, was not the most ancient language of Assyria. The Rev. A. H. Sayce says, in his "Assyrian Grammar, 1872," pages 1 and 10, that the original Assyrian language was more like Hebrew and Phœnician than it was like Syriac. But by degrees the old Assyrian language gave place to Syriac. Mr. Sayce says at page 18, "Assyrian passed away before the encroaching influence of Aramæan."

Before the ten tribes were carried away into Assyria, they had been brought under the power of the Syrians of Damascus, and this may have tended to change their language. While they were in Assyria, they seem to have adopted Syriac wholly, and to have ceased to speak their ancient Hebrew tongue.

DR. ASAHEL GRANT, (M.D.) a modern missionary to that part of ancient Assyria, which is now called Coordistan, published a book, the third edition of which is dated 1844, entitled, "The Nestorians, or the Lost Tribes." At page 55, he says that among the Nestorian Christians whose ancestors dwelt there from before the time of Christ, the worship is still conducted and the Scriptures are read "in the ancient Syriac language," which is now "quite unintelligible to the common people;" so that when the Scriptures are read to them, they have to be translated by the reader into the modernized Syriac, which is now spoken both by these Nestorian Christians, and by the Israelites who are not Christians, who dwell near them in Coordistan. He says at page 149, that this modernized Syriac is "at this day a living language only among the Nestorians and nominal Jews of Media and Assyria; unless an exception be found among the Syrian Christians dwelling west of the Tigris; who may, perhaps, also have a Hebrew origin." He says that both the Nestorian Christians, and the unchristianised Israelites, who use this "vernacular language, peculiar to themselves, must have acquired it at a remote period of antiquity; because an entire want of social intercourse forbids the idea that they have learned it from each other in modern times." Dr. Grant says, that both the Nestorians and the Israelites say that they all speak this modern Syriac language because they have a "common ancestry;" and he thinks that their common and peculiar language "affords convincing proof that they are both alike the children of Israel."

Dr. Grant was fully convinced that the ancestors of these Nestorians "received the gospel from the apostles and immediate disciples of our Saviour," (p. 56); "from Thomas, Bartholomew, Thaddeus, and others; not from Nestorius," from likeness to whom they are called Nestorians, (p. 50.) He says that their Scriptures, which are like other copies of the ancient Peshito-Syriac Bible, have been preserved by them "in manuscript, with great care and purity," (p. 60); that "these Nestorians throughout Assyria and

Media have a general and universally believed tradition that they are descendants of the ten tribes," (p. 110); that the Israelites "admit that the Nestorians are as truly the descendants of the Israelites as themselves, (p. 114); and that the Nestorians have a tradition that they "came from the land of Palestine," (p. 113.) Dr. Grant remarks that both the Nestorian Christians and the Israelites, inhabit the very country where "the ten tribes were placed," (p. 114); that they "are the only people in Assyria who can be identified with the ten tribes, and consequently that they must be their descendants," (p. 140.) He says that Dr. Perkins, another missionary, agreed with him that the body of the modern language now spoken by the Nestorians and Israelites, comes as directly from the venerable Syriac, and as clearly, as the modern Greek does from the ancient, (p. 144.)

Dr. Grant says also, "NAZAREANS is a term very commonly employed by themselves and others to designate the Nestorians. It is never applied to other Christian sects. The term Nazareans has been well defined to mean Christians converted from Judaism, ...who adhered to the practice of the Jewish ceremonies......... Jerome speaks of them as Hebrews believing in Christ. We have good reason from Acts xv. 5, to believe that the Gentiles never adopted the rites of the Jews, nor the name of Nazareans, to whom these rites were peculiar. It must then have been applied exclusively to the Jewish converts. Hence the conclusion that the Nestorians must have been Jews," (pp. 153—4.) By Jews, he clearly means Israelites. Mosheim, in his "Christianity before Constantine," Cent. ii., chap. xxxix., says, "A small band of Christians, who joined Moses with Christ, divided into two sects called Nazareans and Ebionites. The ancient Christians did not class the Nazareans with heretical sects." Dr. Grant says, "It is the simple fact, that the Nestorians are what they profess to be—the children of Israel," (p. 113.)

Concurring proofs seem to make it certain that these Nestorian Christians received the gospel from some of the apostles; that there has been a succession of them from that time to this; that their copies of the Peshito-Syriac Scriptures are derived from copies received at a very early date; that they have been carefully made and preserved, and are of great value in determining the true text and meaning of God's word.

A LIKE SETTLEMENT TO THAT IN COORDISTAN, of Christians and Hebrews dwelling near to each other, has also existed from the time of the apostles until now, IN TRANVANCORE AND THE MALABAR COAST OF INDIA. These Christians, as well as those of Coordistan, use the ancient Peshito-Syriac Scriptures in their worship at the present day. They believe they have had these Scriptures from before A.D. 325, in which year their bishop signed

his name at the council of Nicæa. There is ancient testimony that
the Gospel of Matthew in Syriac was left with them by the apostle
Bartholomew, and that the apostle Thomas preached the gospel
among them. The Hebrews, to whom these Apostles preached,
must have been settled there at a still earlier period. Dr. Asahel
Grant said of the Christians of Travancore, "They may be, in
part at least, a branch of the present Nestorians of Media and
Assyria. We have good evidence that they were formerly of the
Nestorian faith, though they have more recently become connected
with the Jacobite Syrians. It is worthy of inquiry whether they
have not traditions, rites, customs, or other evidence of Jewish
origin," (p. 155.) "That the apostle Thomas preached in India,
we have the testimony of numerous Greek, Latin, and Syrian
authors quoted by Asseman in his Bibliotheca Orientalis, vol. iv.,
pp. 5—25, 435." Grant, p. 156, note.

DR. CLAUDIUS BUCHANAN, of the Church of England, in
1806—8, visited the Christians of St. Thomas in India, and also
the Israelites who dwell near them. He found that the Israelites
"are divided into two classes, called the Jerusalem or White
Jews; and the ancient, or Black Jews." He saw and conversed
with some of both classes. The White Jews delivered to him a
narrative, in the Hebrew language, of their arrival in India. It
stated that their "fathers, dreading the conqueror's wrath, departed
from Jerusalem, a numerous body of men, women, priests, and
Levites, and came into this land after the second temple was
destroyed," which took place A.D. 70. This narrative states that
other Hebrews afterwards joined them from Judea, Spain, and
other places, (pp. 200—2.)

He says of the Black Jews, "It is only necessary to look at
their countenance to be satisfied that their ancestors must have
arrived in India many ages before the White Jews......The White
Jews look upon the Black Jews as an inferior race, and as not of a
pure caste, which plainly demonstrates that they do not spring
from a common stock in India. The Black Jews recounted the
names of many other small colonies of the ancient Israelites
resident in northern India, Tartary, and China; and gave me a
written list of sixty-five places. I conversed with those who had
lately visited many of these stations." Dr. Buchanan seems to
have regarded the Black Jews as part of the ten tribes. Those to
whom the apostle Thomas preached must have been settled there
before his arrival, which probably was many years before the
destruction of Jerusalem, A.D. 70, and the arrival of the White
Jews; so that there is a strong probability that those to whom he
preached were a migratory part of the ten tribes. Dr. Buchanan
says, "I inquired concerning their brethren the ten tribes. They
said that it was commonly believed among them that the great
body of the Israelites is to be found in the very places whither they

were first carried into captivity; that some few families had *migrated* into regions more remote, as to Cochin and Rajapoor in India, and to other places yet further to the East, but that the bulk of the nation, though now much reduced in number, had not to this day, removed two thousand miles from SAMARIA." (pp. 206—7.)

It seems to be certain that in the time of the apostles the language of the Israelites in Travancore must have been Syriac. For although the language now most in use, both among the Israelites and the Christians, is the Malabar, or Malayalim, which is the vernacular language of the country, (p. 99); yet the ancient Peshito-Syriac Scriptures are still used by the Christians in worship, and they have to be "expounded to the people in the vernacular tongue," (p. 100.)

The ancient Christians of Travancore and Malabar are still called, The Syrian Christians of St. Thomas, and have received that name from their use of the Peshito-Syriac Scriptures, and from the fact that their ancestors received the gospel from the lips of the apostle Thomas. Dr. Buchanan says that the apostle Thomas is said by them to have landed at Cranganore, when he first arrived from Aden in Arabia; that not far from Cranganore there is an ancient church which bears his name still; and that the tradition among these Christians is, that he afterwards went to the Coromandel Coast, and was put to death at the place still called St. Thomas's Mount. (Researches, p. 114.) When the Portuguese invaded that part of India, and had established at Goa, what even the Roman Catholic Superintendent of sixty-four R. C. churches called in the presence of Dr. Buchanan, the "horrid tribunal" of the Inquisition; that tribunal used its utmost power to bring the Christians of St. Thomas under the dominion of the Pope. By bitter persecution and condemning some of these Christians to be burnt, it obtained the possession and use of many of their church buildings. The Peshito-Syriac Scriptures which they used, like all copies of the original Peshito, did not contain 2 Peter, 2 and 3 John, Jude, Revelation, and some other passages contained in the Roman Catholic Latin Vulgate. The copies of these Syriac Scriptures were ordered by the Inquisition, at the Synod of Diamper, to be all conformed to the R. C. Latin, and all books containing Nestorian teaching were ordered to be burnt. (Decrees of Synod of Diamper, by Dr. Michael Geddes, pp. 134, 147, 428.)

But even in the buildings which were thus obtained, the Roman Catholic Service was still conducted in Syriac instead of in Latin, as Dr. J. W. Etheridge states in his History of the Syrian Churches, 1846, p. 158.

EUSEBIUS says that in the reign of Commodus, (A.D. 180—192) Pantænus, a Christian who had been a philosopher, went as an evangelist from Egypt as far as India; and was said to have found there "the Gospel of Matthew in Hebrew," that is, in Syriac, then called Hebrew, "among some who there knew Christ; to whom Bartholomew, one of the apostles, had proclaimed Him." Dr. Buchanan says that these Christians now possess the Peshito-Syriac Scriptures of both covenants in writing; that they believe they possessed them "before the year A.D. 325," (p. 118;) that "they have preserved the manuscripts of the Holy Scriptures incorrupt," (p. 124); and with such care that in one written copy which he saw, "the words of every book are numbered." (p. 118.)

Syriac was the native tongue of SYRIA. Two territories were called Syria; one to the east, the other to the west of the Euphrates. The capital of Syria, west of the Euphrates, was Damascus. In 2 Sam. viii. 6, "The Syrians of Damascus" are mentioned. Before the ten tribes were carried captive into Assyria, the kings of Syria had reduced them to long servitude. 2 Kings viii. 12; x. 32; xiii. 4—7. Dr. Grant suggests that this tended to change the language of the ten tribes from Hebrew to Syriac. (p. 147.) Syria, to the east of the Euphrates included the impor- tant city called Edessa. Bar Hebræus, a very learned Syrian of the thirteenth century, said, "Of the Syriac language there are three dialects. Of these the most elegant is the Aramæan spoken by the inhabitants of Edessa and Haran, and Syria the Exterior," that is, Syria in Mesopotamia. (Walton's Poly. Prol. xiii. 4; Asseman's Bibliotheca, Vol. I., p. 476.)

G. AMIRA, a Syrian of note, and the author of a Syriac Gram- mar, made a statement which tends to show how very widely the Syriac language was used. He said that "he was able to define the Syriac or Chaldaic tongue to be that which was born, and had chief rule in the East; which could alike be called Assyrian, Babylonian, Aramæan, Hebrew, or Christian; since it was known by nations of those names, and used by them." (Wichelhaus on N. C. Peshito, p. 21.) Walton also, in his Polyglot, (Prol. xiii. 2) says that the language in which the books of the Old and New Covenants exist in the east, and which to-day is called Syriac, "has been called Chaldaic, Babylonian, Aramæan, Syriac, Assyriac, and even Hebrew." The dialect in which the Chaldeans spoke to the king of Babylon, Dan. ii. 4; and that in which Rabshakeh, the Assyrian, was asked by the elders of Israel to speak to them, Isa. xxxvi. 11, are both called in those passages, Aramæan, a name which includes different Syriac dialects.

DR. J. S. ASSEMAN, the learned author of the great work —Bibliotheca Orientalis, published in four volumes folio; a Maronite Syrian; said in the Prologue to Vol. I. p. 1, that the

Syriac language formerly flourished in the immense empire of the Assyrians and that of the Chaldees, and was brought to the greatest degree of amplitude and elegance; that it was afterwards consecrated by the mouth of Deity incarnate and talking with men; that it was known familiarly by the apostles; that it was used in sacred worship every where in the East; and was made famous by being used by eminent writers of the greatest excellence. It was in this language that the gospel was diffused from Edessa and other places throughout the East, as from Antioch in Syria it was diffused by Paul in Asia Minor and in Europe. Dr. J. S. Asseman, also said in his Prologue, p. 1, "To begin from those things which were first written in Syriac, it is a tradition certain and uniform, which the marvellous agreement of all the eastern nations confirms, and which both Eusebius of Cæsarea, and Jerome, deemed to be established, that Thaddæus, or as the Syrians prefer to call him, Adæus, either an apostle or a disciple of Christ, immediately after His ascension into heaven, went to Abgar, the Toparch of Edessa, and instructed the people of Mesopotamia in the Christian faith; and that king Abgar himself received sacred baptism. The gospel was next openly proclaimed in those places, churches were built,......and the sacred books translated out of Hebrew into Syriac......Very many learned men began by their word, and by their writings, to deliver the divine teaching to the people, and to confute ancient, and more recent errors by their published volumes......Frequent incursions of the Persians, Arabs, and Tartars into Mesopotamia, and the adjoining provinces of the Syrians, followed; by which, cities were overthrown to their foundations, monasteries levelled with the ground, churches consumed by fire, and volumes of the most surpassing worth taken away. If any escaped the hands of the barbarians (as it is certain that very many did) they either feed the book-worms of the desert, or are torn, cut up, and devoted to profane uses by their ignorant possessors." He afterwards refers to later times, to 1555, when the N. C. Peshito was first printed, and to the efforts which have been made to discover, and to make use of, such ancient Syriac copies, both of the Scriptures and of other works, as may still exist.

JOSEPHUS is a very important witness in proof of the extent to which Syriac was known and used in the first century. He took part in the war against the Romans which led to the destruction of Jerusalem, A.D. 70. He was taken captive by them, and was well acquainted with all the events connected with the war. He wrote a history of it in Syriac; and states how great a multitude of people, living in different nations, from near the Caspian Sea to the bounds of Arabia, could read and understand what he had written in Syriac. He afterwards wrote the same history in

Greek, that those who spoke Greek, and those of the Romans, and of any other nation who knew Greek, but did not know Syriac, might read it also. He says, that in order to write the Greek history, he used at Rome the aid of persons who knew Greek; that Greek was to him a "foreign language;" (Jewish Antiquities, Book I.); and that very few of his countrymen knew it well. (Jewish Antiq. Bk. xx., chap. ix.) He says in his two books against Apion, that Apion and others "had undertaken to make false charges against his history." In a long defence of it, he said of the Greeks, (Bk. I, chap. 8,) "They see that some Greeks of the present time dare to write about these things, who neither were present at them, nor have taken care to get information from those who know about them." "But I have written a true history of the whole war, and of the particular events which occurred in it; for I was the general of those whom we call Galileans, so long as it was possible to resist; and I was taken and made captive by the Romans. Vespasian and Titus then kept me in custody, and compelled me to attend them." During the siege of Jerusalem, "Nothing was done which escaped my knowledge; for while I was observing whatever was done by the encamped army of the Romans, I carefully wrote it down; and I was the only person who understood what was told by those who delivered themselves up. Afterwards, having obtained leisure at Rome, the whole of my work being in a state of readiness, I made use of some to work with me in respect of the Greek tongue; and in this way I completed my account of those transactions. I had so strong a conviction of the truth of that account, that the first persons whom I selected to bear witness to it, were the chief commanders of the war, Vespasian and Titus. To them first, I gave my books; and I gave them afterwards to many of the Romans who had fought together in the war." It is evident from this account, that Vespasian and Titus knew Greek, and that if any of the Jews who delivered themselves up to the Romans during the siege, could have spoken Greek, Josephus would not have been the only person who understood them.

Josephus, in the Prologue to his Greek translation of the history of the war, says, "I have proposed to translate into the Greek tongue, and to relate for those who live under the rule of the Romans, what I before composed in the language of my own country, and sent to the upper barbarians." A. M. Ceriani, of Milan, speaks of a part of this history as still existing in the Ambrosian Library of Milan, in Syriac. There is other proof that Syriac must be the language which Josephus calls that of his own country. Josephus says, "I thought it would be unbecoming to overlook the perversion of the truth with respect to events so important, and that Parthians, and Babylonians, and the remotest Arabians, and those of our own race beyond the Euphrates, and those of Adiabene "—a part of Assyria—" should know correctly, by means of my diligence, whence the war began, and amid what great sufferings it proceeded, and how it ended ; and that the Greeks, and those of the Romans who were not in the war, should be ignorant of these things, and should be deceived by flatteries or fictions." If we compare the countries mentioned in this passage of Josephus with those named in Acts ii., as countries from which devout Jews had come who were then " dwelling at Jerusalem," we find in both accounts Parthians, Arabians, and dwellers in Mesopotamia. The words of Josephus prove that Syriac was well understood in these countries as well as in Palestine ; and that the tongues spoken by the apostles, which excited the surprise of those who came from these countries, must have been other tongues than Syriac, which was spoken or read both in Palestine and in these countries. Peter, after the miraculous gift of tongues, addressed " all " these persons then dwelling at Jerusalem, (Acts ii. 5, 14,) and must have spoken in a language which " all " could understand ; for he intreated all to " hearken to his words." (Acts ii. 14.) This is proof that there must have been some language which all understood, and as Josephus states that Syriac was so generally known throughout the East, and there is no proof that any other language was so generally known there, it seems that the language to which Peter intreated all to hearken must have been Syriac. So that the events of that Pentecost concur with the testimony of Josephus to show how widely the Syriac language was understood.

II.—Proof that very few Israelites in the time of Christ understood Greek.

Some have supposed that the language of Palestine in the time of Christ was either wholly, or in part, Greek. Professor A. Neubauer, Reader in Rabbinical Hebrew in Oxford University, published in "Studia Biblica, 1885," an essay " On the Dialects spoken in Palestine in the time of Christ." He says that Isaac Voss, who died in 1689, was the first who supposed that " Greek was the only language spoken in Palestine after Alexander," the Great ; that Diodati in 1767, closely followed Voss, and sought to prove that " Greek was the mother language of the Jews in the time of Jesus ;" that Professor Paulus, of Jena, in 1803, held that an Aramaic dialect was then the current language of the Jews in Palestine, but that Jesus and his disciples had no difficulty in using Greek in their public speeches when they found it convenient to do so ; that Dr. Alexander Roberts, Professor of Humanity in St. Andrew's University, and a Member of the Company of Revisers of the N.C. Scriptures, published in 1881, contends that " Christ spoke for the most part in Greek, and only now and then in Aramaic," (pp. 39–41). Dr. Roberts published in 1859 a work in which he discussed the question relating to "The language of Palestine in the time of Christ." At p. 62, he said that he thought he had "proved that Greek, and not Hebrew, was the common language of religious address in Palestine in the days of Christ and his apostles." He said, at p. 63, "Christ spoke in Greek, and his disciples did the same, when they reported what he said. Their inspiration consisted, not, as some have deemed, in being enabled to give perfect translations, either of discourses delivered, or of documents written in the Aramaic language, but in being led, under infallible guidance, to transfer to paper, for the benefit of all coming ages, those words of the Great Teacher which they had heard from his lips in the *Greek* tongue." Few at present are of Dr. Roberts' opinion. The question does not affect the inspiration of the Greek text, but it has a very important bearing on the value of the Peshito-Syriac books of the New Covenant.

Professor Neubauer's familiarity with the Jewish writings of that time, enables him to discuss the subject with much fulness and force. He gives the following probabilities as the result of his own examination of the subject:—That in the time of Christ, the Galileans understood their own Syriac dialect only, together with a few current expressions in ancient Hebrew ; that in Jerusalem a modernised Hebrew, and a purer Syriac dialect than that of Galilee, were in use among the majority of the Jews ; and that the small Jewish-Greek colony there, and a few privileged persons, spoke a Judeo-Greek jargon, (p. 50.) He says that the Syriac dialect of Galilee was "the popular language;" and that it is the language which is called in the New Covenant, "Hebrew," (John v. 2); and is called by Josephus, and in the Apocrypha, the language of the country ; that "it was in this dialect that Josephus at first wrote his historical work" on the war; that the Syriac words which are recorded in the Greek N. C. Scriptures, prove that this was "a distinct dialect in some respects" from the Syriac of the Syrians, and yet was so like it, that "Josephus says the Jews could understand the Syrians," (p. 53.)

Prof. Neubauer has no doubt that the language used by Jesus was the popular Galilean Syriac dialect, and that in the Greek text we have only a Greek translation of the words which he uttered. He says, "Jesus, as is now generally admitted, addressed himself to his disciples and to his audience in the popular dialect. This appears, not only from the Aramaic words left in the gospels by the Greek translators, but more especially from his last words on the cross, which were spoken under circumstances of exhaustion and pain, when a person would naturally make use of his mother tongue ; and from the fact that it is mentioned that he spoke to Paul in Hebrew, Acts xxvi. 14," (pp. 53, 54.) "The Jews so little knew Greek and so much less cared to know it, that Paul, in order to gain a hearing, was obliged to speak to them in their

Aramaic dialects." "How would the Medes, Elamites, and Arabians have understood Peter at Pentecost, if he had spoken Greek to the 'men of Judea, and all who dwelt in Jerusalem,'" (p. 54.)

Prof. Neubauer gives many reasons for his "belief that few Jews in Palestine had a substantial knowledge of Greek." One of them is, that no events had occurred which could have made "Greek prominent in Palestine," (p. 62); that no nation ever makes so great a change in its language as to adopt "a totally different" one, unless the conqueror transports the greater part of the inhabitants, and introduces foreign colonists who are far more numerous than the remaining inhabitants; and that the Greeks had never this superiority of numbers in Palestine, (p. 64.) He says that few Greek words occur in the Jewish writings such as the Mishnah, the Targums, and the Talmud of Jerusalem; that "no apocryphal book, as far as our knowledge goes, was composed in Greek by a Palestinian Jew," (p. 65); that "so far as he can judge, all that the Jews in Palestine learned of Greek was at most a few sentences, sufficient to enable them to carry on trade, and to hold intercourse with the lower officials; and that even this minimum certainly ceased after the Maccabean victory over Antiochus Epiphanes; because it was the interest of the Asmonean Princes to keep the Jews aloof from the influence of the neighbouring dialects," (p. 66.)

Professor Neubauer thinks that those Hebrews who lived in cities occupied chiefly by Greeks, "may have acquired a fair knowledge of conversational Greek, but not to such an extent as to enable them to speak it in public," (p. 67.) He says that even those Jews of Egypt and Asia Minor who spoke Greek, maintained a connection with the mother-land by going to Jerusalem for feast-days; and that "we may infer that they all still spoke, more or less, their native Hebrew dialect, because no mention is made of interpreters being required for them either in the temple or outside of it," (pp. 62, 63.)

The Greek translation of the Old-Covenant Hebrew Scriptures, called the Septuagint. which was made in Egypt, existed in the time of Christ; but Prof. Neubauer says, "we may boldly state that this Greek translation of the Bible was unknown in Palestine, except to men of the schools, and perhaps a few of the Hellenistic Jews. It is said in the Talmud that when the Greek translation of the Seventy appeared, there came darkness upon the earth, and that the day was as unfortunate for Israel, as that on which the golden calf was made," (p. 67.)

The fact that the Jews at Jerusalem who spoke Greek are called HELLENISTS, that is, GRECIANS, in Acts vi. 1, and ix. 29, shows that their Greek speech made them a peculiar class quite distinct from the rest of the people.

In Antioch of Syria, though it was a celebrated Greek city, Syriac, as well as Greek, continued to be spoken. Professor Neubauer says, " Antioch and other Syrian towns would not give up Syriac," (pp. 63, 70.)

He says also, " Had Greek been generally spoken and taught, why should the Talmud record a general exception, in favour of Gamaliel; and later, in the second century......in favour of the family of Judah the saint, the redactor of the Mishnah," a decision that they " should be allowed to learn Greek, because they had to conduct negotiations with the government," (p. 67.)

The Greek Scriptures record some of THE EXACT WORDS USED BY JESUS. Many of these are words which were used only in Syriac dialects. This fact is often referred to as proof that Christ spoke in Syriac. Bp. Walton, in the 13th of his Prolegomena, sec. 19, says, " There are many purely Syriac words left in the Greek N. T., which cannot be explained without a knowledge of Syriac; as *raca*, Matt. v. 22 ; *momuno*, riches, vi. 24 ; *Bar-de-yauno*, son of a dove, xvi. 17 ; *Kurbono*, offering, Mark vii. 11 ; *shebakthoni*, thou has forsaken me, Matt. xxvii. 46 ; *Benai-Regesh*, sons of thunder, Mark iii. 17 ; *Talitho, kumi,* Damsel, arise ; Mark v. 41 ; *Khekal-demo*, the field of blood, Acts i. 19. Many others occur in Acts v. 1 ; ix. 36 ; John i. 47 ; 1 Cor. xvi. 22,—[*Moran etho*, our Lord has come]; and elsewhere. Indeed *Jesus*, the name of our Lord, is Syriac for Saviour; the name *Messiah* is also Syriac, meaning Anointed......The writers of the New Covenant first made known the heavenly words to the Jews, and to other surrounding populations, in this their native tongue, and afterwards wrote in the Greek language, but in doing so retain everywhere a flavour of Syriac."

Prof. Neubauer says, with reference to 1 Cor. xvi. 22, written to Greeks, " Is not the watchword, *Moran etho*, [our Lord has come], which passed to Greek-speaking populations, a sufficient proof that the speech of the first Christians was Aramaic," (p. 54.) A still more decisive proof that it was so, occurs in a remark made by Luke. He, guided by God's Spirit, said that the word *Akeldama*, (in the Pesthito *Khekal-demo*), the field of blood, was part of the language commonly used in Jerusalem. There is no such word as *Khekal*, field, in Ancient Hebrew. The only languages in which Castle, in his Lexicon of the six related languages :—Hebrew, Chaldee, Syriac, Samaritan, Æthiopic, and Arabic, says it occurs, are Chaldee, Syriac, and Arabic. It does not occur in Gesenius's Lexicon of ancient Hebrew. When therefore Luke says—" And it became known to all the dwellers in Jerusalem, insomuch that in their language that field is called *Akel-duma*, that is, the field of blood," (Acts i. 19), we have infallible proof that the Syriac language was the language of Jerusalem.

JOSEPHUS is a witness of very great importance on this subject also. He was so perfectly familiar with the state of things in Palestine, in the first century, and took such care to give correct information, that his testimony has great weight. At the end of his "Antiquities, (written in Greek,) he said, "I am bold to say that no other person, whether a Jew, or of another race, would have been able, had he wished, to produce this work for Greeks, so accurately; for I am admitted by my own countrymen to excel them far in the learning of our country, and I have applied myself with diligence to obtain a knowledge of Greek literature.........For among us those are not esteemed who learn the languages of many nations; ......but testimony for wisdom is given to those only who understand well our laws, and are able to explain the meaning of the sacred writings. For this reason, out of the many who have toiled at this endeavour, scarcely some two or three have succeeded well." This testimony of the most learned and reliable of unconverted Jews, is proof how few Jews had much knowledge of the Greek language.

Another proof of this, is what he relates of the time when he was a captive in the Roman army on the outside of Jerusalem. In defending himself against Apion (Book I.), he says that he presented his Greek history of the Jewish war "to the chief commanders Vespasian and Titus, and to many Romans who were in the war," and that these all bore testimony to his truthfulness. They all therefore knew Greek, and would have understood what those Jews who came out of the city, and surrendered themselves, said, if these could have spoken only a few words of Greek. But Josephus says,—"The things told by those who surrendered themselves, only I understood." It is impossible therefore that the Jews of Palestine and Jerusalem could have understood either the Redeemer or his apostles, if they had spoken to them in Greek, or in any other language but that which Josephus calls the language of his own country at that time—a dialect of the widely spread Syriac language.

THE CONCLUSION to which such a concurrence of evidence leads is that Syriac was unquestionably the language commonly spoken in Palestine in the time of Christ, and that very few Jews had a good knowledge of Greek.

This conclusion leads almost of necessity to another; namely, that there must have been some provision in writing, made by the apostles for the use of that large body of Christians who knew no language well but Syriac. Whatever was revealed as the will of God, whether written at first in Syriac or in Greek, was to be taught, not to the Jews only, nor to the Gentiles only, but to *all disciples every where ;* that all might know it, and all be guided by

it. Peter, writing to Hebrews, said (2 Epistle i. 15), " Moreover I
will endeavour that ye may be able after my decease to have these
things always in remembrance." This could only be done by writing.
The apostles knew well, and must have remembered as Peter did,
that what they had taught by voice would soon be unknown to most,
unless the disciples were well supplied with it in writing. They
must all, of necessity, have had Peter's desire. They must have
wished to make provision that what they taught by revelation to
some one church might be known to all churches, not only while
they lived, but after they were dead. Paul, who was willing to be
made a curse, with view to the salvation of the Hebrews, must have
desired that what was revealed to him for the guidance of Greeks,
should be known also to Hebrews; and that it was known to
Hebrews in his life time, appears from the remark of Peter, who
laboured chiefly among Hebrews, and who, when writing to
Hebrews, speaks of "all" Paul's letters as well-known writings.
In his 2 Epistle iii. 16, he says of Paul, " As also in all his letters,
speaking in them of these things; in which are some things hard
to be understood, which those who are unlearned and unstable
wrest, as they do also the other Scriptures to their own destruction." His words imply that all Paul's letters had been extensively
read by Hebrew Christians, and that they were treated with the
same supreme regard as "the other Scriptures." They cannot
have been read by more than a few of the Hebrews in Greek; it
seems almost certain that there must have been some Syriac
translation. Such considerations as these prepare us to receive
readily whatever proof may exist, that Greek was not the only
language in which the apostles left written records of God's will.

TREMELLIUS, a Christian Jew, who was a Professor in the
University of Heidelberg, and who published, in 1569, an edition
of the N. C. Peshito, contended that unless God loved *foreigners*
more than Jews he must have provided these, as well as the
Greeks, with the inspired writings in their own tongue. He said
that it seemed to be " wholly in accord with truth, that at the
very beginning of the Church of Christ, the Syriac version was
made either by the Apostles themselves, or by their disciples;
unless indeed we prefer to suspect that, in writing, they intended
to have regard *for foreigners only* ; and to have either no regard,
or certainly very little, for those of their own nation," (Gutbier's
Peshito, p. 29.) We know that the apostles, instead of showing
less regard for the Jews than for the Gentiles, always went to the
Jews first, and showed a surpassing regard for their welfare. It
seems to be extremely probable that Paul himself took care that
most of his epistles should be written *in Syriac as well as in
Greek*, so as to inform his own countrymen everywhere of whatever
was revealed to him for the guidance of all Christians throughout
the world.

III.—THE DIFFERENCE BETWEEN THE SYRIAC OF THE PESHITO-
SYRIAC TEXT, AND THE POPULAR SYRIAC DIALECT OF PALESTINE.

The Syriac words which are retained in the Greek text have a
slight difference, in form, from those of the Peshito-Syriac text ; and
show that the Syriac of Palestine, used by the Redeemer, differed
slightly from that of Edessa, for which city the Peshito-Syriac was
made. Professor Neubauer says, that the Syriac words which are
recorded in the Greek text, show that the Jewish Syriac " was a
distinct dialect, in some respects, from the Syriac of the Syrians,"
(p. 53.) No book of the New Covenant writings has come down to
us, written in the popular dialect of Palestine. The Gospel of
Matthew is said by all the early Christian writers to have been
written for the Christians of Palestine in their own Syriac language.
It has not come down to us in that dialect. But Jerome (who died
A.D. 420) said that he had seen a copy of it. His words are these :—
" Matthew, the first [writer], composed in Judæa, for those of the
circumcision who had believed, a gospel of Christ in Hebrew letters
and words. Who it was who afterwards translated it into Greek is
not sufficiently certain. Moreover the Hebrew gospel itself is
preserved even to this day in the Library at Cæsarea, which
Pamphilus the martyr collected with the greatest diligence," (Jer.
Jones on the Canon, part ii., chap. xxv., sec. 13 ; also Prager on
O. C. Peshito, p. 36.) The siege and destruction of Jerusalem are
probably the cause of its having been so rare even at that time.
It seems also to have been afterwards corrupted and made worthless. But it was much more important that copies of the inspired
books should be preserved in the more widely used Syriac dialect
in which the Peshito is written, than in the local dialect of Palestine. And God so ordered events that though whatever books of
the New Covenant were written in the Syriac of Palestine, seem
to have perished, those of the Peshito in the Edessa dialect were
multiplied exceedingly, and were copied with the utmost care.

The N. C. Peshito-Syriac, properly so called, NEVER CONTAINED
THE WHOLE OF THE BOOKS WHICH WE HAVE IN THE GREEK TEXT.
The books 2 Peter, 2 and 3 John, Jude, and Revelation, were
never regarded as part of it, though these books, in a separate Syriac
translation, were admitted to represent inspired books. The
extraordinary esteem in which the books of the Peshito were held,
shows that the Syriac copies of these were regarded as having had
a far more exalted origin than the Syriac text of the other five.
The fact seems to be, that at the later date at which the omitted five
books were written, no inspired men corrected them in the dialect
of Edessa ; and that for this reason the Syriac translation of these
five books was not permitted to be associated with that of the other
books, to prevent it from being regarded as of the same authority.
Bp. WALTON, in his Polyglot, Prol. xiii. sec. 16, says that

B

"Syriac writers state that 2 Peter, 2 and 3 John, Jude, and Revelation, were not in the ancient edition" of the Peshito.

J. WICHELHAUS says, "It is very well known that the Syrians did not reject" the five books not contained in the Peshito. "We deem the sum of the matter to be that by the tradition of the Syrians, the Peshito version was made in the time of Abgar the King [of Edessa], at the time when the gospel was preached there," (p. 63.) The Nestorian Christians deemed it "to have been written by *Apostolic Authority*," (p. 153.) At p. 85, Wichelhaus says of the five books which are not in the Peshito, that "by the consent of all, they ought to be assigned to the end of the lives of the Apostles;" and that some derive from their omission an argument for the antiquity of the Peshito, as having been "written before the four epistles and the Revelation were published," (p. 85.)

Bp. HUET, in his learned work "On the most illustrious Translators, 1683," remarks that the absence of those five books is "a great proof of the antiquity" of the N. C. Peshito, (p. 126.)

The N. C. Peshito-Syriac IS OF SPECIAL WORTH for two reasons; first, that there is credible testimony that it was made in the lifetime of the Apostles; and next, that the copies of it have been made with the greatest exactness and care. Wichelhaus says "There was no doubt about its truth and perfectness; and on that account the more effort and labour were bestowed on the text of the version, to keep it pure and free from every taint of error and variation," (p. 153.) "All persons testify, and the history of the Syrians itself clearly proves, that the greatest care was taken from the most ancient times, in order that the letter of the *sacred Scripture* might be always perfectly preserved in agreement with itself. For of the Peshito version, there was the greatest veneration," (p. 230.)

IV.—HOW WE MAY KNOW WHETHER BOOKS WHICH ARE SAID TO BE THE WORD OF GOD, ARE SO OR NOT.'

Three things need to be proved to make it certain that any book which we have now, contains, "not the word of men, but the word of God," (1 Thes. ii. 13.) First, proof by miracles that God spoke by the alleged writer, (see John iii. 2; x. 38; Heb. ii. 3, 4.) Secondly, proof by the hand-writing of the alleged author, or other means, that the original copy of the book was declared by him to be "the word of God." Paul gave this token by his hand-writing, in every epistle (2 Thess. iii. 17, 18.) Thirdly, proof that the book which we have now is the same book which he delivered, and has been copied and handed down to us without alteration. The first and second proofs could only be known to those of the first centuries. The hand-writing of the apostles, which proved the divine authority of early copies, soon perished. What we need now is clear and credible testimony that copies, which were in public and private religious use in the early centuries, when their descent from the originals could be traced, and their likeness to them proved, were by most, or universally, believed to be true copies of thĕ books which contained, not the words of men, but "the words" of God. We need also proof that these copies of the first ages were in the following centuries, so exactly copied, that we are assured that the copies we have now, are exact copies of them. It is evident that if copies whose Apostolic descent was firmly believed and well attested in the first ages, have in the following ages, been copied in different places far apart; that, then, if the existing copies of these separate lines of descent agree, it is the most decisive proof possible that they must all have been most carefully made through the ages, or they could not possibly agree thus now. Proof of *exact copying is essential* to our knowledge of what the Apostles wrote. For as, when a witness lies, no one can tell when he is speaking truth; so, when the copy of a book which contained at first the words of God, is proved to be untrue in many places, no one can rely on it as proof of what is true, or what is false, in doubtful readings. Copies proved to be of true descent, and to have been exactly copied from the first, are the only copies fit to be trusted as witnesses on disputed readings; especially because the question at issue is, What words are, or are not, the infallible words of God. The exact copying of the Peshito-Syriac text is one of the things which gives it such great weight.

P. D. HUET, Bp. of Avranches, in France, a scholar of high repute, and chief editor of the Delphin classics, said, with respect to the means of deciding whether a work is really what it is said to be, "That every book is genuine which was esteemed genuine by those who lived nearest to the time when it was written, and by the ages succeeding in a continued series"; and that "this is an axiom which cannot be disputed by those who will allow any thing at all to be certain in history." (See Jeremiah Jones's work on the Canon, 1798, vol. 1, p. 43). Mr. Jones remarks on this axiom, that in the case of Christian books this kind of evidence may be stronger than in the case of other books; that the esteem in which the books from the first were held, the use made of them by religious assemblies, and the translations made from them very early into other languages, may concur to make an imposture in their case "almost impossible;" (pp. 43, 44.)

JUSTIN THE MARTYR, in his second defence of the Christians, written 150 years after the birth of Christ, said that they were an "innumerable multitude," and that every Sunday they met together, and read the "Gospels written by the Apostles" (see his Greek Apology.) Justin describes himself as being " of Palestine," and as writing his address on behalf of those who dwelt there. (See the beginning.) Mr. Jeremiah Jones remarks that as the

B2

language of Palestine was Syriac, the Gospels which were said by
Justin to have been read every Sunday, must have been in Syriac.
He says, "This argument I look upon as conclusive," in proof
that the Gospels then existed in "the Syriac language" (Vol. I.,
p. 97). No other Gospels but those of the Peshito, are proved by
other evidence to have been in general use by those speaking
Syriac. The one Gospel used by the Nazareans, cannot possibly
be meant by Justin when he speaks of the records made by the
Apostles, which are called "*the Gospels*" (Paris edition, 1552,
p. 162).

Proof that the Peshito existed in the time of Justin the Martyr,
and also that it had existed *from before the time when the latest
Apostolic books were written*, seems to be given by the fact that it
does not contain these books. If they had been then *written*, they
could not have been then excluded from fellowship with the other
divine writings without giving the false impression that they were
not of the same divine authority. But there is proof that those
five other books were not kept separate from the Peshito, because
they were *themselves* denied to be of Apostolic authority, but
only because the *Syriac copies of them* were denied to be of
the same authority as the other Syriac books in the dialect of
Edessa. The difference made between those five Syriac books
and the Peshito, was because the five had only some uninspired
translator. It therefore implies belief that the Peshito had
been made by persons who were *more* than mere human translators, such as he was who made the Edessene transcript of
the other books; it implies that the Peshito was made either
by persons who themselves wrote what God directed them to
write, or by others whose work had their oversight and approval. For if all the New Covenant books had been written
in the Edessene dialect by uninspired translators, there is no
known reason why they should have been kept so separate; and
why the Peshito alone should have been treated with such
superior reverence, and with such faith in its *very words*, as sacred,
that it would have been deemed a sin to alter any of them. In
this view Mr. Jeremiah Jones concurs. He says that "it seems
most probable" that the reason why the five books are not in the
[Peshito-] Syriac copies, is "because they were *not written* when the
Syriac Version was made; for had they been written then, those
so useful Epistles would have been translated, for the same
reason as the others. This was the argument which, among
others, convinced Tremellius (see the preface to his Syriac N. T.)
and the learned Bp. Walton (see the Prolegomena to his Polyglot),
that this version was made in the Apostles' time" (Jones, vol.
iii., p. 175).

CANON WESTCOTT, of Cambridge University, says in his work
on the Canon of the N. T. (that is, on what books are really part

of God's Word,) 1875, that to justify the acceptance of any book as infallible, we need evidence similar to that which Bp. Huet says is a sure proof that a book is what it is said to be. Dr. Westcott says at p. 12, " It is impossible to insist too often or too earnestly on this, that it is to the Church, as a witness, and keeper of holy writ, that we must look both for the formation and the proof of the Canon. The written rule of Christendom must rest finally on *the general confession of the Church*, and not on the independent opinions of its members. . . . The chief value of private testimony lies in the fact that it is a natural expression of the current opinion of the time." He applies this rule to the Greek Testament, by showing that its several books were received at an early date, and prized in the following centuries, as divine, by the mass of those Greek Christians, who were not gross corrupters of the truth. He appeals to " common usage," p. 12 ; to the mention of these books as " received by Churches," p. 13, and to proofs of " a belief widely spread throughout the Christian body," as affording decisive evidence that these books are genuine and Apostolic (p. 14).

Dr. Westcott admits that evidence very much like this exists also with respect to the Peshito-Syriac books. He says, " The Peshito Version is assigned almost universally to the most remote Christian antiquity. The Syriac Christians of Malabar even now claim for it the right to be considered as an *Eastern original* of the New Testament, and . . . . their tradition is not, to a certain extent, destitute of all plausibility," " It was in the Aramæn vernacular language of the Jews of Palestine that the Gospel of Matthew was originally written, if we believe the unanimous testimony of the fathers ; and it is not unnatural to look to the Peshito as likely to contain some traces of its first form." (P. 233.) " The dialect of the Peshito, even as it stands now, represents, *in part* at least, that form of Aramaic which was current in Palestine." (P. 234.) " Edessa is signalised in early church history by many remarkable facts. It was called the 'holy' and the 'blessed' city : its inhabitants were said to have been brought over by Thaddeus in a marvellous manner to the Christian faith ; and 'from that time forth,' Eusebius adds, 'the whole people of Edessa have continued to be devoted to the name of Christ.'" " Tradition fixes on Edessa as the place whence the Peshito took its rise. Gregory Bar Hebreus, one of the most learned and accurate of Syrian writers, ... assumes *the Apostolic origin* of the New Testament Peshito *as certain*. . . . He speaks of this *as a known and acknowledged fact*." (Pp. 235—6.) Dr. Westcott says also, " This version was universally received by the different sects into which the Syrian Church was divided [after] the fourth century, and so has continued current even to the present time. All the Syrian Christians whether belonging to the Nestorian, Jacobite, or

Roman communion, conspire to hold the Peshito AUTHORITATIVE, and to use it in their public services. . . . The Peshito became in the East the fixed and unalterable RULE OF SCRIPTURE." (P. 239.) " The respect in which the Peshito was held, was further shown by the fact that it was taken as the basis of other versions in the East. An Arabic and a Persian version were made from it." (P. 240.)

Dr. Westcott has linked the Peshito with the Latin Vulgate in a passage which, if freed from reference to the Latin version, to avoid any discussion respecting it, says of the Peshito, " Its voice is one to which we cannot refuse to listen. It gives the testimony of Churches, and not of individuals. It is sanctioned by public use, and not only supported by private criticism. Combined with the original Greek [and the Old Latin], it represents the New Testament Scriptures as they were read throughout the whole of Christendom towards *the close of the second century*. . . . It furnishes a proof of *the authority* of the books which it contains, widespread, continuous, reaching to the utmost verge of our historic records. Its real weight is even greater than this ; for when history first speaks of it, it speaks as of that which was recognised as a heritage from an earlier period, which cannot have been long after the days of the Apostles." (P. 263.)

Dr. Westcott gives at p. 241, the following information from Dr. Wm. Wright, Professor of Arabic in Cambridge University, one of the best informed persons on this subject. He says, " Of the Syriac manuscripts in the British Museum, the earliest of the N. T. which is *dated*, is A.D. 768." It does not contain the five books last written. "An earlier copy of the 5th or 6th century gives the same books in a different order. . . . The earliest manuscript in which the disputed Epistles occur is dated A.D. 823."

Dr. Westcott gives, under letter D, in his appendix, "The chief catalogues of the Books of the Bible during the first eight centuries." Sixteen out of thirty-two of them are those of the Eastern Churches. No. IV., by Chrysostom, cent. IV., has only " three catholic Epistles," James, 1 Peter, and 1 John. He omits the five books absent from the Peshito. No. VII. is a list by Hebedjesu, about 1318, A.D., from Asseman's Bibliotheca, Vol. iii. Hebedjesu omits the five books above mentioned. He says, "Matthew wrote in Hebrew in Palestine." He describes the three Epistles, that of James, 1 Peter, and 1 John, as " The three letters which have, written in them, writing by the Apostles in every copy and language, namely, those of James, Peter, and John ; and which are called catholic." The statement that these three Epistles were issued by the Apostles in various languages, and authenticated in all of them by the handwriting of the Apostles, is of special importance. In No. XVIII., the list of Leontius, about A.D. 590, seven letters are called catholic, *i.e.*, universal, namely, that of James, 1 and 2 of Peter, 1, 2 and 3 of John, and that of Jude, and the reason given for this name is, "Because they were not written for one nation, as those of Paul were; but universally for all nations;" he means probably for the Hebrew Christians dispersed throughout all nations. The above lists all represent the Eastern Churches.

The Churches which have used the Peshito-Syriac text have borne witness as uniformly to its "Apostolic origin" and authority, as the Churches which have used the Greek text have declared its Divine authority. Too little attention has been given to this admitted fact; and besides this, many modern critics who have treated the Greek text as the only text which has testimony to its Apostolic authority, have rejected the *general testimony* of those *very Churches* which have used the Greek text. These critics have slighted the readings best approved by the mass and long line of those assemblies; and have adopted as chief guides two copies which have *no record whatever* of having been generally approved by those Churches; they have also done this in spite of internal evidence in these two Greek copies, that they have been *carelessly written.* Special attention needs to be given to these facts. Even Canon Westcott, who insists so strongly, in his work on the Canon, p. 12, that we must depend for proof of what "the written Rule of Christendom" is, on the "general confession" of Christian bodies, has adopted in connection with Dr. Hort, and with view to settle the Greek text upon a sure basis, "a system" which, as Dr. Scrivener says, (Introduction, p. 537), is itself "entirely destitute of historical foundation."

CANON WESTCOTT AND DR. HORT have made and followed conjectures equally "destitute of historical foundation," with respect to THE PESHITO-SYRIAC TEXT. One of these conjectures relates to some fragments of an old Syriac translation of the Gospels, discovered by the late Dr. W. Cureton, and published by him in 1858. Nothing is known about it, except that it was brought from Egypt to Britain. I have not been able to get a copy, and know it chiefly by a review of it published in 1859, by Prof. Christian Hermansen, of Copenhagen. This is not the place to discuss the peculiarities of that translation. It is sufficient to quote a few words from Mr. Hermansen. He says that the Peshito and this translation "greatly differ" and in "various ways," p. 7; and that there is "a wonderful agreement between this translation and the Cambridge manuscript called D," (p. 21), of which copy Dr. Scrivener, an able judge, says, "It may be said without extravagance, that no set of scriptural records affords a text less probable in itself, or less sustained by any rational principles of external evidence, than that of codex D, of the Latin codices, and (so far as it accords with them) of Cureton's Syriac. (Introduction to N. T. 1883, p. 510.) Dr. Roberts, of Aberdeen, seems to be justified in saying of Dr. Cureton's fragments, "Never, probably, was there in the whole history of critical publications, such a notable example of self-delusion as that under which Dr. Cureton has laboured in this undertaking;" (Dr. R., on the Original Language of Matthew, p. 131); that is, the undertaking to prove that these fragments "more nearly represent the exact words of Matthew himself than any copy yet discovered," (p. 122). And yet Dr. Westcott and Dr. Hort *assume* that this "Curetonian version of the Gospels" is the first form of the Peshito. Canon Westcott calls it the "Old Syriac," (on Canon, p. 233, note 6.) He says, "It appears to have been afterwards corrected," but "in the absence of an adequate supply of critical materials, it is impossible to construct the history of *these recensions* in the Syriac," (p. 234.) Notwithstanding these conjectured recensions, he speaks of "the present corrupt state of the text" (p. 240.) One is startled, pained, and almost appalled, by finding that a scholar so highly esteemed as Canon Westcott is, can so violate his own rules; by finding that he not only rejects the admitted testimony of "Churches" to the "Apostolic authority" of the Peshito as it now exists, but even invents and follows mere fictions, and these of a kind fitted and seemingly intended to destroy its reputation. Can it be that this amazing inconsistency and impropriety is in some degree due to a fact which Canon Westcott mentions in one of his notes, when speaking of the Peshito? The note is this (in his work on the Canon, p. 238,) "In reference to the phraseology of the Peshito, it is *worthy of remark* that *Episcopus* is preserved in one place only, Acts xx. 28. Elsewhere it is *kashisho* (presbyter) except in 1 Pet. ii. 25." The Peshito has there "care-taker." Dr. Westcott's note directs special attention to the fact that the Peshito has omitted in most places the word, which, by being adopted as the name of the prelates who rule the Church of England, gives them some show, and but a deceptive show, of scriptural origin. It cannot be forgotten that Dr. Westcott has stated that the omission of the word *bishop* from passages in the Peshito, is a fact "worthy of remark."

DRS. WESTCOTT and HORT published in 1881, six years after Dr. Westcott's fourth edition of his work on the Canon, dated 1875, a long and mysteriously made Introduction to a new Greek text, full of strange changes. Both editors are responsible for the principles, arguments, and conclusions set forth in this Introduction, but it was "written by Dr. Hort" (Int. p. 18.) The following suggestions made by them are founded wholly on *imagination*, without one word of proof. "The popular Peshito version, till recently, has been known only in the form it finally received by an evidently authoritative revision. . . . An Old Syriac must have existed as well as an Old Latin. Within the last few years the surmise has been verified. An imperfect Old Syriac copy of the

Gospels, assigned to the fifth century, was found by Cureton
among MSS. brought to the British Museum from Egypt in 1842,
and was published by him in 1858." This is *assumed* by the writers
to be the Peshito "in its original form," and is said to '' render the
comparatively late and *revised* character " of the Peshito, " a matter
of *certainty* " (p. 84.)   Upon this dream of the imagination, continued references are made to the Peshito as "not coming up to
the requirements of criticism," etc. (pp. 84, 92, 136, 156, 158-9.)
Sadly often have " false witnesses risen up."   But it must be
deemed an alarming proof of the diseased state of biblical criticism,
if we find even leading men indulging, not only in wild fancies,
but even in false accusations against the most truthful of witnesses.
The late Dean Burgon in his work, '' The Revision Revised, 1883,''
pp. 273—8, said in reference to these conjectures, '' Not a shadow
of proof is forthcoming that *any such Recension as Dr. Hort
imagines, ever took place at all.*"   He has, '' 1stly, assumed a
'Syrian Recension ;' 2ndly, invented the cause of it ; and 3rdly,
dreamed the process by which it was carried into execution."
After reminding Dr. Hort that Bp. Ellicott has said that, " It is
no stretch of the imagination to suppose that portions of the
Peshito might have been in the hands of the *Apostle John*," the
Dean said, '' The *abominably corrupt* document known as ' Cureton's Syriac,' is by another bold hypothesis, *assumed* to be the only
surviving specimen of the unrevised version, and is thenceforth *invariably* designated by these authors as the Old Syriac."
'' Not a shadow of reason is produced why we should *suppose*, 1st,
that such a Revision took place, and 2ndly, that all our existing
manuscripts represent it."   " These editors even assure us that
' Cureton's Syriac ' renders the comparatively late and 'revised'
character of the Syriac Vulgate," i.e., the Peshito " *a matter of
certainty*.   The very city in which it underwent revision, can, it
seems, be fixed with '*tolerable certainty*.'   Can Dr. Hort be
serious ? "
      These painful details are given for the double purpose of guard-
ing the reader, 1st, against wrong conclusions as to the Peshito
itself ; and 2ndly, against placing confidence, without due examination, in the conclusions of the most influential critics of the day.
The habit of substituting mere conjecture for proof, is far too
common with respect to the Peshito.
      One illustration of the great importance of some of the questions
which these editiors try to decide by the aid of conjecture, is
worthy of special notice.   In John i. 18, they have placed words,
meaning that Christ is " the only begotten God."   They have
placed these words in the main text.   The Revisers of the English
Version have not put these words in the chief place ; but say in
the margin, " Many very ancient authorities read, God only
begotten."   In two of the three creeds in the Prayer-book of the

Church of England the semi-Arian belief is avowed that the Word, the second person of the *Godhead*, was *begotten* by the first. In the Athanasian creed he is said to have been "begotten before the worlds." In the creed used in the communion service he is said to have been "begotten before all worlds, very God of very God, begotten not made." The Peshito has in John i. 18, "the only God," without the word "begotten." He who called himself "I am," declared that, like the Father, he, the Word, is self-existent (John viii. 58.) God tells us by Luke, that Jesus is called the Son of God, in respect of his manhood, not of his Deity (Luke i. 35.) But these eminent scholars, by following corrupt copies, have introduced the false teaching of the creeds, as to the *derived* and *inferior* Godhead of the Word, into the Book of God itself. This false reading not only ascribes to the Redeemer a double Sonship, one, that of his humanity, another, that of his divinity, of which Scripture says nothing ; but it provides a theme for the scoff of infidels; and builds a barrier which prevents the godly from asserting the absolute "oneness," and the underived equality of the Deity of the Father and the Word.

BISHOP HERBERT MARSH, Professor of Divinity in the University of Cambridge, in his "Lectures on the Criticism of the Bible, 1828," maintained, as most persons do, that CONJECTURE must not be "applied to the sacred writings," (p. 26.) It is indeed self-evident that conjecture cannot possibly prove a book to be of Divine origin ; nor can possibly be a fit reason for believing that any words in it have such authority. We have to insist that evidence, not fictions, shall guide those who profess to teach us what words are those of God, that readings approved by the mass of the faithful both of earlier and of later centuries, shall have a full hearing ; that mere foundling copies, without a history, full of copyist errors, and tainted with semi-Arian untruth, shall have a low place and little regard ; that copies exactly written, and well attested, as having descended from the very time of the Apostles, shall be treated with all the honour which is their due.

V.—THE BELIEF OF THOSE CHRISTIAN BODIES WHICH HAVE USED THE N. C. PESHITO-SYRIAC BOOKS.

The fact that the N. C. Peshito Books were never, for many centuries, combined with any Syriac translation of the five omitted books, though the omitted books were also believed to have had a divine origin in some other dialect, is, itself, a proof that the origin of the Peshito text was believed to be so much above any uninspired translation, that it would have been a sin to bind up any uninspired translation with the Peshito. Wichelhaus says, "In all copies of the Peshito version, those [five omitted] books are sought for in vain" (p. 221.) Yet "it is very well known that the Syrians did not reject those epistles (p. 63.)

There is an account of the use of Syriac books called " The New Covenant " by the converts of Thaddeus, one of the seventy who were sent forth by Christ himself in His lifetime. Matthew says that the fame of Jesus " went throughout all Syria " (Matt. iv. 24), and the following are not idle tales, but well authenticated historical facts. Abgar was the king of a small Syrian kingdom called Osrhoene, which, as Gibbon says, " occupied the northern and most fertile part of Mesopotamia, between the Euphrates and the Tigris. Its capital, Edessa, was situated about twenty miles beyond the Euphrates." (Decline, chap. viii.) Eusebius says that he himself, translated into Greek from Syriac, for his history, the account then existing in the public records of that kingdom, of the manner in which the king and many of the citizens became true Christians. Abgar was afflicted with an incurable disease. He heard of the cures effected by Jesus. He sent a messenger to him asking that he would come and heal him. Jesus is said to have replied, that after his ascension to heaven, he would send one of his disciples to heal him, and to teach both him, and those with him, the way of life. Eusebius says that after the ascension of Jesus, the Apostle Thomas, by divine direction, sent thither Thaddeus one of the seventy. Thaddeus did great miracles. Abgar was healed by him, and many others.

Dr. Cureton found among the Syriac manuscripts in the British Museum a very old one, copied, he said, " certainly not later than the beginning of the fifth century." Its title is, " The Teaching of Thaddeus the Apostle." It relates what Thaddeus did and said, and what results followed his teaching, down to the time of his death. The Syriac original, and a translation by Dr. Cureton, are before me ; also the Syriac, and an English translation of another copy published by Dr. George Phillips, President of Queen's College, Cambridge. Thaddeus, whose first address to the citizens is recorded in this document, spoke in a manner which remarkably corresponds with such a divine mission. In the course of it he said, " Though ye were not near at the time when the Anointed suffered, yet by the sun which was darkened, and ye saw [it], learn and understand how great a convulsion there was at the time of the crucifixion of him whose message has been spread abroad through all the earth, by the miracles which his disciples, my companions, are working in all the earth, and who, though Hebrews, who knew only the tongue of the Hebrews, in which they were born, behold! to-day are speaking in all tongues ; that those who are far off, as well as those who are near, may hear, and may believe, that this is he who confused the languages of the arrogant in this region of the ancients; that it is he who teaches by means of us to-day, trust in what is true and

real, by [us] the lowly and uncultured, who are from Galilee of
Palestine. For I also, whom ye see, am from Paneas, from the
place where the river Jordan goes forth : and I was chosen,
together with my companions, to be a bearer of tidings. . . And the
seed of his word I sow in the ears of every man ; and those who
are willing to receive it, theirs will be a good reward of [their]
profession : but against those who obey not, I shake off the dust
of my feet, as he [Jesus] commanded me. Turn, therefore, my
beloved, from evil ways and hateful deeds ; and turn to him
with a good and honest will, as he has turned to you in the
compassion of his rich mercies. . . . . Flee, therefore, from things
made and created, as I have said to you—from things which by
name only are called gods, but are not gods in their nature ; and
draw near to him who, in his nature is God eternally and from
everlasting. . . . Because though he clothed himself in this
body, he is God with his Father." " Get that new mind which
worships the Maker, and not the things made ; [the mind] in
which is to be formed an image of what is true and real—of the
Father, and of the Son, and of the Spirit of holiness, when ye
shall trust, and be immersed in the threefold glorious names."
(See Cureton's Syriac copy, pp. 8, 9, 11.)

Thaddeus was probably not one of the twelve, though he is
called an apostle, but one of the seventy sent forth by Christ to
preach, with power to work miracles, in his life-time. The above
extracts are given as a portrait of his ministry and teaching. He
is the person to whose superintending care Syrian writers ascribe
the formation of the Peshito ; and as he worked miracles, whatever
he sanctioned as part of God's teaching, had the same authority
as that which the twelve said was from God. The above extracts
tend to confirm belief in his fitness to make or obtain for his
converts divinely attested copies of the sacred books so soon as
they were written. It is vain to expect to trace all the means by
which it was effected. It is enough for us to know that those
who knew the result attest it to be, that the Peshito "was
written by apostolic authority," (Wichelhaus, p. 153). Thaddeus
may have died before many of the books contained in the Peshito
were first written. But the Apostle John lived for some time after
they were completed, and, whoever may have written some of these
books in the Syriac of Edessa, it was possible for them to have
been submitted to him for rectification and divine authority. It is
stated by an early writer that some books were really submitted to
John for this purpose. Photius, who is called by Mr. Jer. Jones
a "most accurate and judicious critic" (vol. i. 240), has given an
extract from a very ancient book which states that the Apostle
John, after he had been banished from Ephesus by Domitian,
who died, A.D. 96, returned to Ephesus when Nerva succeeded
him, "took the several books which contained the history of our

Saviour's sufferings, miracles, and doctrines, and which were *now translated into several different languages, reviewed them, rectified them,* and joined himself to the former three evangelists," *i.e.,* by writing his Gospel in Greek. (Jones on Canon, Vol. iii. 2.)

A MANUSCRIPT OF THE FOUR GOSPELS IN SYRIAC, BEARING DATE A.D. 78, is mentioned by J. S. Asseman, in his Bibliotheca. The manuscript was preserved at Bagdad on the river Tigris; at the end it had these words under written; " This sacred book was finished on Wed., the 18th day of the month Conun, in the year 389," that is of the Greeks, which was A.D. 78, " by the hand of the Apostle Achæus, a fellow labourer of Mar Maris, and a disciple of the Apostle Mar Thaddeus, whom we intreat to pray for us." This prayer implies that the statement was written after the time of Achæus (who is probably the person called also Aggæus), and Dr. Glocester Ridley says that Achæus died A.D. 48. For this and other reasons J. D. Michaelis says that the statement "is of no authority." (Marsh's Michaelis, 1823, vol. ii., p. 31.)

THE GREAT NUMBER OF CONVERTS made by Thaddeus, needed to be supplied immediately with WRITTEN DIVINE RECORDS IN SYRIAC, to teach them what to believe and what to do. Greek books would not have been suitable, for their language was Syriac. The ancient Syriac copy of "The Teaching of Thaddeus," from which the above extracts are taken, states that not only King Abgar, and many of the people of that city, were converted, but many also throughout " all Mesopotamia, and the regions round about it." It says that Thaddeus "received all those who trusted in the Anointed, and immersed them in the name of the Father, and of the Son, and of the Spirit of Holiness "; that the king gave money with which a house of worship was built; that in it they " offered praises all the days of their lives ;" that in the worship conducted there, the teachers " read in the Old Covenant and in the New, and in the Prophets, and in the Acts of the Apostles every day." By the New Covenant seems to be meant the Gospels; for the N. C. is distinguished from the Acts of the Apostles, and a little afterwards it is said that many people assembled from day to day, and came to the prayers of the service, and the [reading of the] Old Covenant and of the New in four parts. (See Syriac, pages 13, 15.) The Syriac of this narrative is like that of the Peshito itself; a fact which corroborates the statement that the Peshito was made by the care of Thaddeus.

SOME DOUBT, however, attaches to some of the above statements, because " The Teaching of Thaddeus " has at the end, received forged additions. Dr. Glocester Ridley says that Achæus (sometimes called Aggæus) a disciple of Thaddeus died A.D. 48. Serapion was bishop of Antioch about A.D. 192—214 ; Zephyrinus was bishop of Rome 202—217. Yet in this record it is said that when Aggæus died, " Palut received the hand of priesthood from Serapion, bishop of Antioch, which hand Serapion received from Zephyrinus, bishop of Rome, from the succession of the hand of priesthood of Simon Cephas." So that though the above extracts do not seem to be corrupted, some of them may be so.

BARDESANES was a Syrian writer of note in cent. II. Cave says that he flourished about A.D. 172. Dr. Nathaniel Lardner, in his Credibility, 1735, vol. ii., p. 673, says, "Eusebius speaks favourably of him, though most later writers call him a heresiarch," Eusebius says that he was "a most eloquent writer in the Syriac language"; and that he wrote several dialogues in his own language against Marcion and other authors of different opinions." (See Eusebius' Hist., Cent., iv., ch. 30.) Also that he was at first a follower of Valentinus, and that though he gave up some of his errors, he did not get rid of all the filth of his former heresy. Epiphanius says that he was a native of Edessa and very intimate with the king then reigning there, who was also called Abgar, and a professed Christian; that Bardesanes "went into several great errors but continued to use the Law and the Prophets, both the Old and *the New Covenant*, joining with them some apocryphal books. (Lardner ii. 677—8.) This is evidence that at that time a Syriac "New Covenant" existed. Canon Westcott says also of the controversial writings of Bardesanes that they "*necessarily imply*" the existence of a Syriac Version of the Bible." (On the Canon, p. 237.)

HEGESIPPUS lived in the latter part of the second century. Eusebius, bk. iv., ch. 22, says, "He sets forth some things from the Gospel according to the Hebrews, and *from the Syriac*, and from the Hebrew dialect as his own, showing that he was one of the Hebrews who had trusted. Dr. Westcott (on Canon, p. 238) says, "This testimony is valuable, as coming from the only early Greek writer likely to have been familiar with Syriac literature." The bare reference of Hegesippus to "the Syriac," leaves it uncertain to what part of the Scriptures in Syriac he referred; but it shows that he made use of some Syriac copy, and the Peshito is the only one which can be supposed to be intended.

APHRAATES, a Persian sage, wrote twenty-two Syriac homilies, A.D. 337—45. The citations from the gospels met with in these homilies, are said by Professor Wright to be very loose; to have some occasional resemblance to Cureton's Syriac, but to be on the whole, much nearer to the text of the Peshito. (Scrivener's Int. p. 323, note.)

EPHRÆM, of Edessa, was a very eminent Syrian writer. He died A.D. 373. J. S. Asseman devotes 140 folio pages to extracts from his writings, and to comments on them. They are in the same Syriac dialect in which the Peshito is written. Dr. Westcott (on Canon, p. 238) says, "Ephrem treats the version in such a manner as to prove that it was already old in the fourth century."

One of Ephrem's similes will show the beauty of his style, and though it does not prove that he believed the N. C. Peshito to have divine authority, yet his constant use of it seems to imply that he was referring to it when he spoke of the New Covenant as a harp, the notes of which have been played by the finger of God. He said, "Praise be to the Lord of all, who framed and fitted for himself two harps, those of the Prophets and of the Apostles ; but it is the same finger which has played upon the two, the different notes of the two covenants." (Asseman's Bib. Or., vol. i., p. 103.)

IN THE FIFTH CENTURY, those who used the Peshito began to be divided into different sects. But, as Dr. Westcott observes, the Peshito has continued to be "universally received" and used by these different sects down to the present time. He says, "All the Syrian Christians, whether belonging to the Nestorian, Jacobite, or Roman communion, conspire to hold the Peshito *authoritative*, and to use it in their public services. . . . The Peshito became in the East the fixed and unalterable RULE OF SCRIPTURE." (On the Canon, p. 239.)

THE THREE CHIEF SECTS which, to this day, continue to use the N. C. Peshito-Syriac books, are the Nestorians, Jacobites, and Maronites. Their names are derived from Nestorius, Jacob Baradæus, and Maron.

NESTORIUS, or NESTORE, became Patriarch of Constantinople, A.D. 430. An absurd custom had arisen of calling Mary who was the mother of Jesus, " The Mother of God." Nestore objected to it, and said, as Mosheim relates, that she "was rather to be called the mother of Christ; since the Deity can neither be born nor die; and only the Son of Man could derive his birth from an earthly parent." (Cent. v.) The Emperor Theodosius called a council of bishops which met at Ephesus, A.D. 431. This council, one of " lawless violence," defended the false title given to Mary. Nestore was condemned. He resigned his bishopric, and was afterwards banished. Many agreed with him, and held that his sentiments had been taught by Scripture from the beginning. They were called Nestorians, not because they derived their sentiments from him, but because he was one of the chief defenders of those sentiments. Amrus, a Nestorian, about A.D. 1340, said, that " Nestore, whose name was imposed on them, was a Greek, but they were Syrians; they had never seen him, nor had he ever trod their lands" (Patriarchs, by Aloys Asseman, p. 206). Another council of bishops (for prelates had then assumed to themselves the right to rule the churches, and pretended that their decisions were laws given by the will of God,) met at Chalcedon in Asia Minor, not far from Constantinople, about A.D. 451. This Council, by its decrees, said that some had dared to corrupt the mystery of the gospel, and were denying the application of the word "*Theotokos*—

mother of God, to the Virgin;" that this Council held that the Son, is "true God and true man......*begotten* by the Father before the ages as to his *Deity*.....but of Mary, virgin and *deipara*— Mother of God, as to his *humanity;* one and the same Jesus Christ, Son of God, Lord and only begotten, made manifest in two natures," which two natures "concur in *one person*," who is "one and the same only begotten Son, the God-Word" (Magdeburg Centuriators, cent. v., col. 531.) It is self-evident that things which differ so much as Godhead does from manhood, are not "one and the same." The first evident error in the above statement is that the Divine Word is a *begotten* Deity. The next is that the Deity of this begotten God, though declared to be quite distinct in nature from the humanity begotten of the Virgin, is nevertheless so "one" with it, that because Mary was mother of the manhood, she therefore was *mother of the Godhead also.* A greater absurdity is impossible. Yet this is still called, not only by Roman Catholics, but by a member of the Church of England, the orthodox faith of the true church. It was this absurdity which Nestore denied. For doing so, he is still called by many a heretic. Gibbon remarks, that the doctrine of the Council of Chalcedon, namely, that in Christ there is but "one person in two natures," was received by Europe during ten centuries of servitude to the Vatican, and was then "admitted without dispute into the creed of the Reformers." (Decline, ch. xlvii.) Is it difficult to form a correct opinion on this point? The statement that the Deity and manhood of Christ formed but "one person" seems to mean that they had only one capability of personal action. In Christ "dwells all the fulness of the Godhead bodily;" Col. ii. 9. Did this indwelling make the Godhead and the manhood to be so one, that when the manhood was crucified the Godhead was crucified? God dwells, in an inferior degree, in his saints; does this make them to be so one in person with God that when they pray and sing, God prays and sings? And yet for denying that God was born of Mary Nestorians are counted heretics.

Nestorians were also charged with making the SONSHIP OF CHRIST DOUBLE. (See Magdeburg Centuriators, cent. v., col. 334, F.) Almost all the ancient creeds do this, by teaching that even the Deity of Christ was begotten, as well as his humanity. Nestore's opponents held this creed. But they seemed to have imagined that by calling the Godhead and the manhood "one person," they made the divine Sonship, in respect of which the Creed of Chalcedon says he was "begotten before the ages," to be one and the same with the sonship of his humanity. The charge against the Nestorians was that by denying Christ to be "one person," they left the double sonship unresolved into oneness. Nestore and his opponents both held that the Divine Word was a begotten Deity; but his opponents added absurdity to error when they imagined that the words "one person" converted two sonships into one. The word of God says nothing of a begotten God. "I am," which denotes underived existence, was used by Christ of his Godhead, as well as by God of himself when he spoke to Moses. (Ex. iii. 14; John viii. 58.) Oneness with the Father is the oneness of self-existence. God tells us that Christ is his Son because begotten by him of Mary, Luke i. 35.

ANOTHER CHARGE brought against Nestore was that he made FOUR PERSONS in the Godhead. (Mag. Centuriators, cent. v., col. 335 F., 338 F.) As if it were impossible to believe that the Deity of Christ differs from his manhood, without converting his manhood into a second Deity. Such absurdities seem to be intended to show that if men assume a lordship which God forbids, he makes their wisdom folly.

These facts are proof that the Nestorians, who suffered the loss of all things, and preferred to be under the ban of perpetual excommunication, rather than admit the untruth that Mary was the mother of God, gave far better proof of being trustworthy witnesses as to the origin of their Scriptures, than those of the Greek and Roman bodies who asserted that untruth.

THESE CHARGES HAVE BEEN MENTIONED because they help to account for the unwillingness, so strong in some quarters, to receive THE TESTIMONY OF THE NESTORIANS respecting their Peshito Scriptures. For, strange as it may seem, even Dr. Liddon, a Canon of St. Paul's Cathedral, London, in his Bampton Lectures on the Divinity of Christ, 9th ed., 1882, defends the false title "mother of God," (p. 261.) He pleads that it has been used by those whom he calls "the whole church, since the Council of Ephesus," and justifies them in "attributing to God birth of a human mother," (p. 261, note.) He calls the rejection of that false title by Nestore, a "vital heresy," (p. 123.)

PENAL LAWS drove most of the Nestorians out of the Roman empire (Gibbon, chap. xlvii.) But ELSEWHERE THEY INCREASED EXCEEDINGLY. A large majority of the people of Persia became Nestorians. Cosmas, who is called the Indian navigator, and was a Nestorian, said of them, in the sixth century, that Christianity was successfully preached by them to the Bactrians, Huns, Persians, Indians, Medes, and Elamites; and that the number of churches from the Gulf of Persia to the Caspian sea, was almost infinite. Gibbon says that, in a subsequent age their missionaries pursued without fear the footsteps of the roving Tartar; that some of them entered China, and that under the Mohammedan Caliphs, "their numbers, with those of the Jacobites, were computed *to surpass the Greek and Roman communions.*" (Gibbon, ch. xlvii. Nestorians.) All these churches used the Peshito.

THE BEST CHARACTERISTICS of the Nestorians are their LOVE AND USE OF THE PESHITO, and THEIR GREAT CARE TO KEEP IT

PURE. From the first they shared the corruptions of Christianity which prevailed in the fifth century; and Wichelhaus says, in reference to about the year 600, "They were often contentious, ambitious, covetous; doctrines were adulterated," a hierarchy had been founded and was promoted; they corrupted and depraved the doctrines and precepts which they had received pure from the Apostles, not less than the Roman Catholics did. "This thing only is to be praised in them, that they always used the Bible, and greatly valued learning," (p. 130.) He says that from the eighth century, slaughter and desolation overwhelmed both the Nestorians and the Jacobites; that some of the Nestorians fled for refuge to the mountains of Coordistan, and some of the Jacobites, partly to the mountain regions of Mesopotamia, and partly to the solitudes of Lebanon; (p. 205—6). J. Aloys Asseman (a nephew of J. S. Asseman, who wrote the Bibliotheca) wrote a history of the Nestorian Patriarchs, published A.D. 1775, and showed a constant succession of them down to that date. He gives an account also of some of their chief writers. One of these, Jesudadus, mentions the belief of the Syrians as to the origin of the Peshito.

JESUDADUS, who is sometimes called SOADEDUS, lived during the Patriarchate of Theodosius, A.D. 852—858. He said of the Syriac version, "The translation of the sacred books into the Syriac language was in this order; the Pentateuch, and Joshua the son of Nun, and Judges, and Ruth, and Samuel, and David, and Proverbs, and Ecclesiastes, and the Song of Songs, and Job, were translated in the time of Solomon, at the request of Hiram, king of Tyre, his friend. But the rest of the books of the Old and those of the New Covenant, in the time of Abgar, king of Edessa, by the care and solicitude of Thaddæus and other apostles." (J. A. Asseman's Patriarchs, p. 102, note 1.)

Thaddæus, who worked miracles, could give the same authority to what he approved, as the twelve apostles did. The belief of the Syrians, therefore, about 800 years from the time of the Apostles was that the N. C. Peshito was made under such apostolic care that it had the same authority as the gospels of Luke and Mark had from being made under the care of Paul and Peter.

EBEDJESUS, who became Metropolitan of Soba, that is, of Nisibis, A.D. 1290, was a Nestorian of great eminence. His works were very numerous. The list which he gave of the sacred books of the N. T. was that of the Peshito, not of the Greek. He states that the Gospel of Matthew was " written in Palestine in Hebrew," that is, in Syriac, then called Hebrew; and that the reason why the epistles of James. 1 Peter, and I John, were called catholic, was because " they had in them words written by the apostles in every copy and *in every language.*" The Syriac books of which he was speaking were those contained in the N. C. Peshito. His statements imply the general belief of Syrians that those four books, at the least, were written in Syriac, and that the Peshito contained true copies of them. (See Westcott on Canon, p. 540, and Dr. Badger's Nestorians, 1852, vol. ii., pp. 361—3.)

EBEDJESUS gives the following account of the origin of the Nestorians, the Jacobites, and the Melchites, in his work called "The Jewel," which is translated by Dr. Badger, vol. ii., p. 380. Ebedjesus says that Cyril maintained that we ought to call the Virgin, "Mother of God," and wrote twelve sentences, excommunicating all who should draw any distinction between the Godhead and humanity of Christ after their union. Nestorius shewed that these sentences were erroneous; that the appellation "Mother of God," is unscriptural. He called her "Mother of the Anointed," the Anointed being the word used by prophets and apostles. From this difference of creed came slaughter, exile, imprisonment, and great persecution. The Council of Chalcedon decided that there are *two natures* in Christ, and *two wills*, and anathematised all who should deny the two natures; but decided that there is but *one person*. The party of Cyril objected to "two natures;" that of Nestorius to "one person." An imperial edict degraded from their dignity all who did not agree with the decision, that there are two natures and one person. Some submitted. Others did not. Hence arose three sects. Those who held *one nature and one person in Christ*. This sect included the Copts, Egyptians, and Abyssinians. This is called the Jacobite sect, from a Syrian teacher called Jacob. The second sect held that there are *two natures and one person* in Christ. These are called Melchites—the king's party, because this creed was imposed forcibly by the king. It is received by the Romans called Franks, by those of Constantinople who are Greeks, and by all the people of the West, such as Russians, Circassians, Georgians and their neighbours. The Jacobites and Melchites accept the appellation "mother of God." The Jacobites have added the declaration that "God was crucified for us." The third creed is that of the Nestorians, that there are *two natures and two persons* in Christ. The Easterns have never changed their faith, but have kept it as they received it from the apostles, and therefore are unjustly called Nestorians, because he was not their patriarch, nor was his their language. Nestorius followed *them*, not they *him*, and more especially, as to the appellation "Mother of the Anointed." Such is the account given by Ebedjesus of the three sects. It shews how well informed he was, and how important his testimony is as to the books of Scripture.

THE CHRISTIANS OF ST. THOMAS, in India, whose profession of Christianity dates from the time of the apostles, maintain that Syriac was the original language of Scripture. Dr. Westcott says, "The Syriac Christians of Malabar even now claim for the Peshito the right to be considered as an Eastern original of the New Testa--

ment." (On the Canon, p. 233.) "How shall we know," said one of them, speaking to Dr. Claudius Buchanan about the Greek Testament, "that your standard copy of the Bible is a *true translation?* We cannot depart from our own Bible. It is *the true book of God,* without corruption; it is that book which was first used by the Christians of Antioch. What *translations* you have got in the West, we know not; but the true Bible of Antioch we have had in the mountains of Malabar for fourteen hundred years, or longer." Another of these professed Christians said, "If the parables and discourses of our Lord were in Syriac, and the people in Jerusalem commonly used it, is it not marvellous that his disciples did not record his parables in the Syrian language, and that they should have recourse to the Greek? Surely there must have been *a Syriac original.* The poor people in Jerusalem could not read Greek. Had *they* no record in their hands of Christ's parables which they had heard, and of his sublime discourses recorded by John after his ascension? You admit that Matthew was written originally in Syriac; you may as well admit John. Or was one Gospel enough for the inhabitants of Jerusalem?" (Dr. Etheridge's Syriac Christians, pp. 166—7.)

THE NESTORIANS NEVER TREATED THE GREEK TEXT AS OF HIGHER AUTHORITY than that of the N. C. Peshito. Wichelhaus says (p. 187,) that "the Nestorians had no social union with Western Christians; and that they held the text of the Greek New Testament in almost no esteem, and deemed the ancient Peshito to be in all things authentic." At p. 153 he says, "In the history of the Nestorians, it was never found, so far as I know, that learned men took the trouble to compare the Syriac text of the New Testament with the Greek, and to conform it to that." (Also p. 266.)

THE TERMS APPLIED TO THE PESHITO prove the general belief of its divine origin. Wichelhaus says, (p. 153), "It was extolled with the greatest praises; it was esteemed to be exactly what was written in the first times BY APOSTOLIC AUTHORITY; it was called, not only ancient, but SACRED AND BLESSED."

THE EXTREME CARE taken to preserve its text in purity implies that every part of it was believed to be from God. The care taken was like that which the Jews took of their inspired Hebrew text. Wichelhaus says, "It is a proof of the extreme accuracy of the Syrians in treating the sacred text, that, like the Jews, they have their Masora," a collection of critical comments on correct readings; "not only do they divide the text into chapters and lections, but they also number the comma-divisions of each book." (P. 156.) Monasteries abounded in the East from the fourth century. When the city of Edessa was taken by the Saracens, 300 monasteries were found in it, (p. 126.) The monks of that period devoted their time chiefly to copying the scriptures, and making known the gospel. Wichelhaus attributes the great accuracy of the copies of the Peshito, and especially of the Nestorian copies, to the following causes. 1st. Many copies were written in monasteries, by skilled men, from approved examples, and with the utmost care and attention. 2ndly. Those copies were read and examined many times by ministers and monks. 3rdly. In the time of Ephræm, cent. iv., deep interest was taken in the letter of Scripture, and many Syrians are mentioned who had committed almost the whole New Testament to memory. 4thly. In schools, in church-assemblies, and in monasteries, there was such constant communication between the teachers and the taught, that if any differences crept into the text, they could scarcely escape notice, nor become fixed by custom. 5thly. A large part of the Christians of that region had been Jews, they were compelled to discuss points with Jews, they had Jewish schools near them, and were thus accustomed to consider the words of sacred scripture, to be themselves sacred and inviolable, and almost to number the very letters." (P. 151.)

THE NESTORIANS WERE FAMOUS FOR THEIR SCHOOLS. In these schools the copying of the scriptures was a first part of the education given. For instance, in the school or college at Nisibis, A.D. 490, the rules required that " the brethren admitted to it, should not, except from urgent necessity, cease from writing, reading, and expounding " Scripture. As to the writing of Scripture, they were " in the first year to write the Pentateuch, and a book of Paul ; in the second, the Psalms and Prophets; in the third, the New Testament." (p. 125.) There were secular studies, but the young had to begin with the study of Scripture.

AS TO THE AGREEMENT OF DIFFERENT COPIES: most of those which have been brought to Europe, are not Nestorian, but Jacobite copies. But so far as the Nestorian and the Jacobite copies differ, the greater reverence which the Nestorians had for the Peshito, justifies a higher esteem for the exactness of their text. Wichelhaus says, " Testimonies prove that the text of the Nestorians is altogether the same as that of the ancient Peshito version." But the differences between their early texts, and other texts of early date, are so little, that Wichelhaus says, " The texts of copies written in cents. v. and vi., in Mesopotamia, and which bear the date when they were written recorded upon them, and the text of copies written at a later time, alike of Jacobites and of Maronites, of Nestorians, and of Melchites, is a text so entirely the same, and with such constancy of likeness, that, in the Syriac version, *no place was given for Recensions*, such as are said to have been made in the *Greek text*, even in the first centuries." (pp. 150, 151.) This answer, by the voice of fact, denies almost the possibility of such a recension of the Syriac text, as Dr. Hort, in his Introduction to the Greek Testament of Drs. Westcott and Hort, 1881, first conjectures, and then treats as "certain." (p. 84.)

2. THE JACOBITES BEAR LIKE TESTIMONY, as to the origin of the Peshito. They are called Monophysites, that is, persons who believe that in Christ there is but one *nature*, as well as one person. Apollinaris, bishop of Laodicea, had taught, before the time of Nestore, that Christ had *no human mind*, that he was only Deity and a human body. About A.D. 448, Eutyches, an abbot of Constantinople, spread this belief, while opposing the Nestorians. (Mosheim, cent. v.) At Ephesus, where the Council of 431 condemned Nestore, another Council in 449, condemned Flavian, Patriarch of Constantinople, and others, for excommunicating Eutyches. The Greeks called this Council " a band of robbers," because it " carried everything by fraud and violence." (Mosheim.) Gibbon says, " It is certain that Flavian, before he could reach the place of his exile, expired on the third day, of the wounds and bruises he had received at Ephesus. The synod has been justly branded as a gang of robbers and assassins." (Decline, ch. xlvii.) Wichelhaus (p. 134) says that the Emperors Zeno and Anastasius were favourable to the Monophysites, (A.D. 474—518); but that when the Emperor Justin (518—527), began to remove the Monophysite bishops from their sees, the Monophysites, chiefly by the influence of Jacob Baradæus, separated themselves from the Greek church, and became a distinct body, thenceforth called Jacobites, from their connection, it is said, with Jacob Baradæus. The Nestorians more abounded in the East of Asia ; the Jacobites in the West, and in Egypt.

A body with such an origin, and such a creed, cannot be said to have much claim to general confidence ; but Gregory Bar Hebræus, one of their learned men, is much relied on. Dr. Westcott calls him "one of the most learned and accurate of Syrian writers." (On the Canon, p. 236.)

" GREGORY BAR HEBRÆUS," Dr. Westcott says, " relates that the New Testament Peshito was made in the time of Thaddæus and Abgarus, king of Edessa, when, according to the universal opinion of ancient writers, the Apostle went to proclaim Christianity in Mesopotamia. This statement *he repeats several times*, and once, on the authority of Jacob, a deacon of Edessa, in *the fifth century*. . . It is worthy of notice that Gregory assumes *the Apostolic origin* of the New Testament Peshito *as certain ;* for while he gives three hypotheses as to the date of the Old Testament Version, he speaks of this as *a known and an acknowledged fact.*" (On the Canon, p. 236.) Bp. Walton said that if the Peshito was " made by some one of the Apostles, it would have divine and equal authority with the other sacred books." It is therefore worthy of special notice that, according to Bar Hebræus, the Peshito was "known" to be of "Apostolic origin," and therefore was known to be of the same authority as the Greek Text. Even Canon Westcott calls attention to the unwavering and unqualified nature of this testimony to a "known fact."

BAR HEBRÆUS was born 1226, and died 1286. He said, speaking first of the O. C. Peshito-Syriac,—"Respecting this Syriac translation, there were three opinions; the first, that it was translated in the time of kings Solomon and Hiram; the second, that Asa the priest translated it, when the Assyrian sent him to Samaria; the third, that it was translated in the days of Thaddæus the apostle, and of Abgar, the king of Edessa, when also they translated the New Covenant in the same Peshito form;" that is, in the same simple or faithful manner. (See the Syriac words in Prager, on O. C. Peshito, p. 7; and a Latin translation in Wichelhaus, p. 61.)

BAR HEBRÆUS records also, in another place, the fact that JACOB OF EDESSA says, "that translators were sent by Thaddæus the apostle, and Abgar, the king of Edessa, into Palestine, and translated the Scripture from Hebrew into Syriac." (See the Syriac words in Walton's Prol. xiii. 16.) The words of Jacob of Edessa refer to the O. C. Peshito; but Bar Hebræus in the above extract says that the N. C. Peshito was made at the time when Jacob of Edessa said, in this passage, that persons were sent into Palestine to translate the O. C. Scriptures.

THE JACOBITES SEEM TO HAVE ALTERED TWO PASSAGES in some of their copies of the Peshito, to justify such expressions as that "God was crucified for us," a statement which Gibbon says was "imagined by a monophysite bishop." (Decline ch. xlvii. The Trisagion.)

In ACTS xx. 28, most of their copies have "the church of *the Anointed*, which he purchased with his blood :" which is in agreement with other copies of the Peshito. But Wichelhaus says that Sabarjesus, a Nestorian Presbyter, mentions Jacobite copies which had "the church *of God;*" and that Asseman found in the Vatican library a monophysite copy which has "of God." (p. 150.) Our common English Version has "of God;" but Griesbach and Tischendorf adopted "of the Lord," as the true Greek text. The general testimony of the Syriac copies is that "of the Anointed" is the true text of the Peshito.

In HEB. ii. 9., most of the Jacobite copies say of Jesus, "He, God, in his merciful favour, tasted death on behalf of every man." This reading could be used to defend the statement that God was crucified. The Nestorian copies have, "For he [Jesus], apart from God, (or the Godhead)," etc. Origen, nearly 200 years before Nestore lived, mentioned Greek copies which had a like reading. He died about A.D. 254. Theodore bishop of Mopsuestia, a celebrated Greek writer, who died about A.D. 429, said that some persons had removed the reading, "without God," and had substituted,

" by the merciful favour of God." He said also that the context shows that the apostle was not speaking of God's mercy, but of the relation between the Deity and manhood of Christ. (See Tischendorf's 8th edn., under Heb. ii. 9.) Tischendorf says, " From these testimonies, it is *certain* that the reading, without God, did not originate with the Nestorians; for Origen found it in his copies." There is no reason, therefore, to suppose that the Nestorian text of the Peshito in Heb. ii. 9, is the result of any change made by them; but there is reason, on the contrary, to regard it as part of the original text of the Peshito; and a proof that the Greek copies which had the same reading in the time of Origen were correct.

THE JACOBITES DID NOT CONTINUE, as the Nestorians did, to treat the Syriac as BETTER THAN THE GREEK TEXT. About A.D. 616, a new Syriac version of the N. C., was made by them. It was from the Greek text, and followed it closely. It is called the Philoxenian Syriac, from Philoxenus, its patron. Wichelhaus says that the Jacobites seem to have thought that it would be wicked to supplant the Peshito, and yet to have preferred the new version. He thinks that the name Peshito came into use at this time, and among them, because the Nestorians had no need of a distinct name for the Peshito. They had not, as the Jacobites had, a second Syriac version.

Wichelhaus says also, that all the Jacobite teachers took delight in making changes, called corrections and emendations, (p. 205); and that after the Philoxenian version was made, they began to conform, even their copies of the Peshito, to the Greek text, so that, in estimating the worth of copies written after that date, inquiry needs to be made whether they are Jacobite or Nestorian. (p. 231.)

3. THE MARONITES GIVE LIKE TESTIMONY RESPECTING THE ORIGIN OF THE PESHITO. Bp. Walton says, " The Maronites were so called from Maro, an abbot. They were reconciled to the Pope, and to the church of Rome, A.D. 1182. They have a college of Maronites at Rome, founded by Gregory 13th," (who died in 1585), " from which priests and bishops are sent into their country." (Walton, Poly. Prol. xiii. 2.) They are an offshoot from the Jacobites. About the close of the seventh century many of the Jacobites fled, to save their lives, partly to mountains in the north of Mesopotamia, and partly to Mount Lebanon. Those who fled to Lebanon divided into two parties; one party submitted to the emperors of Constantinople, and were called Melchites, that is, Imperialists; the other party maintained a more independent existence, and were called Mardaites, that is, Rebels. Of this party John Maro became a leader, and a Patriarch. J. S. Asseman, in his Bib. Or., vol. i. p. 517., shows that Maro opposed

both the Monophysites and the Nestorians. Maro seems to have been a Monothelite, that is, one who held that in Christ there was only *one will*. J. S. Asseman contends that he held the creed of Rome,—that of two natures and one person ; but Gibbon says that the Maronites, before they joined Rome, were Monothelites. He says of them, "The unfortunate question of *one will*, or operation in the two natures of Christ, was generated by their curious leisure. . . . Their country extends from the ridge of mount Libanus to the shores of Tripoli. . . . In the twelfth century the Maronites, abjuring the Monothelite [—the *one will*] error, were reconciled to the Latin Churches of Antioch and Rome. . . . The learned Maronites of the college of Rome have vainly laboured to absolve their ancestors from the guilt of heresy," that is, of Monothelism. (Ch. xlvii.)

GABRIEL SIONITA, is one of the many learned Maronites who have become eminent since the erection of the Maronite college at Rome. Ancient Syriac writing was a kind of short-hand, in which there was little more than the consonants written. While it was a living language, the vowels could be supplied by the reader, though not without liability to error. By degrees, signs were used, placed at the top and bottom of the consonants, to indicate the true vowel sounds. Bp. Walton, speaking of the Peshito, says, "That most illustrious man, Gabriel Sionita, first put vowel-points to the Syriac ; for before that time all manuscripts were destitute of vowel-points," or nearly so. This was done by him for Michael de Jay, in his splendid work, the Paris Heptaglot, A.D. 1628—45. Bp. Walton gives the following testimony of Sionita to the Peshito.

SIONITA, says Walton, " testifies that the Peshito has always been held in the greatest veneration, and held to be of *the greatest authority* by all the populations which use the Chaldaic or Syriac language, and has been publicly accepted and read in all their most ancient churches, formed in Syria, Mesopotamia, Chaldæa, Egypt, and finally, in those which are dispersed and spread throughout all parts of the East. In this language they read, not only the Scriptures, but liturgies also, and celebrate divine worship, even in those places where Syriac is not to-day the mother-tongue; although from those liturgies, and the longer responses of the people, it is sufficiently evident that those liturgies were commonly known and understood *when they first began to be used*." (Prol. xiii. Sec. 18.) In reference to Scripture, " the greatest authority " is *divine authority*.

FAUST NAIRON, a Maronite, is often referred to by J. S. Asseman as a writer of eminence. He was one of the two editors of the edition of the Peshito Syriac Version, printed by the side of an Arabic Version of the N. T., in 1703, by command of the Roman Congregation *De propaganda fide*, for the use of the Maronites.

He also wrote the preface. In this he said, (p. 2.) "The Syriac text *excels in antiquity all other texts*. By it very many places which in these are obscure, may be made plain." He proceeds to endeavour to prove that the Syriac text is more ancient than the Greek text of the Gospels. He mentions the common opinion that the Syriac Gospels were translated from the Greek, and says that there are better reasons for concluding that the Greek Gospels were translated from the Syriac. The weak part of his argument is, that he considers it certain that the sacred writers could not have given details of words and events so numerous and so varied as to time and place, unless they had made a *written record* of them, when they heard, saw, or were first informed of them. He says, that if they did make such a record, it must have been in their own language, Syriac. To this it may be replied, that we have very little evidence that any of them did make such records in the Saviour's life-time; and that they had no need of them, because the Holy Spirit brought all things to their remembrance. (John xiv. 26.) But the events which occurred were so extraordinary, and Christ so often called attention to his teaching, by saying, " He that has ears to hear, let him hear," that those who could write, would of necessity think it worth while to keep a written record of what they heard and saw, as Josephus did of the events of the Jewish war. Evidence that this was done by some persons appears from what Luke says of the many who had " set forth in order " the events of the gospel history, (Luke i. 1) ; and when he says of himself, that he had " closely followed up with exactness *from the first* what had been *delivered* by those who, from the beginning, were eye-witnesses ;" he seems clearly to intimate that what he wrote was from written records made by himself *from the first* of what those eye-witnesses had told him ; so that F. Nairon has, in these words of Luke, some support for his remark, that the sacred writers in order to construct with accuracy, as witnesses, what they knew of the " parables, miracles, and sayings of Christ," may have done so, unless the Holy Spirit's aid dispensed with ordinary means, from records made in the life-time of Christ; and that as they then knew no language but their own native Syriac tongue, these records must have been made in Syriac. (Introduction, pp. 2, 3, 4.)

Of MATTHEW, F. Nairon says, and correctly, that "all the ancients bear witness that he wrote his Gospel in Syriac." (pp. 3, 4.) He states also that Theophilact says the apostle John translated it into Greek. He notices the singular fact that Matthew does not record the ascension of Christ to heaven, and he draws from this the conclusion that the gospel was completed before that event took place. (p. 6)

Of JOHN's GOSPEL, F. Nairon says that Alexander, (who was bishop of Rome about A.D 109 to 119), stated that John opposed and confuted the error of Cerinthus, who in Jerusalem, Cæsarea, and Antioch, denied the Deity of Christ. F. Nairon says, that for this purpose John's Gospel must have been first written in Syriac. He says that Cerinthus afterwards went into Asia Minor. Irenæus, who died about A.D. 200, says that John "published a Gospel while he dwelt at Ephesus, in Asia." (Lardner's Credibility, bk. i. ch. xvii.) F. Nairon suggests that this may mean that John, to meet the error of Cerinthus there, re-issued his Gospel, and in Greek. He says that John, like Matthew, does not mention the ascension, and that this implies that his Gospel was written before it took place. He says also, that the Syriac modes of speech in John's Greek Gospel, imply that it was first written in Syriac. (p. 4.)

Of MARK, F. Nairon says that he preached the gospel in many regions, and that some writers say that he wrote his Gospel in *three languages* ; Greek, Latin, and Syriac. (p. 5.)

OF THE GOSPEL OF LUKE, F. Nairon says, that from the writings of Origen, Ambrose, Theophilact, and Epiphanius, it appears that Luke was a Syrian from Antioch, and sent his Gospel first to his own countrymen in Antioch, to oppose some false teachers there; that for this purpose it needed to be written in Syriac, as well as in Greek ; because, though Greek had been introduced by the Greek rulers of Antioch, it was not the common language of the citizens. He says also, that Greek was not the native language of Luke himself, but acquired by him afterwards; that this appears from the statement of Jerome, that he was "a physician of Antioch, and not ignorant of Greek." F. Nairon says, that the many Syriac idioms in Luke's Gospel show that he was a Syrian.

OF THE ACTS OF THE APOSTLES, F. Nairon says that Jerome states the book was written in Greek, but that Metaphrastes says, Luke also wrote it in the language of his own country, which was Syriac.

OF 1 JOHN, he says, that it was sent to Hebrew Christians who lived beyond the Euphrates under the rule of the Parthians, that it was anciently called, The Epistle to the Parthians, and must have been written in Syriac, the native tongue of the Hebrews there. (p. 8.)

OF HEBREWS, JAMES, and 1 PETER, F. Nairon makes no special mention ; but his remark, that all the epistles must " of necessity have been written in the languages of those to whom they were sent, or they could not have been understood by them," applies specially to these epistles ; for their contents prove that they were written to Hebrew Christians, and their native language, as F. Nairon says, was Syriac. (p. 9.)

OF THE EPISTLES OF PAUL, he says, that to them, as well as to all the epistles, the rule must be applied, that they must have been written in the language of those to whom they were sent. We

have Paul's letters in Greek, and we have them also in Syriac, with
abundant evidence that they were written in Syriac in the time of
the apostles. From what Peter says of Paul's Epistles, it seems
probable that they were circulated among Hebrew Christians in
Syriac, very soon after they were written. Syriac was the only
language, as we have found, which was *generally*, and well understood by all the Hebrews. Yet Peter, writing to the dispersed
Hebrew Christians of Asia Minor, speaks of *all* " Paul's Epistles,
as if well known among them, and not only those which Paul had
written " to them." (2 Pet. iii. 15, 16.) This reference to " *all* his
Epistles," seems to imply that those which he had written in Greek
were well known to Hebrews who knew little of any language but
Syriac ; and tends, by its agreement with the Syrian testimony, to
show that *all the letters of Paul in the Peshito*, were written in Syriac
in the time of the Apostles.

F. Nairon says in proof that THE PESHITO, AS A WHOLE, IS
NOT A MERE TRANSLATION OF THE GREEK COPIES, that the *number*
of books in it is different from that of the Greek text, which has
2 Peter, 2 and 3 John, Jude, and Revelation. That the *order* of
books is also different from their order in most Greek copies ; for
James, 1 Peter, and 1 John, follow the Acts ; and that the Greek
text has passages which the Peshito has not.

He says that Luke xxii. 17, 18, is not in most copies of the
Peshito. " And he took the cup, and gave thanks, and said, Take
this, and divide it among yourselves; for I say unto you, I will
not drink of the fruit of the vine, until the kingdom of God shall
come." Bishop Walton says, " These verses are not found in the
Vienna manuscript, nor in the one which we have mostly used."
They are placed in brackets by Dr. Lee, 1816, and in the Ooroomiah edition, to show, apparently, that they were not in the copies
followed.

The account of the adulteress, John viii. 1—11, which is in many
Greek copies, is absent from most of those of the Peshito. Bishop
Walton printed it in Syriac from a copy in the library of
Archbishop Usher, but said that it was absent from all preceding
printed editions. In Dr. Lee's edition, and that of Ooroomiah,
lines are placed across the page at the beginning and end of the
passage, with evident intention to show its absence from the copies
followed.

Acts xxviii. 29 : " And when he had said these words, the
Jews departed, and had great reasoning among themselves," is not
in the Peshito.

Nor is 1 John v. 7 : " There are three who bear witness in heaven,
the Father, the Word, and the Holy Spirit, and these three are
one."   F. Nairon remarks that this verse is quoted by Cyprian,
(bishop of Carthage, 247—258), when writing on the unity of the
the Church, and that this was before Arius was born. (See the

edition of Cyprian's work by Le Preuse, 1593, p. 297.) Cyprian says, "Respecting the Father, and Son, and Holy Spirit, it is written, And these three are one." F. Nairon suggests that this verse was probably added to the epistle when published in Greek, with view to meet more fully the denial of the Deity of Christ by Cerinthus; and that its appearance in the Greek text, though absent from the Syriac, tends to show that the epistle "was first written by John in Syriac." (Nairon, p. 8.)

F. NAIRON's belief that A RECORD WAS MADE IN SYRIAC by Matthew, Mark, Luke, or John, of events in the Saviour's history, DURING HIS LIFE-TIME, receives some support from the contents of the first three Gospels. It has been observed, that there are passages in some of the Greek copies of these three Gospels, which are in *exactly the same words* as passages in others. Bishop Herbert Marsh, in his translation of the Introduction of J. D. Michaelis, vol. iii. pp. 160—409, prints an elaborate treatise on the origin of the first three Gospels, and gives in Greek many instances of these identical Greek passages. He says that it is "wholly impossible" that these three historians, if they had no connexion with each other, should have written *in Greek*, passages so identical, (p. 168); and that "we are reduced to this dilemma, Either the succeeding Evangelists copied from the preceding, or that all the three drew from a common source." (p. 170.) After examining various attempts made by others to account for this identity of Greek words, he comes to the conclusion that internal proofs show that these three writers did not copy words one from another. (pp. 320—330.) At p. 361, he says that the verbal agreements and disagreements of these three Gospels, can be solved in a manner which is perfectly consistent with the inspiration of the Greek Gospels, by admitting that "all three writers used copies of *a common Hebrew*," that is, *a Syriac "document."*

STEPHEN EVOD ASSEMAN, Archbishop of Apamea, a third Syrian of the name of Asseman, in answer to an inquiry made by Dr. Glocester Ridley, who published a work on the Peshito in 1761, said,—"The first [Syriac] version of the N. T., is called the Peshito; the Syrians believe that its translation of the Gospels was made either by the Apostles themselves, or at least by the Apostle Thaddæus; that the Acts and Epistles were made by Apostolic men, and that Ephraem, and other fathers, who flourished in the third and fourth centuries, used that version." (Wichelhaus, p. 68.) Dr. N. Lardner defines the meaning of "apostolical men," to be "disciples of the Apostles, intimately acquainted with them," (Credibility, book i., chap. xxii. p. 536); men like "Mark and Luke, companions of the Apostles." (chap. xxvii. p. 576.) Such men could obtain from the apostles their correction of and authority for what they wrote.

TRANSLATIONS MADE FROM THE PESHITO FOR CHRISTIAN BODIES are themselves testimonies that its authority was deemed as great as,

or greater than that of the Greek text.   F. Nairon, in the Introduction already named, refers, as Bishop Walton has done also, to
a Syrian Commentator on Psalm xix., who asserts, in reference to
the "New Covenant," that "though the Armenians translated
from the Greek, they afterwards compared their copy with the
Syriac, and made it agree with the Syriac in particular places."
(p. 9.) An Arabic version in part, and a Persian version, were made
from the Peshito. (Wichelhaus, p. 214, also p. 152.)

In the above testimonies, NO ELEMENT IS WANTING OF PROOF
HELD TO BE DECISIVE, that a book is what it is said to be. They
give, by their universal and continuous harmony, from very early
to the present time, proof that the Peshito had its origin in the
time of the Apostles, and was made under their care.   They fully
satisfy the rule of Bishop Huet.   They equally satisfy the rule laid
down by Dr. Westcott in his book on the Canon.   They are testimonies respecting the belief of large Christian bodies ; a belief
attested by the treatment of the book as "sacred," and as a Divine
Rule of faith and practice.   The Peshito is a witness, such as the
utmost efforts have failed to find in Greek copies of early date.
Vain, as yet, has been every attempt, by means of Greek copies,
to give a text which is proved to be "brought back to the condition in which it stood in the sacred autographs." (Scrivener, Int.
pp. 6, 520.) But the Peshito, in the opinion of Wichelhaus, who
has studied it and its history with the greatest care, possesses a
Syriac text so ancient and so well preserved, that even if it were
due only to a human translator, it would be proved to represent,
with a few exceptions, a Greek text "most like to the autographs
of the apostles." (Wichelhaus, p. 264.) Canon Cook also, the
Editor of the Speaker's Commentary, says that the Syriac Peshito,
is the version which probably *comes nearest to the autographs* of the
Evangelists, especially in Matthew;" and that to it, and some
other authorities, "a higher value is to be assigned in some
cases," than to any Greek copies, because this version is "*more
ancient*, and *better attested* than any manuscripts." (First Three
Gospels, p. 143.)

VI. INTERNAL EVIDENCE THAT THE PESHITO WAS MADE IN
CENT. I., AND IS NOT A MERE TRANSLATION OF THE GREEK.

JESUDAD said that the N. C. Peshito is "a translation made by
the care and solicitude of Thaddæus and other Apostles."   Books
written, as the Gospel of Matthew was, in the Syriac of Palestine,
needed very little change when translated into the Syriac of Edessa.
Paul's letter to the Hebrews, the letter of James, the first of Peter,
and the first of John, were all addressed to Hebrews, and probably,
therefore, were first written in Syriac, the language of the Hebrews;

and needed but few changes when translated into the dialect of
Edessa. These few changes were probably what Jesudad called a
"translation," so far as the word had reference to these books.
The Apostles, when taking the care and oversight of the translation
of all the books in the Peshito, were not bound as an uninspired
translator would have been, to follow always the exact words of
what was translated. They had divine authority to use whatever
difference of expression the Holy Spirit might guide them to adopt,
as better fitted for use in the translation.

If, therefore, in comparing the Syriac with the Greek text, we
find that they both express nearly the same *meaning*, but that in
places a supposed Greek original so differs *in words* from the Syriac,
that if the Syriac had been made by an uninspired translator, he
would be justly condemned for licentious departure from his Greek
copy, the reason may be, that the inspired translator has been
divinely guided to make that difference; and if, in some of these
cases of different wording, the Syriac meaning be more clear, or
exact, or better adapted for Syrian readers than the Greek wording
is, those very differences become evidence of the correctness of
the Syrian belief that the Peshito was made " by the care and
solicitude of Apostles." For it is evident that an uninspired
translator could not, as a rule, bring light out of darkness, clearness out of obscurity, exactness and correctness out of ambiguity
and uncertainty. Persons familiar with the Peshito admit the
truth of Faust Nairon's remark, that the Peshito does really sometimes "make clear, things difficult or doubtful in the Greek."
(Introduction, p. 9.)

Bishop Walton quotes with approval the remark of De Dieu,
that "the true meaning of phrases which often occur in the N. T.,
can scarcely be sought from any other source than the Syriac.
(Polyg. Prol. xiii. 19.)

J. D. Michaelis says, "the Syriac Version leads us sometimes
to just and beautiful explanations, where other help is insufficient."
(Marsh's Michaelis, vol. ii. p. 44.)

WICHELHAUS REJECTS THE SYRIAN TESTIMONY that the Peshito
was made by "the care of Apostles," and gives this reason for
doing so,—that it "does not in all things express and religiously
follow the Greek text;" (p. 259.) But these differences, according
to Syrian testimony, are differences made BY SOME OF THE APOSTLES
THEMSELVES, in writing or revising the same things in two
different languages. If, in some places, the expressions in the
Syriac are more exact, and make the meaning more clear, than
the Greek does, the fact that they differ from the Greek more than
a faithful translator from the Greek would have dared to differ,
favours the Syrian belief that they are due to that apostolic
authority which had a right to vary the mode of verbal expression,
where this was thought to be desirable, in a different language.

The following are specimens of those differences which Wichelhaus mentions, and which, as he contends, *compel* the conclusion
that the Syrian belief which has existed from the first ages till
now, is a complete delusion. The reader will probably think that,
instead of proving this, there is nothing in them which is inconsistent with that belief.

The passages which ARE NOT IN THE SYRIAC, are not on that
account to be deemed of doubtful authority ; for if they are well
sustained by Greek copies, that is evidence that they were afterwards added by Apostolic authority. Dr. Scrivener says that some
various readings are probably due to additions made by the sacred
writers themselves to some copies of their writings after these were
first issued. He says, '' It may be reasonably thought that a portion
of the variations [in ancient copies], and those among the most
considerable, had their origin in a cause which must have operated
at least as much in ancient as in modern times, the changes
gradually introduced after publication, *by the authors themselves*,
into the various copies yet within their reach. Such revised copies
would circulate independently of those issued previously, and now
beyond the writer's control, and thus, becoming the parents of a
new family of copies, would originate and keep up diversities from
the first edition, without any fault on the part of transcribers.''
(Intro., p. 18.)

In MATTHEW, six differences named by Wichelhaus as proof of
bad translation, are certainly not so. They are cases in which the
common Greek text is admitted to be corrupt, and the Revisers of
the E. V. have followed the Peshito readings. They are v. 27 ;
ix. 13 ; xxii. 44 ; xxvi. 9, 60 ; xxviii. 9. In xiv. 24 also, some
Greek copies have, as the Peshito has, '' many furlongs distant
from the land,'' instead of, '' now in the midst of the sea ;'' so
that it is doubtful whether the true Greek text differs from the
Syriac there. In vii. 14, the Syr. has, how narrow ; the Gk. has,
for narrow. In x. 10, Syr., staff ; Gk., some copies, staves ; some,
staff. xiii. 18, Syr., seed ; Gk., sower. xiv. 13., Syr., on dry land;
Gk., on foot. xvi. 27, Syr., holy angels ; Gk., angels. xxi. 34,
Syr., that they should send ; Gk., to receive. xxii. 23, Syr., the
Sadducees were saying ; Gk., the Sadduces who say. xxii. 37,
Syr., and with all thy might ; Gk. has it not. xxvii. 9, Syr.,
by means of the prophet ; Gk., by means of the prophet Jeremiah.
An error, for the words are in Zech. xi. 12, 13. In Matt. xxvii.
60, Syr., was hewn ; they rolled, placed, departed ; Gk., he had
hewn ; he rolled, and departed. xxviii. 18, Syr., And as my
Father sent me, so I send you ; Gk. has it not.

In LUKE, ix. 34, Syr., And they feared when they saw that
Moses and Elijah entered the cloud ; Gk., and they feared when
those, (some copies have, when they) entered the cloud.

In JOHN, vii. 39, the Syr. has, The Spirit was not yet given ; the Gk., The Spirit was not yet. In viii. 1—11, the Syr. has not the account of the adulteress. In the Gk., some copies are without it; but others have it. It probably is due to an addition made by John himself after his Greek Gospel was first issued. (See the remark of Dr. Scrivener, quoted p. xlviii, from his Introduction, p. 18.) It has in itself strong evidence of Apostolic origin.

In ACTS, iii. 21, Syr., until the completion of the times of all those things of which God has spoken ; Gk., until the times of the restoration of all things, of which God has spoken. v. 37, Syr., in the days in which men were enrolled for the head-tax ; Gk., in the days of the enrolment. x. 22, Syr., in a vision by a holy angel ; Gk., by a holy angel. xii. 1, Syr., Herod the king, who is surnamed Agrippa ; Gk., Herod the king. xii. 10, Syr., the iron gate ; Gk., the iron gate which leads into the city. xiii. 13, Syr., Paul and Barnabas ; Gk., those around Paul. xvii. 19, Syr., to the house of judgment which is called Areopagus ; Gk., to the Areopagus. xviii. 5, Syr., was restricted in speech ; some Gk. copies have, was pressed in spirit ; others, was hindered in word ; rendered in R. E. V., was constrained by the word. xviii. 7, Syr., Titus ; Gk., Justus. xx. 4, Syr., Timothy, who was of Lystra ; Gk., Timothy. xxviii. 13, Syr., Puteoli, a city of Italy ; Gk., Puteoli. xxviii. 29, Syr., nothing ; Gk., some copies, And when he had said these words, the Jews departed, and had great reasoning among themselves. Other Gk. copies, and R. E. V., have nothing.

In ROMANS i. 1, Syr., Paul, called, and a Chief Messenger. The Gk. has not the word and. The Gk. meaning is uncertain. The Common and Revised E. Vs. have, called [to be] an Apostle ; but the Gk. may be rendered, One called, an Apostle. v. 9, Syr., how much more shall we now be declared just ; Gk., how much more, having now been declared just. xv. 6, Syr., God the Father ; Gk., the God and Father. So also in 2 Cor. i. 3 ; Eph. i. 3 ; 1 Pet. i. 3.

In 1 Cor. vii. 35, Syr., but that ye may be faithful to your Lord in a comely manner, not setting thought on the world ; Gk., but for what is comely and serviceable to the Lord, without interruption. x. 2, Syr., were immersed by means of Moses ; Gk., were immersed into Moses.

In PHILIPPIANS, ii. 13, Syr., to will and to do that which ye wish ; Gk., to will and to do on behalf of [his] good pleasure. ii. 15, Syr., pure sons of God, who dwell among ; Gk., children of God without blemish, in the midst of.

2 Thess. 1. 7, Syr., with the power of his angels ; Gk., with the angels of his power.

1 Tim. ii. 15, Syr., but she is to have life [-bliss] by means of her children, if they, [the women], etc. Gk., but she will be saved by means of the bearing of children, if they, [the women], etc.

D

In HEBREWS, ii. 6, Syr., the Scripture; Gk., one somewhere. vi. 2, Syr., the teaching of immersion; Gk., the teaching of immersions. vi. 4, Syr., have gone down into immersion ; Gk., have been once enlightened. vii. 3, Syr., neither his father, nor his mother, was written in family records, nor the beginning of his days, nor the end of his life ; Gk., without father, without mother, without family record, having neither beginning of days, nor end of life. x. 32. Syr., in which ye received immersion ; Gk., in which, having been enlightened.

IN THE WORDS USED TO DESCRIBE CHURCH ELDERS, there is evidence that the Peshito is not a mere word-for-word translation, as some imagine, of the Greek Text. The Syrians sometimes used the Greek word *episcopos*, in the form of *episcope*. It is used in Acts xx. 28, ''The church—the assembly, over which the Holy Spirit has made you *overseers* ;'' for overseer is the meaning of *episcopos*, anglicised in the word bishop. But in 1 Tim. iii. 1. where the Greek has '' the office of overseer,'' the Peshito has, '' the office of elder.'' In verse 2, the Greek has overseer; the Peshito, elder. In Phil. i. 1, the Greek has, overseers, the Peshito, elders. In Titus i. 7, the Greek has overseer, the Peshito, elder. In 1 Pet. ii. 25, the Greek has overseer, the Peshito, care-taker. So that the difference of the words used for the same office in all these cases but one, shows that the Greek was not a mere translation of the Syriac.

IN THE NAMES OF PLACES, the Peshito shows the same independence of the Greek. In Matt. iv. 13, the Gk. has Capernaum ; the Syr. has, The village of Nahum. In John iii. 23, the Gk. has, Ænon ; the Syr. has, The Fountain of the Dove. In John xix. 38, the Gk. has Arimathea ; the Syr. has, Romtho ; in Acts xxi. 7, the Gk. has, Ptolemais ; the Syriac has, Acu.

Mr. Jer. Jones, in his work on the Canon, 1798, contends that the use of the name ACU, for Ptolemais, is a decisive proof that the Peshito must have been made not far in time from A.D. 70, when Jerusalem was destroyed. (vol. i. p. 103.) He says that the most ancient name of this place among the Israelites was Aco, or Acco, Judges i. 31 ; that this name was afterwards changed to Ptolemais; that some say it had its new name from Ptolemy Philadelphus, about 250 B.C. He says it is certain that the old name Aco, was antiquated and out of use in the time of the Romans, and that the use of the old name Acu, in the Peshito, can be accounted for in no other way, but by supposing that the persons for whom the version was made were more acquainted with it, than with the new name Ptolemais; that upon any other supposition it would have been absurd for him to have used Acu. He says, that until the destruction of Jerusalem, one may suppose that the Jews may have retained the old name Aco still, out of fondness for its antiquity ; but, he says, '' how they, or any other part of Syria, could, after the Roman conquest, call it by a name different from the Romans, seems to me impossible to conceive. . . To suppose, therefore, that this translation, in which we meet with this old name, instead of the new one, was made at any great distance of time after the destruction of Jerusalem, is to suppose the translator to have substituted an antiquated name known to but few, for a name well known to all." (pp. 104, 105.)

Mr. Jones says that a similar proof that the Peshito cannot have been made much after A.D. 70, is found in the fact that the Peshito often calls the Gentiles, as the Jews were accustomed to do, *profane persons*, where the Greek calls them *the nations*, that is, the Gentiles. The Peshito calls them profane, in Matt. vi. 7; x. 5; xviii. 17; Mark vii. 26; John vii. 35; Acts xviii. 4, 17; 1 Cor. v. 1; x. 20, 27; xii. 2; 1 Pet. iv. 3. The expression is used, therefore, throughout the Peshito. Mr. Jones says, that it shows that the writer was a Jew, for no other person would have called all the world profane; and that after the destruction of the temple, all Hebrew Christians must have seen that other nations were not to be reckoned unclean and profane in the Jewish sense, and that therefore this version must have been made either before, or soon after, A.D. 70. (On Canon, Vol. i., pp. 106—110.)

It must be admitted, I think, that the above differences are not inconsistent with the proof given by Syrian testimony that "the Peshito was written by Apostolic authority." (Wichelhaus, p. 153.) Those differences seem to indicate that the Apostles, who had authority to deviate from their own words in one language, when writing or revising copies in another, did so deviate with respect to the Peshito text, and the Greek text. And it is evident that Wichelhaus and others, not only reject the evidence on which we must rely in order to know the true origin of the Peshito, but also create for themselves a difficulty which they do not solve; namely, that an uninspired translator, whom they praise for his great general exactness, has to be accused by them of practising, in some places, a "licentious" freedom of which no mere translator, if faithful, can be supposed to have been guilty.

VII. CHARACTERISTIC DIFFERENCES BETWEEN THE PESHITO-SYRIAC AND THE GREEK.

The following passages, as well as the preceding, tend to illustrate differences between the Syriac and the Greek. In some of them, it will probably be thought that the Syriac has the truer meaning, or expresses the true meaning more clearly than the Greek does. The translation of the Greek is that of the Revised E. Version, the marginal readings of which imply some obscurity or ambiguity in the Greek text.

The Peshito-Syriac. | The Greek.

The Peshito-Syriac.	The Greek.
Heb. v. 7. Also when he was clothed with flesh, he offered up prayer. . . . to him who was able to bring him to life from death.	Who, in the days of his flesh, having offered up prayers . . . . unto him that was able to save him from death. Margin, or out of death.
VI. 2. The teaching of immersion.	The teaching of baptisms. Margin, or, washings.
IX. 28. The Anointed was offered up once, and in himself he slew the sins of many; and the second time he is to appear without the sins, etc.	Christ, having been once offered, to bear the sins of many, shall appear a second time, apart from sin, etc.
X. 5. But with a body thou hast clothed me.	But a body didst thou prepare for me.
X. 12. This [Priest] offered up one slain offering on behalf of sins, and sat down at the right hand of God for ever.	He, when he had offered one sacrifice for sins for ever, sat down on the right hand of God. Margin, or, for ever sat down.
X. 38. He who is righteous will have life [-bliss] through trust in me.	My righteous one shall live by faith. Margin, Some ancient authorities read, The righteous one.
XI. 1. Trust is persuasion about things hoped for, as if they were things done; and it is a revealing of those things which are not seen.	Faith is the assurance of [things] hoped for, the proving of things not seen. Margin, assurance of, or, the giving substance to. Proving, or test.
XI. 12. Abraham, who was incapable from age.	As good as dead.
James I. 18. The Father of lights willed, and begat us by the word of truth.	The Father of lights, of his own will, brought us forth by the word of truth. [An incredible statement. The falseness of it is self-evident. W.N.]
II. 10. He who sins in one thing is condemned by the whole law.	Whosoever shall stumble in one point, he is become guilty of all.
II. 13. Ye are to be exalted by mercy above condemning judgment.	Mercy glorieth against judgment.
III. 6. The tongue is a fire, and the world of sin is like a wood; and the tongue being itself in the midst of our members, blackens our whole body.	The tongue is a fire; the world of iniquity among our members is the tongue, which defileth the whole body. Margin. Or, a fire, that world of iniquity: the tongue is among our members that which, etc. Or, that world of iniquity, the tongue, is among our members that which, etc.
IV. 5. Or think you that the Scripture has said without reason, that the spirit which dwells in us, covets eagerly through envy?	Or, think ye that the Scripture speaketh in vain? Doth the spirit, which he made to dwell in us, long unto envying? Margin. Or, The Scripture saith in vain, the spirit which he made to dwell in us, he yearneth for, even unto jealous envy? Or, That spirit which he made to dwell in us, yearneth [for us], even unto jealous envy? Or, instead of, he made to dwell, some ancient authorities read, dwelleth in us.
V. 11. Ye have seen the ending which the Lord worked out for Job.	Ye have seen the end of the Lord.

The Peshito-Syriac.

1 Pet. ii. 24. And he bore our sins, all of them, and carried them up in his body to the cross, that we might be dead to sin, and have life [-bliss] by his righteousness.

III. 20, 21. Into which [ark] only eight persons entered, and were kept alive by the waters. In likeness to which example, ye also have life[-bliss]through immersion, (not when ye wash the body from filth, but when ye profess God with a pure conscience,) etc.

V. 2. Take care [of the flock] spiritually.

1 John iii. 1. Who has called us sons, and has also made us sons.

The Greek.

Who his own self, bare our sins in his body upon the tree, that we, having died unto sins, might live unto righteousness. Margin. Or, carried up our sins to the tree.

Wherein few, that is eight souls, were saved through water; which also, after a true likeness, doth now save you, [even] baptism, not the putting away of the filth of the flesh, but the interrogation of a good conscience toward God, etc. Margin. Were saved, or, were brought safely through water. Interrogation, or inquiry, or appeal.

Exercising the oversight.

That we should be called children of God.

The different translations given by the Revisers, show how unable they were to decide what is the right meaning of the Greek in some of the above passages. The different meanings given, leave the reader in utter uncertainty as to what the right meaning is. The meanings given by the Peshito are not only clear, but most of them have the appearance of being also correct.

VIII. THE RESULT OF TRUSTING CHIEFLY TO CERTAIN FAULTY GREEK COPIES, AND SLIGHTING THE PESHITO-SYRIAC.

The Greek copies, from having been less carefully written than those of the Peshito, abound with various readings, some of which make the meaning of important passages uncertain. The result is, that the infallible teaching of those parts of Scripture is said to be destroyed.

Dr. PHILIP SCHAFF, who was President of the American committee which took part in preparing the Revised English Version of 1881, says in his Companion to it, 1883, that, as "most of the variations" of the Greek text "date from early transcription in the first two centuries, AN INFALLIBLE TEXT IS IMPOSSIBLE." (p. 420.) He says this, as one who believes that the Scriptures were given to be an "Infallible Guide in all matters of Christian faith and duty." (p. 494.)

Dr. SCRIVENER suggests, that in the 2094 Greek manuscripts now known, the variations may amount to more than 100,000. Comparatively few of them affect the meaning of Scripture on points of great importance. But a sufficient number of them do so, to afford those who undermine the authority of Scripture, some seeming reason for saying that if Divine guidance made it infallible at first, it has ceased to be so now. The aim of Biblical critics has been, as Dr. Scrivener says, "to bring back the Greek text to the condition in which it stood in the sacred autographs, by separating the pure gold of God's word, from the dross which has mingled with it through the accretions of so many centuries." (Introduction, 1883, p. 5.)

Dr. SCRIVENER admits, that notwithstanding the greatness of past efforts, difficulties still "defy all our skill and industry to detect and estimate aright." (P. 520.) All these difficulties arise, either from wilful alterations, or from THE WANT OF EXACT COPYING, especially in the second century. Hence the extreme value of copies of the Peshito, which are proved to have been made with the greatest care and exactness from the first. This proof exists in the marvellous agreement of all early copies, wheresoever and by whomsoever made.

As DR. SCHAFF says, to restore infallibility to the Greek text, in doubtful places, BY MEANS OF GREEK COPIES, SEEMS TO BE "IMPOSSIBLE." The only hope of knowing, in such places, what is true, and what is false, seems to arise from the exactness of the Peshito copies. Even the penmanship of some specimens of these, as given by Professor Adler, is of great exactness and beauty ; and the Rev. D. T. Stoddard, an American missionary at Ooroomiah, in Persia, says of the Nestorian copies, " They are sometimes very beautifully written, and the best type can never exceed, and perhaps not even rival them in elegance." (Grammar of Modern Syriac, p. 21.) This is no slight proof of the care with which they have been written.

Dr. SCRIVENER says, " The Peshito-Syriac has not yet received that critical care on the part of *editors* which its antiquity and importance so urgently demand," and " with such full means of information within our reach, it will not be to our credit if a good critical edition of the Peshito be much longer unattempted. (pp. 317-8.) But though a good critical edition is much to be desired, there is far greater need of readiness on the part of Biblical critics, to give to the Peshito the attention due to it, and the influence which it ought to exercise. No great changes are to be expected from a new critical edition, though such an edition is so much to be desired.

The Rev. G. H. GWILLIAM, M.A., of Oxford University, will, it is to be hoped, be enabled to complete his new critical edition of the Gospels of the Peshito, "based on a number of copies of very great antiquity, and high critical value." (Studia Biblica, 1885, pp. 153-4.) He has kindly told us in advance, that in this new edition, "A certain number of corrections will be made, but that these, for the most part, will be in comparatively unimportant points of grammar and orthography." (Same, p. 161.)

Most critics of the Greek text have been TOO INDIFFERENT TO THE TESTIMONY OF RELIGIOUS BODIES, in reference to Greek manuscripts. They have trusted too much to copies which have no known support from the approval of any such societies. The result is, that instead of establishing a Greek text upon a sound historical basis, they have given us the result of *theories*, of *speculations founded on probabilities*, and on a comparison of copies which, as Dr. Scrivener says, " are *perpetually at variance with each other*," and " *scarcely ever in unison*," (Introd., p. 523.) These copies have been unreasonably supposed to be of supreme authority, because *the substance on which they are written* has survived that of other copies more in use, and has brought them down from times when Greek manuscripts, instead of being pure, were full of the errors, both of those, and of preceding centuries.

The lamentable result is, that by the latest Greek Text, Drs. Westcott and Hort seem to have done more harm than any earlier Greek editors, by the selection of wrong readings, and by corrupting still more a text which they profess to improve. The statement of Dean Burgon may, with apparent reason, be regarded as lamentably true, that this text is " the most depraved which has ever appeared in print." (Revision Revised, 1883, p. xxx.)

THE GREEK COPIES CALLED ALEPH AND B, are those on which Drs. Westcott and Hort chiefly rely. They say that the readings of these " should be accepted as the TRUE READINGS, until strong internal evidence is found to the contrary." Yet, as Dean Burgon has said, these copies " have come to us without a character, without a history, without antecedents of *any* kind," (p. 14); except, indeed, such antecedents as Canon Cook, in his " First Three Gospels, (1882)," has shown to be almost ascertained facts. He has shown it to be in the highest degree probable, that these Greek copies were made when Arianism was in high favour, and under the superintendence of Eusebius of Cæsarea, whom Jerome calls " The standard-bearer of the Arian faction." (Cook, pp. 151, 164, 183.) Canon Cook says that the omissions and corruptions of these two Greek copies are " logically incompatible with an entire faith in the Saviour's proper and true Divinity." (p. 177.) He says also, that these two oldest manuscripts, Aleph and B, " are responsible for nearly every change which weakens or perverts the record of sayings and incidents in our Lord's life." (p. 142.) Among these changes Canon Cook mentions the following. Drs. Westcott and Hort omit the leading point in the title of Mark's Gospel, " ' Son of God,' an act of singular temerity." (p. 35.) They reject, as a forged addition, the account of our Lord's bloody sweat in Gethsemane ; Luke xxii. 44. They omit the doxology in the Lord's prayer, Matt. vi. 13, " For thine is the kingdom," etc. They reject the first words uttered by the Redeemer on the cross, Luke xxiii. 34, " Father forgive them, for they know not what they do." (Cook, p. 106.) They omit the last 12 verses of Mark, which Canon Cook calls a mutilation without parallel in the critical history of the New

Testament," (p. 120); and one which removes Mark's account of
the ascension, removes the only statement in the Gospels that
Christ is seated at God's right hand; removes an emphatic statement of the necessity of faith, "and the most emphatic statement
in the New Testament as to the importance of baptism." (pp. 121-2.)

The following eminent critics have endeavoured to CORRECT THE
TEXT OF THE GREEK TESTAMENT, and have published editions of
it. John Mill, 1707; John Jacob Wettstein, 1751-2; Griesbach,
1771-5; Lachmann, 1842-50; Tregelles, 1857-1879; Tischendorf,
8th ed., 1869-1872; Westcott and Hort, 1881. Most of these have
treated the Peshito-Syriac as of little importance.

Dr. JOHN MILL, 1707, is spoken of by Dr. Scrivener as having
rendered "services to Biblical criticism, which surpass in extent
and value those rendered by any other, except, perhaps, one or
two men of our time." (Intro. p. 448.) He did not know Syriac,
but he collected the readings of the Peshito, relying on translations of it, and was sometimes misled. (Wichelhaus, p. 246.)
He speaks of the Syrians as gloryifing their version too much in
saying that it was made "*by Thaddæus and other Apostles;*" but
he seems to concur with Bishop Walton and many of the learned,
in conjecturing that it was "made by *Apostolic men* in the age next
to that of the Apostles." He says that "beyond all doubt it was
used by the Syrians not long after the beginning of their church,"
which must have been begun about A.D. 35. (Prol., sec. 1237.) He
trusts to *conjecture*, and rejects *Syrian testimony.*

WETTSTEIN says, that "if you listen to some men, this version
is the most ancient of all, and made by an Apostle, or Apostolic
man. . . . This is untrue, as will appear from what I subjoin."
His proofs consist of differences between it and the Greek text.
He regards it as the work of an uninspired translator, who, instead
of always following "the Greek text closely, used licentious
liberty in substituting some things for others, and in too frequently
giving a paraphrase." (Prol., p. 109.) The insufficiency of such
reasons has been shown in the preceding section, with reference to
like objections by Wichelhaus.

GRIESBACH supposed that there had been three recensions, or
rectifications of the Greek text, one of which he calls Alexandrian,
another Western, and the third Constantinopolitan. He says of
the Syriac Version, "As printed, it is like none of these recensions,
and yet it is not wholly unlike any of them. In many things it
agrees with the Alexandrian, in more with the Western, in some
also with the Constantinopolitan. . . . It therefore seems to
have been *again and again revised* at different times, according to
very different *Greek copies.* (Prol., sec. iii. 15 pp. lxxi.-ii.) These
revisions of the Syriac are all *pure conjectures;* and he admits that
his whole Greek text "is only his *own judgment* of various readings." Wichelhaus says, "Ought not Griesbach to have distrusted

his recensions, when he found that the text of the Syriac version combined the readings of those three recensions ? a version which is held to be *older than the time when those recensions had their origin ?* But men are accustomed to distrust all things rather than their own opinion of them." (p. 240.)

LACHMANN did not know Syriac, and he asks, "Of what use would it have been to me to have learned the language of the Syrians, while the most ancient copies of the Peshito, and those worthy of trust, have not yet been classed and presented to view, in the way in which I have divided the Latin ones ?" (Pref. p. 24.) This question has for suitable answer, that those who know Syriac, have not only printed editions, but access also to ancient manuscript copies. Wichelhaus says of those who act thus, "Even those who appear to have laid up all store of learning, and to have searched all library-shelves, that nothing may adhere which is false or foreign to the text of the Bible, care not to study that version of it, which all those who are most skilled in it say is most ancient; the numerous copies of which are of wonderful age, and easily viewed, and which has been found to be *equally one and the same*, not only in printed editions, but in manuscript copies, and throughout the churches of the whole East." (p. 240.) Lachmann says of the Received Greek Text, that no learned man deems it genuine. How is it then, asks Wichelhaus, that the Ancient Syriac Version does not represent those readings which our critics call ancient, genuine, best and true, but represents the Received Greek text ? (p. 268.) "Lachmann praises what is ancient; he wishes that nothing be received which is not proved to be ancient. I wonder, therefore, why he does not think it worth while even to refer to our [Syriac] Version. If his will is to form a [Greek] text by readings from Origen, and the most ancient Greek copies ; he will not deny that if we produce as a witness the Eastern Syriac Version, we have in it documents more ancient still." (p. 268.) Wichelhaus gives cases from Luke, in which he contends that the Peshito is right, and Griesbach and Lachmann are evidently wrong. (pp. 268-9.)

Dr. TREGELLES is more daring still. He makes a statement which Syriac copies prove to be utterly groundless, namely, that "The Peshito-Syriac was frequently modernized from time to time." (Gk. Test. Introductory Notice, p. v.)

TISCHENDORF said in an edition of the Gk. T., dated 1858, that "The Peshito was made in the second century." Of this he gives no proof, nor have I seen any clear evidence of it given by others.

Drs. WESTCOTT and HORT assert in their Gk. T., that a foundling Syriac fragment which has no known, nor seeming connection with the Peshito, "renders its revised character *a matter of certainty.*" Dean Burgon's rebuke of this untruth has already been given at p. xxv. Dr. Scrivener says, "Of this formal transmutation of the

Curetonian Syriac into the Peshito, (for this is what Dr. Hort means, though his language is a little obscure), ... not one trace remains in the history of Christian antiquity ; no one writer seems conscious that *any modification of this translation was made in or before their times.*" (Introduction, p. 533.) On Dr. Scrivener's testimony we may fully rely.

This, then, is the state of the conflict :—These critics have ALL REJECTED the uniform Syrian testimony on a question of fact,— the very testimony on which the rules of evidence teach us to rely, as the only sure means of knowing the truth on points which we cannot ourselves investigate.   Dr. JOHN MILL "was a friend of truth," and he received the Peshito as a witness of what the Greek copy was, from which, as he supposed, it was made, and said, that except in some passages, "there could be seen in it, as a mirror, the natural face of the Greek text, from which it was formed." (Prol. sec. 1243.)   But most of the other Greek editors speak evil of the Peshito, though they give no proof of the evil; this evil-speaking is disproved by known facts.   These charges being all both unproved and disproved, the Peshito ought to be free from suspicion of being marred and mis-shapen, as it has been said to be.   Meanwhile the Syrian testimony in its favour, remains uniform and universal.   "No clear evidence is adduced against that testimony," as Bishop Walton says. (Prol. xiii. 16.)   The credit of the Peshito stands in reality all the higher, for its having passed through the ordeal of having had to meet many charges, and being untouched by any of them.   The conduct of the accusers is viewed with surprise and indignation.   The harm they thought to do it, falls on their own heads.   They are distrusted.   They are felt to be unsafe, if not even dangerous guides.

On the other hand, THE MOST ELABORATE ATTEMPTS TO RESTORE THE GREEK TEXT TO PURITY by the comparison chiefly of Greek copies, is admitted to have been hitherto a failure.   Dr. Scrivener asks, as if almost in despair, " Is it true that we are thus [by past failures] cast upon the wide ocean, without a compass or a guide ? Can no clue be found that may conduct us through the tangled maze ? Is there no other method of settling the text of the New Testament than by collecting, and marshalling, and scrutinizing the testimony of thousands of separate documents, now agreeing, now at issue with each other."   "Elaborate systems have failed, as might have been looked for from the first.   It was premature to frame them in the present stage of things."   "The delicate and important process, whereby we seek to determine the *comparative* value, and trace the mutual relation, of authorities of every kind, upon which" the attempt to restore " the original text of the N. T. is based, . . . will (as we trust) gradually develop facts which will eventually put us on the right road, although, for the present, we meet with much that is uncertain, perplexing, ambiguous." (Introduction, 1883, pp. 520-1.)

IX. TESTIMONIES FOUNDED ON KNOWLEDGE AND ESTEEM OF THE PESHITO-SYRIAC.

Bishop WALTON, 1657, had some degree, but only some degree, of reliance on Syrian testimony respecting the Peshito. He said that "much is to be yielded to the general tradition of the Eastern Churches, because no clear evidence is adduced in opposition to it, and it is sustained by internal evidence in the Peshito, which proves its great antiquity ; for 2 Peter, 2 & 3 John, Jude, and Rev. are not extant in the old issue." The real Syrian tradition is, that it was made not only in the time of the Apostles, but by *the care of Apostles* ; as that tradition is related by Jesudad. But as related by Bishop Walton, "The constant and uninterrupted tradition is, that the Peshito was made in the time of the Apostles, either by some of their *disciples*, or by *Apostolic men*." Even this version of it, implies that the *disciples*, or the *companions*, of the Apostles, would, in the time of the Apostles, submit to them what they wrote, for their correction, that it might have, as the writings of Luke and Mark have, Apostolic authority. Bishop Walton admits, that if " it were made by any of the Apostles, it would have an authority which is Divine, and equal to that of the other sacred books," and he says that therefore " he would not readily admit that it was made by any one of the Apostles." He says also, that " no one up to that time had affirmed its Divine authority ;" and yet this is the very authority which the Syrians seem to say it has. (See Chap. v., especially the words of Jesudad, and of the Indian Christians.)

The Syrians have a tradition that the Peshito was made chiefly by MARK. Bishop Walton thinks this incorrect, because "many parts of the N. T. were written after his death, which Jerome and others say took place in the eighth year of Nero," that is, in 62. (Prol. xiii. 16.)

The great utility of the Peshito, in the view of Bishop Walton, is, that Syriac was the language spoken by Christ and his Apostles, and that the meaning of many expressions which occur in the Greek N. T., can scarcely be discovered, except from the Syriac. (Prol. xiii. 19.)

JACOB MARTINI was Professor of Theology in the University of Wittenberg, and wrote a preface to the N. T. Peshito-Syriac, in which he said, " It is a version, but of all, it is the first and most ancient. . . It is a version, but made either by one of the Evangelists, or at least, of those who . . . had the Apostles themselves present, whom they could consult and hear, respecting many of the more obscure places. To this *only*, therefore, when some obscurity or difficulty occurs in Greek copies, can we safely go. This *only*, when doubt arises respecting the meaning or translation of any passage, can be consulted with safety and freedom from error. By this *only*, the Greek Text is truly illustrated, and rightly understood." (See Gutbier's Preface to his Syriac N. T., 1663, p. 26.)

J. D. MICHAELIS, in his Introduction to the N. T., 1787, chap. vii., sec. 4., says, "The Syriac Testament has been my constant study." In sec. 8., he says, "The Peshito is the very best translation of the Greek Testament that I have ever read. . . . . Of all the Syriac authors with which I am acquainted, not excepting Ephræm and Bar Hebræus, its language is the most elegant and pure. . . . It has no marks of the stiffness of a translation, but is written with the ease and fluency of an original." "What is not to be regarded as a blemish, it differs frequently from the modern modes of explanation; but I know of no version that is so free from error, and none that I consult with so much confidence in cases of difficulty and doubt. I have never met with a single instance where the Greek is so interpreted, as to betray a weakness and ignorance in the translator; and though in many other translations the original is rendered in so extraordinary a manner as almost to excite a smile, the Syriac version must be ever read with profound veneration." "The affinity of the Syriac to the dialect of Palestine is so great, as to justify, in some respects, the assertion that the Syriac translator has recorded the actions and speeches of Christ in the very language in which he spoke." "The Syriac New Testament is written in the same language [as that of Christ], but in a different dialect, . . . in the purest Mesopotamian."

The question is, whether the contents of the Peshito are inconsistent with what the Syrians state to be a known fact ; namely, that it was made in the time of the Apostles, and by the care of the Apostles. J. D. Michaelis did not give the above testimony with view to answer that question ; yet, what he says, shows that he found the Peshito to be as accurate as it would be, if made under Apostolic care. He had found "no version so free from error." He found that "this must ever be read with profound veneration." And owing to some unexplained cause, when he had "difficulty and doubt" as to the Greek, he could with "much confidence consult" the Peshito.

The Rev. JEREMIAH JONES said, "The Primitive Christians are proper judges, to determine what book is Canonical, and what is not." (On the Canon, vol. i. p. 43.) "The Greek copies, and the Syriac ones, were both esteemed the Word of God, though in different languages." (p. 103.)

Professor WICHELHAUS, 1850, dwells much on the worth of the Peshito. He calls it, "The most ancient witness, a version most accurate, untouched and untarnished, ever transcribed and preserved by the Syrians with the greatest care." (p. 236.) He did not see why, with some few exceptions, it should not be "most like to the autographs of the Apostles." (p. 264.) He said, as Dr.

G. Ridley had done, "The Peshito is older and better than all the ancient Latin versions." (p. 77.) The Common English Version is from a Greek text much like the Peshito. Wichelhaus remarks, that "the ancient Syriac version represents the Received Greek Text." (p. 268.) This is a point of deep interest to all to whom the Common English Version is dear.

He asserts that, with certain exceptions, the Peshito "is to be esteemed to be amongst the best and firmest aids for the right construction of the [Greek] text." (p. 270.)

The Rev. EZRA STILES, D.D., President of Yale College, in the United States of America, said, in an Inaugural Oration, "In Syriac, THE GREATER PART of the New Testament (I believe) was ORIGINALLY WRITTEN, and not merely translated, IN THE APOSTOLIC AGE. . . . . The Syriac Testament, therefore, is of high authority; nay, with me, of THE SAME AUTHORITY AS THE GREEK." (Appendix to Dr. Murdock's English Translation of the Peshito, New York, 1851, p. 499.)

Dr. JAMES MURDOCK, Professor of Ecclesiastical History, at New Haven, Connecticut, U. S., America, and Author of an English Translation of the Peshito, 1851, says that Dr. Ezra Stiles was not the only person who believed that " the books of the greater part of the New Testament WERE ORIGINALLY WRITTEN in Syriac." He thinks that the Peshito " may be something more than a mere translation; that it may have nearly, or quite equal authority with the Greek." (P. 500.)

DEAN JOHN W. BURGON, B.D., was the author of three articles in the Quarterly Review, which, he says, were " wrung out of me by the publication on May 17th, 1881, of the Revision of our Authorised Version of the New Testament." In compliance with much solicitation, he published them separately in 1883, under the title of "The Revision Revised." (Pref. p. ix.) He felt conscious, after the publication of his first article in October, 1881, that enough was even then on record, " to secure the ultimate rejection of the Revision of 1881," and that "in the end, it must be universally regarded as—what it most certainly is—the most astonishing, as well as the most calamitous literary blunder of the age." (Pref. pp. x.—xi.) He knew that " by demonstrating the worthlessness of the new Greek text of the Revisionists," he had proved that " the English translation of it must be incorrect." He soon found that " the Revised English, would have been in itself intolerable, even had the Greek been let alone." (p. xii.)

Dean Burgon says, " I am able to prove that this Revision of the Sacred Text is untrustworthy from beginning to end." (p. v.) " The systematic depravation of the underlying Greek, is nothing but a poisoning of the River of Life at its sacred source. Our Revisers, (with the best and purest intentions, no doubt), stand convicted of having DELIBERATELY REJECTED THE WORDS OF

INSPIRATION in every page, and of having substituted for them
fabricated readings, which the church has long since refused to
acknowledge, or else has rejected with abhorrence, and which only
survive at this time in *a little handful of documents of the most
depraved type*. . . . . The Revisers have, in fact, been the dupes of
an ingenious Theorist. . . . . If any complain that I have sometimes hit my opponents rather hard, I take leave to point out, that
. . . . when THE WORDS OF INSPIRATION ARE SERIOUSLY IM-
PERILLED, AS NOW THEY ARE, it is scarcely possible for one who
is determined effectually to preserve the Deposit in its integrity,
to hit either too straight, or too hard." (pp. vi.—viii.) " I traced
the mischief " (done by the New Greek Text of the Revisers) " home
to its true authors,—Drs. Westcott and Hort, a copy of whose
unpublished text of the [Greek] N. T., *the most vicious in existence*,
had been confidentially, and under pledges of the strictest secrecy,
placed in the hands of every member of the revising Body."
(p. xi.)

In answer to Dean Burgon, it was insinuated that he could not
disprove *the theory* of Drs. Westcott and Hort. This, he says,
compelled him to demonstrate that " in their solemn pages," there
is only " a series of *unsupported assumptions*; . . . . a tissue as
flimsy and as worthless as any spider's web." (p. xiv.)

Dean Burgon says that the Greek Text, which is commonly called
" THE RECEIVED GREEK TEXT," is confessedly, at least 1530 years
old." (p. xx.) Dr. Hort admits (see his Intro. to Gk. T., p. 92),
that " The fundamental text of late extant Greek manuscripts
generally," that is, of copies which have had *the approval of
Christian bodies*, on which bodies we have to rely, as on well-
informed and credible witnesses to the truth; he says that the text
of their " manuscripts generally, is, beyond all question, identical
with the dominant Greco-Syrian text of the second half of the
fourth century;" that is, with the text approved by both Greeks
and Syrians, from A.D. 350 to 400. Of this text the Peshito is one
member. This is the text which Dean Burgon says is 1530 years
old.

But the *theory* or *conjecture* which it has pleased Drs. Westcott
and Hort to adopt, is, that the original Greek text was VERY
DIFFERENT FROM THIS, and is contained in *a few copies* of the
fourth, or next following centuries, which are not known to have
been *approved by any large bodies* free from serious error. To
account for the fact that the text of these few copies was " generally " rejected by Greeks and Syrians, Drs. Westcott and Hort
gamble with conjecture. They cannot find history to quote, and
therefore invent fictions. Their chief fiction is, that " a *new* text "
was formed, " different from all " preceding texts, of which there
had grown up three; and that this new text was " a work of
attempted criticism, performed deliberately by editors," (Intro. to

Gk. T., p. 133) ; that there was "an authoritative revision of *Greek*
texts at Antioch, which revision was then taken as a standard for
a similar authoritative revision of *the* [*Peshito*] *Syriac* text; that the
Greek text was itself at a later time subjected to a second authoritative revision ; but that the Vulgate [Peshito] Syriac. did not
undergo any corresponding second revision." (Intro. to Gk. T.,
p. 137.)
    The invention of what is unsaid in history, under pretence of
proving the facts of history, and with respect to infallible truth, is
as rash as it is wrong. But the use made of this invention of revisions which never took place, is more rash still, for it is assumed
that the best text of Greek and Syriac copies was rejected by the
Revisers in both cases ; that the purer texts were abandoned, and
the more corrupt adopted throughout both Greek and Syrian bodies
in all following ages.   Drs. Westcott and Hort conjecture that the
leading Christians in those bodies were so weak, or so wicked, that
they preferred "acceptability" to "purity of text," and were so
"capricious," that their "new interpolations," their forged additions, "were abundant." (pp. 134-5.)   On the ground of this
slanderous assumption, they please to decide, that any reading
which is "distinctly Syrian, is to be rejected at once," (p. 163);
and that the whole line of Greek and Syriac manuscripts in which
this alleged "new" text is found, is to be rejected also. What evil
influence can possibly have so possessed and blinded minds trained
to reason rightly, that they can say what is so unreasonable ?
    On this subject Dean Burgon says :—"We are invited to make
our election between FACT and FICTION." (p. 293.) If there had
been such a revision, "we should insist that no important deviation
from such a *Textus Receptus* as *that*, would deserve to be listened to.
In other words, if Dr. Hort's theory about the origin of the *Textus
Receptus* have any foundation at all in fact, it is 'all up' with Dr.
Hort. He is absolutely nowhere." (p. 293.) But no such authoritative revision is recorded as having ever occurred. "As a mere
effort of the imagination," says Dean Burgon, "it is entitled to
no manner of consideration or respect at our hands." (p. 277.)
But if it had occurred, then, according to Dr. Hort's theory, we
should behold *on one side* the "choice representatives of the
wisdom, the piety, the learning of the Eastern Church, from A.D. 250
to A.D. 350. *On this side* sits Dr. Hort. An interval of 1532 years
separates these two parties." (P. 288.) "According to Dr. Hort,
by a strange fatality,—a most unaccountable and truly disastrous
proclivity to error,—these illustrious fathers of the church have
been at every instant *substituting the spurious for the genuine*,—a
fabricated text in place of the Evangelical verity. Miserable men !"
(p. 289.) "The self-same iniquity [was] perpetrated," Dr. Hort
supposes, in the case of the Peshito, as in the case of the Greek
text. "One solitary witness" to the true text, "Cureton's frag-

mentary Syriac, is suffered to escape,and alone remains to exhibit to mankind the outlines of primitive truth ;" a fragment which is in reality "utterly depraved." (R. R., pp. 279, 289.) "Who is it who gravely puts forth all this egregious nonsense ? It is Dr. Hort, at pp. 134, 135," of his Introduction. According to him, those primitive fathers have been the great falsifiers of Scripture, have proved the worst enemies of the Word of God. And (by the hypo- thesis), " Dr. Hort, at the end of 1532 years, aided by codex B, and his own self-evolved powers of divination, has found them out, and now holds them up to the contempt and scorn of the British public." (R. R. p. 290.)

Dean Burgon says that the admission by Drs. Westcott and Hort of " the practical identity of 99 out of 100 of our extant Greek manuscripts," with what they call " the Greco-Syrian text of the second half of the fourth century," makes the following the only question to be answered, "How is this resemblance to be accounted for ?" and he replies, " Certainly not by putting forward so violent and improbable—so irrational a conjecture as that . . . an authoritative standard text was *fabricated* at Antioch;" but by owning that in the similar text of those Greek copies of 350—400 A.D., and of the Peshito-Syriac version, and the mass of Greek manuscripts, there is probably a *"general fidelity to the inspired exemplars themselves*, from which remotely they are confessedly descended." (R. R., p. 295.)

" THE VERY LITTLE HANDFUL " of Greek copies to which Dean Burgon refers as those on which Drs. Westcott and Hort chiefly rely in opposition to all other sources of information, are those four which are called B, Aleph, C, and D. He says, it matters nothing to these editors " that all four are discovered, on careful scrutiny, to differ essentially, not only from 99 out of 100 of the whole body of other extant manuscripts, but even *from one another ;* the last circumstance being obviously fatal to their cor- porate pretensions," because it proves that "in different degrees they all exhibit a fabricated text." He says, " that when compared with *the Commonly Received Greek Text*, B and Aleph have 8972 omissions, additions, substitutions, transpositions, and modifica- tions ; that these are by no means the same in both ;" and that " these four codices, be it remembered, come to us without a character." (R. R., pp. 11, 12, 14.)

The Rev. F. C. COOK, M.A., Canon of Exeter, and Editor of the Speaker's Commentary, published in 1882, a valuable work on " The Revised Version of the First Three Gospels." He mentions the Peshito thus :—" The Peshito, an independent version, and of *the highest value.*" (p. 37.) "Occupying the highest place among ancient versions." (p. 81.) He names it as being one of the " authorities to which, in some cases, *a higher value is to be assigned, than to any manuscripts,*" because it is " more ancient, and better attested" than these. He says that it is "the version which probably comes *nearest to the autographs* of the Evangelists, especially of Matthew;" and that "It supports the old Received [Gk.] Text in the passages which he dwells upon, as of special importance." "For my own part," he says, "I do not doubt that this version is more trustworthy than manuscript B, especially as evidence against omissions. In fact, in the great majority of disputed readings, that which has its decided support, has a *prima facie* claim to *preference, if not to absolute acceptance.*" (pp. 143-4.)

His remarks on the two Greek copies, B and Aleph, which are relied on as the chief foes of the Peshito-Syriac text, are *very important.* He says that they "were certainly written at a time when Arianism was in full ascendancy; when Eusebius of Cæsarea was the most prominent and the most influential leader of that party," (p. 244); and that a "combination of facts, external and internal, appears to be incompatible with any other hypothesis, than that these two manuscripts which have furnished the Revisers of the E. V. with their new Greek text, were among those which Eusebius prepared by the order of Constantine." (p. 243.) He says that the Peshito-Syriac Version "must surely be regarded as *the most trustworthy witness* to the state of the text, as received from the beginning in Palestine, and all the adjoining districts; that it gives us distinct intimation of the existence of words, clauses, entire sentences, which are obliterated or mutilated in those two manuscripts;" and he asks whether "we can hesitate as to which testimony has THE BEST, THE ONLY RIGHTFUL CLAIM TO ACCEPTANCE?" (p. 245.)

Of B, Aleph, C and D, Canon Cook speaks as Dean Burgon does. He confirms "the charges of corruption and depravation made against B, Aleph, C and L," (p. 229); and says that D is, "of all manuscripts, the least trustworthy." (p. 214.)

Of B and Aleph he says, "I hold it as *all but certain* that they were written at Cæsarea, between 330 and 340 A.D., under the direction of Eusebius," (p. 245); whom Jerome called "the standard-bearer of the Arian faction." (p. 166, note.) He says that the Greek Text followed by the Revisers, as well as by Drs. Westcott and Hort, is "virtually identical with B." (pp. 133, 149.)

Manuscript A differs in character from the rest of "the oldest five Greek manuscripts; Aleph, A, B, C and D." (Dr. Scrivener's Intro. 523.) "Manuscript A is the representative," says Canon Cook, "according to Westcott and Hort, of their [imaginary] Syriac recension. It actually represents the text which was adopted and used, without the slightest indication of doubt, by the great divines, the masters of early Christian thought in the fourth century," (p. 217); it is the text "generally followed" in the later manuscripts, "especially in those which appear to have been the chief authorities for what is called the *Textus Receptus,* which, as Dr. Scrivener and others have shown, is the foundation of our Authorised Version." (P. 133.)

Canon Cook says of the general mass of Greek manuscripts, which many critics despise, that " they ought not to be disregarded on the mere score of inferior antiquity. Because they record *the tradition of the churches* for some ten or twelve centuries, and, as Dr. Hort admits, represent the fathers of the fourth century, including Chrysostom, and those who lived after him." (P. 228.)

The testimony of Canon Cook, therefore, to the value of the Peshito-Syriac, is *very strong* ; and he represents that testimony, as others do, to be in harmony with the Greek copy called A, with the text approved by early Greek writers, with the text of the mass of Greek copies, and with that followed in the Common English Version ; and also as being opposed to that of Drs. Westcott and Hort, and of the Revised E. V.

Dr. Scrivener, Prebendary of Exeter, is said by Dean Burgon to be " *facile princeps*, without question first, in Textual Criticism." (R. Rd. vii.) He is also named by Canon Cook as " that most cautious and judicious critic, the very foremost among those who in England combine reverence for God's Word with the most thorough appreciation of every point bearing upon the criticism of the New Testament." (On R. Vn. p. 120.)

Dr. Scrivener says in his Plain Introduction, pp. 312, 313, " The grievous divisions of the Syrian Christians have now subsisted for fourteen hundred years, and though the bitterness of controversy has abated, the estrangement of the rival churches is as complete and hopeless as ever. Yet the same translation of Holy Scripture is read alike in the public assemblies of the Nestorians among the fastnesses of Coordistan, of the Monophysites who are scattered over the plains of Syria, of the Christians of St. Thomas, along the coast of Malabar, and of the Maronites on the mountain-terraces of Lebanon. Even though the Maronites acknowledged the supremacy of Rome in the twelfth century, and certain Nestorians of Chaldæa [did so] in the eighteenth, both societies claimed at the time, and enjoy to this day, the free use of their Syriac translation of Holy Scripture. Manuscripts too, obtained from each of these rival communions, ... *all exhibit a text in every important respect the same.*"

Dr. Scrivener says that " The mere fact that the Syriac manuscripts of the rival sects, whether modern, or as old as the seventh century, agree with each other, and with the citations from [the Syriac Gospels by] Aphraates, A.D. 337-45, in most important points, seems to bring the Peshito text, SUBSTANTIALLY IN THE SAME STATE AS WE HAVE IT AT PRESENT, UP TO THE FOURTH CENTURY OF OUR ERA. . . . Of this version there are many codices, of different ages, and widely diffused. Of the Curetonian but one."

" Adler (p. 3) describes a copy of the Peshito in the Vatican, dated,

A.D. 548. From the Peshito, as the authorised version of the Oriental church, there are many quotations in Syriac books, from *the fourth century* downwards." (P. 322.) "We are sure that Christianity flourished in these regions [that is, the regions of Antioch and Edessa] at a very early period. . . . . The universal belief of later ages, and the very nature of the case, seem to render it *unquestionable* that the Syrian Church was possessed of a translation, both of the Old and New Testament, which it used habitually, and for public worship exclusively [of any other], from THE SECOND CENTURY of our era downwards. As early as A.D. 170, *the Syriac* is cited by Melito on Gen. xxii. 13. See Mill, Prol.ᵛ 1239." (P. 312.)

In strong contrast with this proved agreement of all Syriac copies from all quarters, from the fourth and six centuries till now, is Dr. Scrivener's reliable account of THE CORRUPT STATE OF THE GREEK COPIES. He says at p. 532, "During THE FIRST HALF OF THE SECOND CENTURY," that is, between A.D. 100 and 150, " must have originated the *wide variations* from the prevailing text, which exist in primary authorities, both manuscripts and versions; variations which survive in D, of the Greek, and in some of the old Latin codices. The text they exhibit is distinguished as Western." Its readings are " the *earliest* which can be fixed chronologically. . . . The chief and most constant characteristic of the Western readings is a love of *paraphrase*. Words, clauses, and even whole sentences, were *changed, omitted*, and *inserted*, with astonishing freedom. . . . There was a disposition to enrich the text, at the cost of its purity, by alterations or additions taken from *traditional*, and perhaps from apocryphal, and other non-biblical sources." (Dr. Hort, pp. 120,—2-3, quoted by Dr. Scrivener, pp. 532-3.) Dr. Scrivener gives passages from B and Aleph, the oldest copies now existing, in proof of their corrupt state, (pp. 543—552); and says that the text which Drs. Westcott and Hort have built chiefly on them, "is destitute, not only of *historical foundation*, but of *all probability*," (p. 542); that it is "*even visionary*." (P. 531.)

Dr. Scrivener says that " During *the whole of the third and fourth centuries, changes* appear to have been going on without notice;" those of them which are ·called Western, in Africa, France, and North Italy ; those of another kind, in Egypt and its neighbourhood ; and of a third kind, in Syria, Antioch, and Constantinople, (p. 554); and that "*all* that can be inferred from searching into the history " of the Greek text, "amounts to *no more than this* :— that *extensive variations* . . . . subsisted in it *from* the earliest period to which our records extend," (p. 519); and that " beyond this point our investigations *cannot be carried*, without indulging in *pleasant speculations*, which may amuse the fancy, but cannot inform the judgment." He says that he is " brought reluctantly to this conclusion after examining the principles laid down by Bengel,

E2

Griesbach, Hug, Scholz, Lachmann, by his disciple Tregelles, and by Professor Hort and Canon Westcott." (pp. 519-20.) He says, "Elaborate systems have failed," (p. 520); "for the present, much is uncertain, perplexing, ambiguous." (p. 521.) He knows of no means of *giving sure proof*, by means of Greek copies, of what readings are true, and what false.

The result of comparing Greek copies, is, in many cases, nothing but an *opinion about probability*; and Dr. Hort admits that these fallible opinions show "great diversity of judgment." (Scrivener, p. 541.) It is self-evident that decisions of this kind fail utterly to establish A SURE TEXT, such as God's book must have, to be infallible. The attainment of such a text in many places, from the mere study of Greek readings, seems to be a forlorn hope.

. HOW IMMENSELY IMPORTANT, therefore, is the certainty given by the agreement of Syriac copies! They retain almost throughout, their *first form*, and are, as Dr. Scrivener says, "IN EVERY IMPORTANT RESPECT THE SAME." (p. 313.) He states that, "Literary history can hardly afford a more powerful case than has been established for THE IDENTITY of the Syriac Version NOW CALLED the Peshito, with that used by the Eastern church long before the great schism had its beginning;" that is, long before A.D. 431. (p. 313.) He says, "The Peshito has well been called the Queen of versions of Holy Writ, for it is at once the oldest, and one of the most excellent." "It is composed in the purest dialect of a perspicuous and elegant language. . . . No version can well be more exempt . . . from stiffness of expression; yet, while remarkable for its ease and freedom, it very seldom becomes loose or paraphrastic." (p. 319.) "It is assigned by eminent scholars to *the first century*, undoubtedly it is not later than the second." (Contributions, 1859, p. 14.)

As to THE RESEMBLANCE of the Peshito to other texts, Dr. Scrivener says that "It habitually upholds the readings of A, one of the oldest uncial copies, those of the later uncials, and of the vast majority in cursive characters." "I claim for codex A and its numerous companions, peculiar attention by reason of their striking conformity with the Peshito Syriac." (Contributions, 1859, p. 14.) "Beza was the true author of what is called the Received Text." (Intro. p. 441, note.) "Beza's text of 1598 is found on comparison to agree more closely with the Authorized Version than any other Greek Text." (See Greek Text with variations of Revised Version, 1881; preface, p. 8.)

THE UNTRUTH OF STATEMENTS AND CONJECTURES made by Dr. Tregelles, Dr. Westcott, and Dr. Hort, against the Peshito, in order to sustain their own Greek texts, is fully shown by Dr. Scrivener. Dr. Tregelles collated a Nestorian manuscript of the Peshito called Rich, 7157, and has said in Horne's Introduction, p. 264, that the greater part of the materials afforded by a comparison of manuscripts with the printed text, for a critical revision of it, "relate to

grammatical forms and particulars of that kind." (Scrivener's Int.
p. 318.) Yet Dr. Scrivener, writing in 1859, said, that though
"this precious document [Rich, 7157] had been collated throughout
by Dr. Tregelles, together with several other manuscripts of high
antiquity in the Museum," and though Dr. Cureton, Mr. Ellis,
and two German scholars, had found that these "venerable manuscripts exhibit a text singularly resembling that of the printed
editions," Dr. Tregelles had spoken of the Peshito, in his "Printed
Text of the Greek N. T., 1854," p. 170, as "the version *commonly
printed as the Peshito.*" "He would persuade us," says Dr.
Scrivener, that the sects of "the whole Eastern Church, distracted
as it has been, ... have laid aside their bitter jealousies in order
to substitute . . . . a spurious version, in the room of the Peshito,
—that sole surviving monument of the first ages of the gospel in
Syria ! Nay more, that this *wretched forgery* has deceived Oriental-
ists profound as Michaelis and Lowth." (Contributions, pp. 14, 15.)
    Drs. Westcott and Hort have represented the Peshito, in the
Introduction to their Greek Testament, as made in the third or
fourth century out of a corrupt text called the Curetonian Syriac, and
have implied that all the Syrians have been deceived as to its origin.
(Intro. p. 84.) Dr. Scrivener says, " Of this two-fold authoritative
revision of the Greek text, and of this formal *transmutation of the
Curetonian Syriac into the Peshito, . . . not one trace remains in the
history of Christian antiquity ;* no one writer seems conscious that
any modification, either of the Greek Scriptures, or of the vernacular
translation, [the Peshito], was made in, or before their times. . . .
Yet Dr. Hort regards his *speculative conjecture as undoubtedly true;*"
and, though he believes that this recension was "made deliberately
by the authoritative voice of the Eastern Church," he declares that
all readings so made "must be at *once rejected,* (p. 119) ; thus
making a clean sweep of all critical materials,—Fathers, versions,
manuscripts uncial and cursive, comprising about *nineteen-twentieths
of the whole mass,* which do not correspond with his *preconceived
opinion* of what a correct text ought to be," p. 163. (Scrivener's
Intro., p. 533-4.)
    These last remarks apply equally to the untruthful statement of
Dr. Tregelles, in the Introduction to his Greek Testament, that
"The Peshito-Syriac was frequently modernized from time to
time." (p. v.)
    When the word of God is in question, it is necessary to know
and show who are trustworthy, and who are not.
    THE ABOVE STATEMENTS, made by persons well informed and of
faithful mind, will aid some, it is hoped, to arrive at the truth, by
as short a path as the breadth of the field permits. Most of these
witnesses reject the Syrian testimony that the Peshito was made in
the time, and by the care of the Apostles. But they give no good
reason for doing so, nor is it easy to see why, if Greek testimony

is accepted as proof of the Apostolic origin of the Greek text, Syrian testimony should not be received as proof of the Apostolic origin of the Syriac text. But it is evident that even on the supposition that the Syriac is but a man-made translation, the three facts, that it was made at so early a date, that there is no proof that it was greatly altered in the first centuries, as the Greek copies were, and that the agreement of existing copies, and of quotations from it, show that it has remained without material change from the fourth century till now; these facts prove that its text has a purity and a stability which are not only peculiar to it, but are providential gifts exactly suited to our present need. They prove that it is able to restore to God's word much of that certainty which some have impaired, and to affirm parts of it to be genuine which they would take away.

X. CHIEF PECULIARITIES OF THE TEXT OF THE PESHITO-SYRIAC.

1. Books, passages, and words, NOT CONTAINED IN IT.

2 Peter, 2 and 3 John, Jude, Revelation.

Matthew x. 8. Raise the dead.

,,   xxvii. 9. Jeremiah, not named.

,,   xxvii. 35. That it might be fulfilled which was spoken by the prophet, They parted my garments among them, and upon my vesture did they cast lots.

Luke xxii. 17, 18. And he took the cup, and gave thanks, and said, Take this and divide it among yourselves : for I say unto you, I will not drink of the fruit of the vine, until the kingdom of God shall come.

John vii. 53—viii. 11. The account of the adulteress.

Acts viii. 37. And Philip said, If thou dost trust with all the heart, thou mayest. And he answered and said, I believe that Jesus the Anointed is the Son of God.

Acts xv. 34. But it pleased Silas to remain there.

,,   xviii. 6. Your blood is on your own heads.

,,   xxviii. 29. And when he had said these things, the Jews departed, and had much reasoning among themselves.

1 Tim. iii. 16. The word "God" is not expressed, though evidently understood in the words, "He was revealed in flesh."

1 John v. 7, 8. In heaven, the Father, the Word, and the Holy Spirit; and these three are one. And there are three that bear witness on earth.

The absence of a passage from the Peshito, is not, of itself, evidence that it is not a part of God's word ; for the passage may have been added by the inspired writer to a Greek copy issued afterwards, If Greek authorities give strong evidence that such a passage is of divine origin, its absence from the Peshito implies that the Peshito was made in the life-time of that sacred writer, and before he wrote those words. But if the evidence from Greek authorities is not decisive, then the absence of the passage from the Peshito strongly implies that it is an unauthorized addition.

2. Readings which DIFFER from the Common Greek text.

In Acts xx. 28, some Jacobite copies have, "The assembly of *God*, which he purchased with his own blood." But most Syriac copies have "The assembly of *the Anointed*," etc. Wichelhaus says, "If I mistake not, all the Nestorian copies have, 'of the Anointed;' some Jacobite copies have, 'of the Anointed;' some of them have, 'of God.'" (p. 150.) Some Greek authorities have "of the Lord," others, "of God." Those Greek authorities which have "of the Lord," are, on the whole, the more trustworthy.

In 1 Cor. v. 8, some Syriac copies have, "with the *leaven*," instead of, "with the *unleavened* [bread]," etc.

In Heb. ii. 9, the Nestorian copies have, "For he, *apart* from Godhead, tasted death," etc. The Jacobite copies have, "For he, God, in his merciful favour tasted death," etc. Dr. Lee, 1816, without giving any authority, has placed the word "God" after "favour," and has made the passage read thus, "He, by the merciful favour of God, tasted," etc. But unless manuscript authority can be produced in proof that such a reading existed, it has no title to be considered part of the Peshito. Greek copies had "without God," as early as the time of Origen, and as the Nestorian copies are, as a rule, so correct, there seems to be no reason for doubting their correctness in this instance.

XI. The Design of this Work.

THE CHIEF DESIGN has been to aid in defending THE TRUE TEXT OF GOD'S WORD, by means of the Peshito-Syriac. God has preserved the Peshito from being corrupted as Greek copies have been. The use recently made of some of these corrupt copies has undermined belief in some parts of God's Book. The testimony of the Peshito-Syriac tends to re-establish confidence in most of these parts, whether they have been set forth as doubtful or rejected. By comparing the translation here given of the Syriac text, with that of the Received Greek text, printed by the side of it, the reader can see how very much the two agree, and how they tend to fix the true meaning of both. The Received Greek text agrees in most places with the Peshito, in opposition to the new Greek text constructed by the Revisers of the English Version. The Common English Version is also proved to be, as a rule, more in accord with the Peshito, than the Revised English Version is.

A hope has also been entertained of making THE WAY OF SALVATION MORE CLEAR. In the common version the verb *to believe* is used where a verb is needed which agrees with the noun *faith*. The Greek noun *pistis* is sometimes translated *belief*, sometimes *faith*, and correctly so. But the Greek verb *pisteuo* is translated *believe*, even when it means *to have faith ;* and this leaves the impression that belief of *the truth of words* is meant, when the real meaning is that of trust on God himself, or on Christ Jesus. The word *believe* means, indeed, to trust ; but only to trust in the truth of words. The Hebrew, Syriac, and Greek words, which sometimes mean to trust in the truth of words, are used also to express trust in persons ; and the word *believe* cannot express this trust with clearness and full effect.

In the Common English Version, those passages in which the idea of trusting ought to be clearly expressed, often fail to convey that meaning, from the unfitness of the word *believe* to do so. We do not, in the language of daily life say we *believe in*, or *believe on* a person, when we wish to express full trust in him, with view to some benefit. We say then that we trust in him.

Who is there who has not felt the difficulty of defining how a person must *believe*, so as to be saved ? Some have said that no one really believes a thing to be *true* who does not act accordingly. But this is plainly contrary to fact ; for we may believe a thing to be good and right, and yet resolve to have nothing to do with it. Others, when asked what it is to believe so as to be saved, say that the word believe must be understood in Scripture to have the unusual meaning of rely on. But this is a poor remedy for a faulty translation. The mass of readers and hearers have to trust to the impression given by the word *believe* itself, which impression, in most cases, is likely to be, that to believe in the truth of facts and doctrines, and in the reality of the Saviour's history, if this belief be connected with morality, makes salvation sure.

Some may perhaps ask for PROOF that the Greek word *pisteuo* does ever mean to trust.

One proof is, that other passages require repentance, devoted love, and unreserved obedience, as necessary to salvation ; and that these would not be necessary if salvation were promised to those who only *believe.*

ABRAHAM is often referred to in the New Covenant, in order to show how we may be declared just, and saved. The words in Gen. xv. 6, which describe how Abraham came to be declared just, are quoted in three places in the N. C. Scriptures; in Rom. iv. 3 ; Gal. iii. 6 ; and James ii. 23. In each of these three quotations the Common Version says, " Abraham *believed* God." It may be asked, perhaps, how these passages can possibly mean more than that Abraham *believed the truth of God's words.* It is true that the English version of these passages *does* convey this meaning ; and yet this meaning implies that salvation is sure to all who believe the truth of what God says, even though they should live in sin, and care nothing about him.

But these three passages must, in reality, have the same meaning as Gen. xv. 6, of which they are a quotation. What do those Hebrew words really mean? The word *aman* is there used in its Hiphil form, of which Gesenius says in his Hebrew Lexicon, "It often means to have faith in, as in Job iv. 18; xv. 15; xxxix. 12; Psalm lxxviii. 22, 32; cxix. 66. In Gen. xv. 6, [it means] he had faith in God," that is, he trusted in God. In Gen. xv. 6, the word meaning to trust is followed by the preposition *in*; and the trust is said to be, not in the words of God, but "in Jehovah" himself. In the following passages the same word with the same preposition *in*, can have no other meaning than *trust in*. Job iv. 18, "Behold, he put no trust in his servants. Job xv. 15, "Behold, he putteth no trust in his saints." Job xv. 31, "Let not him who is deceived trust in vanity." Micah vii. 5, "Trust ye not in a friend." In these passages the evident meaning of *aman* with *in* could not be expressed by *believe*. They prove that the meaning of Gen. xv. 6, may be, and *seems* to be, "Abraham trusted in Jehovah." If we substitute "believed in Jehovah," the meaning is, that Abraham believed Jehovah to be what he really is. But is it not evident that "trusted in Jehovah," must be the *real* meaning? Therefore, as Gen. xv. 6, not only may mean, but so far as evidence goes, does mean, "Abraham trusted in God;" each of the passages, Rom. iv. 3; Gal. iii. 6; and Jas. ii. 23, must have the same meaning; and this meaning is one which agrees with what all other passages say of the way of salvation. It does not convey the false impression which *believe* does, namely, that to believe the truth of what is true, saves. The word trust implies the existence of love and obedience, which other passages make necessary to salvation.

ANOTHER PROOF that *pisteuo* means to *trust*, when it refers to the way of salvation, is the description given by Paul of what it meant in his own case; (see 2 Tim. i. 12,) the committing or intrusting of himself to God. He says, "I know in whom *pepisteuka* I have *trusted*, and am persuaded that he is able to guard my deposit,—what I have intrusted to him, against that day."

In many passages *pisteuo* means to INTRUST SOMETHING to the care of another. This shows that the idea of trust is really in the word. It is used in this sense in Luke xvi. 11, "Who will commit or intrust to you the true riches?" Rom. iii. 2, "Because they were intrusted with the words of God." (See also 1 Cor. ix. 17; Gal. ii. 7; Titus i. 3.)

THE PESHITO-SYRIAC uses a word which means to trust where the Greek has *pisteuo*. For instance, in John iii. 36, "He who trusts in the Son has eternal life." John vi. 29, "This is the work of God, that ye trust in him whom he has sent." Acts xvi. 31, "Trust in our Lord Jesus the Anointed, and thou shalt have life-bliss." The Syriac word is the same as the Hebrew word used in Gen. xv. 6. It has in Syriac the same meaning which it has in Hebrew. It means in Syriac to trust. Wichelhaus says of the noun *haimonutho*, which is derived from the verb *aman*, to trust, " It expresses much more fully than the *pistis* of the Greeks, the true idea of faith ; for it denotes that state in which . . . . the reliance of the heart is placed on that which is most firm and certain." (On Peshito, p. 329.)

A FEW PASSAGES WITH THE WORD TO TRUST SUBSTITUTED FOR TO BELIEVE, will show how correctly and how clearly the way of salvation is thus described ; and how fully the wrong or imperfect idea which the word *believe* conveys, is thus removed. No one can say that this result is one of slight importance ; for nothing can possibly be more harmful than that an English word should be used to describe the way of salvation, which may lead some to believe that *a sound creed* is meant, instead of a change of heart, and which is the cause to others of ceaseless difficulty, when trying to find out the true meaning of Scripture, or when trying to prove to others that the belief which has salvation, is not what is commonly called belief, but something quite different from it. The following pass- ages are selected from those in which the Greek word *pisteuo* is used with *in*, with *on*, with *a dative case*, and without *in*, *on*, or *a dative case*.

PISTEUO followed by IN. Matt. xviii. 6, " Whoso shall make stumble one of these little ones who trust in me." John iii. 15, " So must the Son of man be lifted up, that everyone who trusts in him may not perish, but have eternal life." John vi. 40, " And this is the will of him who sent me, that everyone who sees the Son, and trusts in him, shall have eternal life, and I will raise him up at the last day."

PISTEUO followed by ON. Acts xi. 17, " Since, therefore, God gave the same gift to them as he gave to us, who have trusted on the Lord Jesus, the Anointed," etc. Rom. iv. 24, " It was written also because of us, (that trust was reckoned to Abraham), of us who trust on him who raised up Jesus our Lord from among the dead."

PISTEUO followed by A DATIVE CASE. John v. 24, " Verily, verily, I say unto you, that he who hears my word, and trusts on him who sent me, has eternal life." John viii. 31, " Jesus said to those Jews who had trusted on him, If ye continue in my word, then are ye my disciples indeed."

PISTEUO WITHOUT IN, ON, OR A DATIVE CASE. Mark xvi. 16, " He who shall trust, and be immersed, shall be saved ; he who shall be trustless, shall be condemned." Acts xviii. 8, " And many of the Corinthians heard, trusted, and were immersed.

Another wish has been, TO CONNECT BY LIKENESS OF WORDS, what is said of ATONEMENT in the New Covenant, with what is said of it in the Old. The importance of this is evident from the fact that what was written in the Older Scriptures, was written in part for our benefit. (1 Cor. x. 11) ; and that what was said to be effected by the old sacrifices, which could not take away sins, is of special use to teach us what was really accomplished by the sacrifice of Christ, which could take away sins. This use of the older Scriptures is partly destroyed by the carelessness of translators, when they destroy that likeness of words by which God has linked the Older Scriptures with the New. The English word used about fifty times in the Old Covenant writings, to describe the efficacy of slain offerings, is the word ATONEMENT. But in our New Cov. version that word is used but once, and then wrongly ; for it represents in Romans v. 11, a Greek word which means *reconciliation ;* and reconciliation is *the result* of atonement, not atonement itself. Atonement is the cause of forgiveness or reconciliation. In the Revised Version, the word atonement is not, I think, used at all. There are four passages in which the Syriac and Greek words used to describe the efficacy of the sacrifice offered by Jesus, are of the same meaning as the Hebrew word which is represented by the English word atonement, in the O. C. Scriptures. They are Rom. iii. 25 ; Heb. ii. 17 ; 1 John ii. 2 ; iv. 10.

In Rom. iii. 25, the word *propitiation* is used both in the common and in the revised version. If the word *atonement* be used, the English word has the same relation to the English word used in the Old Covenant, which the Syriac and Greek words have to the Hebrew word. The passage then reads thus. "Whom God appointed beforehand [to be] an atonement, by means of faith in his blood."

In HEBREWS ii. 17, the common version has, "to make reconciliation." The revised version has, "to make propitiation." If the word atonement be used, the passage reads thus, "That he might become a merciful and faithful High Priest in things relating to God, to make atonement for the sins of the people."

In 1 JOHN ii. 2, both English versions have "propitiation." If atonement be substituted, the meaning is, "And he is the atonement for our sins."

In 1 JOHN iv. 10, both English versions have propitiation. If atonement be used instead, the words mean, "God loved us, and sent his Son to be an atonement for our sins."

The English reader, on meeting with the word atonement in these four passages, is reminded of the word atonement in the older Scriptures, and there he finds that when it is said that an atonement was made for any sin, the words often follow, "and it shall be forgiven him." (See Lev. iv. and v.)

Another passage in which the word atonement should occur, is Heb. ix. 5, "The cherubim of glory overshadowing the place of atonement."

Another wish has been to use words, the meaning of which is known to the unlearned by their own DAILY USE OF THEM, instead of words which are less known, or which are but partly understood

by those who do not know Latin and Greek. There are many
Latin-English words in the Common version. Those who have
never learned Latin, have scarcely any *clear* idea of what some of
these mean. These words are little better to them than words
translated out of one foreign language into another.

Words which do not express their meaning clearly, may also be
made strongholds of error. They permit a false meaning to be
given them, and become a storehouse of untruth. Thus the word
church, which ought always to mean, as the Greek word does, an
assembly, is constantly applied to bodies which never assemble.

In the next section a list of words is given which, though well
understood by very many, are wanting in clearness to a large
number of people. Their meaning is given in words more familiar
to most.

The desire has been to use the English language ACCORDING TO
ITS USE IN DAILY LIFE. In the Greek and Syriac texts, the words
used are those which were used about the things of this life. And
to use in any translation of them forms of speech, which differ from
those in common use, is to distort and disfigure God's word, instead
of giving its true likeness. How absurd and unseemly it is to
prefer to call a person *which*, instead of *who*, as the revised version
does; and to suppose that " she *runneth*," is a more holy expression
than " *she runs*."

XII. WORDS IN THE COMMON VERSION NOT WELL UNDERSTOOD
      BY SOME, IN WORDS MORE FAMILIAR.

Acceptance of persons, wrong regard for persons.   To adjure,
to command to answer on oath.   Ado, outcry.   Adversary,
foe.   Adversity, affliction, distress.   Advocate, pleader.
Allegory, description of one thing by another.   Alms, gifts.
Anathema, a setting aside under condemnation.   Angel,
[heavenly] messenger.   Apostle, chief messenger.   Apparel,
clothes, clothing.   Appease, quiet.   Appertains, belongs or
relates to.   Array, dress.   Archangel, chief [heavenly] messenger.   At hand, has come near.   Audience, to give; to listen
to.   Austere, harsh.   Avenge, punish for injury.

Babble, prate, talk foolishly.   Backbite, slander.   Baptism,
immersion.   Baptize, immerse. (1.)   Barbarians, people of
foreign race and language.   Beguile, deceive.   Behoved him,
it was due that he; or he was bound.   Believe, the Greek and
Syriac words often mean to trust. (2.)   Believer, he who trusts,
one trusting.   Betroth, engage to be married.   Bewray, betray.
Bishop, overseer. (3.)   Blaspheme, speak evil of, revile.   Born
of water and of the Spirit. John iii. 5.   Christians are not *born* of
the Spirit, but *begotten* by him; nor are they begotten by means of
water, but by means of God's word. 1 Peter i. 23.   The Greek

word used in John iii. 5, is *gennaomai*, which sometimes is applied to birth of a mother, and then means to be born, as in Matt. ii. 1, "when Jesus was born in Bethlehem;" and sometimes to origin from a father, when it means begotten, as in Matt. i. 2, "Abraham begat Isaac." In John iii. 5, this word must of necessity be used in both of these senses. It must mean *born*, as to water, which does not beget; and *begotten*, as to the Holy Spirit, of whom no one is *born*. So that the correct English translation must be, "Be born of water, and begotten by the Spirit." By and by, immediately.

Note 1. The Syriac word used where the Greek word means "was baptized," is *amad*. Wichelhaus says, "It means, was immersed, and admirably expresses what baptism properly is; it explains what the Apostles teach, that we are immersed, and buried with Christ," (p. 308.) He says also of Heb. vi. 4, where the Greek has, "were once enlightened," "The Syriac has 'they descended to immersion,' from which it appears, first, that the recently baptized were said to be enlightened; and next, that those who were baptized descended into a bath." (p. 332.) He says also, "It appears from the Syriac words of 1 Peter iii. 21, meaning, 'when ye profess God with a pure conscience,' that a profession of God was made in baptism." (p. 332.)

Note 2. Wichelhaus remarks, that the Syriac word *haimonutho*, which is used where the Greek has *pistis*, expresses "much more fully than" this Greek word does, "the true idea of faith; it denotes that state of mind, in which . . . . the heart places *trust* in what is most firm and certain." (p. 329.) John xiv. 1, is an illustration of the manner in which the Syriac sometimes gives a meaning which is without ambiguity, when the meaning of the Greek is uncertain. A Greek word is twice used, which in each case may either be a statement or a command. In the common version it is once translated as a statement, once as a command:— "Ye *believe* in God, *believe* also in me" The Syriac has, "Trust in God, trust also in me," which commends itself as being probably the true meaning.

Note 3. Wichelhaus says, "To all men who love truth, it is sufficiently evident that in the letters of Paul, the office of bishop does not differ from the office of elder. This is proved most clearly by the Syriac, in which [the Greek words for] both bishop and elder are translated by the Syriac word *koshisho*, elder. By this testimony of the Syriac, those are refuted who say, persuading themselves I know not how, that [modern] episcopacy was instituted by John. It is most certain that in the time of the Syriac translator there was no episcopal authority in the church." (p. 331.)

Candlestick, Heb. ix. 2, lamp-stand. Carnal, fleshly. Carriages, Acts xxi. 15, baggage. Centurion, captain of a hundred foot-men. Chambering, Rom. xiii. 13, deeds of bed-lust. Charger, Matt. xiv. 8, dish. Charity, love. Chasten, punish.

Christ, the Anointed.   Church, (both in Syriac and Greek), assembly. (4.)   Circumcise, to cut the foreskin around.   Cloven tongues, Acts ii. 3, tongues divided into parts.   Commend, Luke xxiii. 46, yield up ; Rom. xvi. 1, recommend.   Commit, 1 Peter iv. 19, intrust.   Commune, to share in common, but in Luke vi. 11 ; xxii. 4 ; xxiv. 15, talk, converse.   Communicate, Gal. vi. 6, Heb. xiii. 16, give gifts ; Gal. ii. 2, to state something to (others.)   Communication, 1 Cor. xv. 33, companionship ; Eph. iv. 29, talking with.   Communion, 1 Cor. x. 16, [sign of] common interest in ; 2 Cor. vi. 14, in common; xiii. 14, gift of, or fellowship of (the Spirit.)   Compassed with, Heb. v. 2, clothed with. Compassed about, Heb. xi. 30, gone round.   Comprehend, John i. 5, Eph. iii. 18, perceive ; Rom. xiii. 9, sum up.   Conceive, James i. 15, become pregnant.   Concision, Phil. iii. 2, those who cut and kill.   Conclude, Rom. xi. 32, Gal. iii. 22, inclose, shut up.   Concupiscence, Rom. vii. 8, covetousness, lawless desire. Conditions, Luke xiv. 32, terms.   Confer, take counsel with. Confess, sometimes, profess.   Confirm, Acts xiv. 22, make stead-fast.   Consecrated, Heb. vii. 28, perfected ; x. 20, newly made. Consorted, Acts xvii. 4, joined their lot with.   Constrain, Gal. vi. 12, compel ; 2 Cor. v. 14, presses us on.   Contain, 1 Cor. vii. 9, have self-control.   Conversation, 1 Peter i. 15, conduct, course of conduct.   Conversion, Acts xv. 3, turning to God.   Convert, James v. 19, to turn a person to God.   Covered, Rom. iv. 7, (sins) forgiven.

Note 4.   The Syriac word, as well as the Greek word, for what is commonly called a *church*, means an assembly. Wichelhaus says that the Peshito describes it to be " a congregation, an assembly, a meeting, in which some fill the office of elders, others of servants."

Deacon, servant.   Dearth, famine.   Dedicate (a covenant), Heb. ix. 18, to make binding, by killing and dividing some living creature. (5.)   Defer, Acts xxiv. 22, to delay, to adjourn. Deliver to Satan, exclude from the Christian assembly. (6.) Descent, Heb. vii. 3, family-record.   Desolate, of a person, Rev. xvii. 16, in want.   Desolation of a country, Matt. xii. 25, like-ness to a desert.   Despiteful, Rom. i. 30, full of spite or scorn. Determinate counsel, Acts ii. 23, fixed design.   Devotionr, Acts xvii. 23, objects of worship.   Discern, judge of, or between. Disciple, a submissive learner.   Dispensation, stewardship. Disputation, debate.   Dissemble, feign.   Dissimulation, pre-tence.   Divination, pretence to foretell events.   Doctors, Luke ii. 46, teachers.   Doctrine, teachment, what is taught.   Domin-ions, Col. i. 16, Lords.   Draught, seat of relief.   Dureth, continues.

Note 5.   See the custom in Gen. xv. 9—18.   Wichelhaus says,

" The ancients threatened men, that if thoy broke a covenant, they would be cut in pieces, as the animals were cut in pieces over which it was customary to take the oath." He suggests that the words " shall cut him asunder," Matt. xxiv. 51, probably refer to this custom.

Note 6. The Greek, of 1 Cor. v. 3—5, implies that the *whole assembly* was to deliver the person to Satan. Wichelhaus remarks that the Syriac uses the words, " that ye deliver ;" showing more fully that the act was to be that of the whole assembly.

Earnest, a gift given to prove fulfilment sure, sure pledge. Easter, Passover. Edify and edification, build up, building up. Effeminate, 1 Cor. vi. 9, men-harlots. Elect and election, choose, choice. Emulation, Rom. xi. 14, zeal; Gal. v. 20, rivalry. Ensample, example. Ensue, 1 Peter iii. 11, pursue. Epistle, letter. Eschew, 1 Peter iii. 11, depart from. Espouse, 2 Cor. xi. 2, engage to be married. Establish, Heb. xiii. 9, make firm. Estate, low, Luke i. 48, lowly state. Estates, chief, Mark vi. 21, first men. Eunuch, a stoneless man. Evangelist, one who tells good tidings. Exorcists, Acts xix. 13, those who pretended to cast out devils. Expedient, 2 Cor. viii. 10, useful, of advantage. Extortion, unjust exaction.

Fables, 2 Tim. iv. 4, fictions. Faithless, be not, but believing; John xx. 27, be not trustless but trustful. Fashion, Luke ix. 29, and James i. 11, appearance; Acts vii. 44, pattern ; 1 Cor. vii. 31, plan ; Phil. ii. 8, form. Fellowship, Phil. iii. 10, sharing in ; Acts ii. 42, probably, the giving of gifts; 1 Cor. i. 9 ; 1 John i. 3, association with. Flux, bloody ; a flow of blood from the bowels. Froward, 1 Pet. ii. 18, perverse.

Gainsay, Luke xxi. 15, reply to. Gainsayers, Titus i. 9, those who speak in opposition. Gainsaying, Acts x. 29, objecting ; Jude 11, opposing speeches. Gangrene, in margin of 2 Tim. ii. 17, a deadly sore. Garner, granary. Garnish, put in order, adorn. Gatherings, 1 Cor. xvi. 2, collections. Gender, beget. Genealogies, 1 Tim. i. 4, family-records. Generation, Matt. i. 1, parentage; Matt. i. 17, men of like age, or of the same period ; Matt. iii. 7, offspring; Matt. xii. 39, men of like character. Gentiles, the nations, other than the Hebrews. Gift, Matt. v. 23-4, gift-offering. Glistering, Luke ix. 29, flashing like lightning. God forbid, by no means. Gorgeous, splendid. Gospel, good tidings, good message. Grace, Rom. v. 20, merciful favour ; 1 Peter iv. 10, gifts of merciful favour. Grounded, having a foundation on. Guile, deceit.

Hallowed be, Matt. vi. 9, be held holy. Halt, Matt. xv. 31, xviii. 8, lame ; those named with the lame seem to be the crippled in hand, from xviii. 8, "hand or foot." Handmaid, Luke i. 38, 48, bond-servant. Heathen, those of the nations not

Hebrews. Heirs, sometimes, as in 1 Peter iii. 7, inheritors, in possession. Hell, sometimes not the place of torment, but, as in Acts ii. 31, of spirits absent from the body. Heresy, a self-willed plan. Heretic, one who follows a self-willed plan. Heritage, 1 Peter v. 3, inheritance, possession. Holy Ghost, Holy Spirit. Honour, sometimes, as in 1 Tim. v. 3, honour with a gift. Hospitality, love shown to strangers. Husbandman, one who tills the ground, farmer. Husbandry, God's, 1 Cor. iii. 9, God's tilled field. Hypocrisy, false show. Hypocrite, one who makes a false show.

Idol, image. Idolatry, the worship of images. Illuminated, Heb. x. 32, enlightened. Immortality; in 1 Cor. xv. 53, this dying [body] must put on life which cannot die. Immutability, Heb. vi. 17, changelessness. Impenitent, Rom. ii. 5, unrepenting, without change of mind. Implacable, Rom. i. 31, never at peace. Implead one another, Acts xix. 38, prosecute one another. Importunity, shameless begging. Impotent, John v. 3, sick people; Acts xiv. 8, strengthless. Impute, reckon. Incontinence, want of self-restraint, Incorruptible, which cannot perish. Incorruption, 1 Cor. xv. 53, life which cannot perish. This perishing [body] must put on [life] which cannot perish. Infirmity, weakness. Infidel, 2 Cor. vi. 15, 1 Tim. v. 8, one who does not trust. Infirmity, weakness. Iniquity, Matt. xiii. 41, what is unlawful; xxiii. 28, law-breaking, lawlessness; Acts i. 18, unrighteousness. Inordinate affection, Col. iii. 5, passionate desire. Instant, Rom. xii. 12, persevering. Instantly, Luke vii. 4, Acts xxvi. 7, earnestly. Insurrection, uprising, rebellion. Intercession, intreaty on behalf of others. Interpret, Acts iv. 36, translate. Interpretation, 2 Peter i. 20, prophetic meaning. Issue, Matt. xxii. 25, offspring.

Jeopardy, danger. Judgment, sometimes as in James ii. 13, condemning judgment. Justify, declare righteous. Justification, the declaring a person to be righteous.

Kindred, relations of the same family, tribe, or race. Kinsfolks, Luke ii. 44, xxi. 16, relations. Kinsman, John xviii. 26; Rom. xvi. 11, a relation.

Lasciviousness, lustfulness, gratified lust. Laud, extol. Lawyer, a teacher of the Law of Moses. Lewdness, reckless wrong-doing. Life, often a life of blessedness; as in the words, eternal life. In Syriac, *life* is used where the Greek has *salvation*, and means a life of blessedness. Lineage, line of descent. Low estate, Luke i. 48, lowly state. To lust, to long for eagerly. Lust, strong and wrong desire.

Magnificence, Acts xix. 27, great glory. Magnify, Luke i. 46, praise greatly. Majesty, Heb. i. 3, greatness. Malefactor, wrong-doer. Malignity, Rom. i. 29, crafty malice. Manifestation, Rom. viii. 19, revealing to sight. Manifold, Luke xviii. 30, many times; Eph. iii. 10, very much varied (wisdom); 1 Peter i. 6, iv. 10, various. Martyr, a witness-bearer. Master, often, teacher. Meat, food. Mediator, one who stands between God and man; to stay, as Aaron did, in Num. xvi. 48, God's anger. For a memorial, to bring to memory. Messiah, a Hebrew word, like Christ in Greek, the Anointed. Minister, servant. Ministration, serving. Ministry, service. Mortal, dying. Mortality, that which dies. Mortify, put to death. Multiply, to increase in number, or, Acts xii. 24, in effect. Mystery, a secret.

Nations, the; Luke xii. 30, those not Hebrews. Nay, no. Noisome, Rev. xvi. 2, hurtful. Nurture, Eph. vi. 4, instruction.

Observation, Luke xvii. 20, outward watching for. Occasion, opportunity. Offence, sometimes sin, as in 2 Cor. xi. 7; transgression, as in Rom. v. 15; sometimes a cause of stumbling, as in Rom. xvi. 17, and 1 Peter ii. 8. Offend, often, to make stumble, as in Matt. v. 29; sometimes, to stumble, to be faulty, as in James ii. 10; iii. 2. Omnipotent, almighty. Oracles, words. Ordain, 1 Cor. vii. 17, Titus i. 5, arrange, appoint. Ordinances, commands. Overcharged, Luke xxi. 34, be weighed down.

Palsy, now called paralysis. A parable, a comparison. Passion, after his; Acts i. 3, after he suffered death. Pastor, shepherd. Patience, sometimes as in Rom. ii. 7, patient continuance; sometimes, as in 2 Cor. i. 6, bearing patiently. Pentecost, fiftieth day after the Passover; the feast of harvest-thanksgiving. Perdition, destruction. Phylacteries, words of scripture worn on the dress. Potentate, mighty. Preach, Luke viii. 1, to tell good tidings; Luke ix. 2, to proclaim, to make proclamation; Luke ix. 60, and Acts iv. 2, to make known; or announce; Acts viii. 25, to speak. Predestinate, Rom. viii. 29, to destine beforehand. Prevent, Matt. xvii. 25, to speak or act in advance of another. Prophesy, 1 Cor. xiv. 3, to build up, admonish, or comfort by means of a miraculous gift. Propitiation; Rom. iii. 25, Heb. ii. 17, 1 John ii. 2, iv. 10, atonement. Proselytes, converts to the law of Moses. Provoke, to make angry; but in Heb. x. 24, to urge onward; in Rom. x. 19, xi. 14, to excite to jealous zeal. Publican, a tax-collector. Purloin, Titus ii. 10, pilfer.

Quicken, to make alive, give life to.

Receive, Rom. xiv. 1; Phil ii. 29, embrace. Recompence of reward for transgression, Heb. ii. 2, just repayment of punishment. Recompense to no one evil for evil, Rom. xii. 17, repay, etc., also repay in 2 Thess. i. 6; Heb. x. 30. Redeem, set free by ransom; Tit. ii 14; 1 Pet. i. 18; Rev. v. 9, to buy; and in Gal. iii. 13, iv. 5, to buy out (of curse.) Redemption, Heb. ix. 12, freedom by ransom. Regeneration, begetting again. This English word is used only twice in the N. C. Scriptures, and both times *wrongly*, instead of *new birth.* The Greek word in Matt. xix. 28, means the new birth (of the new creation.) In Titus iii. 5, it also means new birth :—" By means of the bath of new birth." The words probably refer to baptism, as the birth or manifestation of that new life which the Holy Spirit begets beforehand, by means of God's *word.* See 1 Peter i. 23, James i. 18. The divine act called begetting by Peter and James in these passages, is called in Titus iii. 5, the renewing of the Holy Spirit. The false rendering, "*regeneration,*" claims *special attention.* Because, by means of it many teach that new life is *begotten by baptism,* and deceive many fatally. Re-mission, forgiveness (of sins.) Remnant, Rom. xi. 5, those who are spared, a spared number ; in Matt. xxii. 6 ; Rev. xi. 13 ; xii. 17 ; xix. 21, the rest. Repent, follow a new mind. Reprobate, false, counterfeit. Respect of persons, wrong regard for persons. Restitution, Acts iii. 21, restoration. Resurrection, rising up (from death.) Revenge, 2 Cor. x. 6, punish. Rudiments, Col. ii. 8, low-grade lessons.

Lord of sabbaoth, Lord of armies. Sabbath, (day of) rest. Sacrifice, a slain-offering. Sacrilege, robbing a temple. Saints, holy ones. Salvation, the Syriac uses the word *life,* where the Greek has *salvation.* This shows how great is the error of those who say that the promise of eternal life is merely the promise of eternal existence, instead of the promise of a life of bliss. Sanctify, make holy ; the death of Christ is said to make holy by the efficacy of his sacrifice, Heb. ix. 13 ; x. 10 ; the Spirit is said to make holy, 2 Thess. ii. 13 ; and by means of God's truth, John xvii. 17. Sanctification, the being made holy. Sanctuary, a holy place. Savour, sweet smell. Eph. v. 2, an odour of sweet smell. Savourest not, Matt. xvi. 23, do'st not approve of. Schism, 1 Cor. xii. 25, division, split. Scribes, learned writers. Scrip, bag for food. Scripture, the writing ; some word like " holy," as expressed in Rom. i. 2, and in 2 Tim. iii. 15, is under-stood when the words " the writing " refer to God's book. Secure you, Matt. xxviii. 14, free you from anxiety. Sedition, Acts xxiv. 5, rebellion. Senate, the body of elders. Servant, sometimes a bond-servant. Paul calls himself a bond-servant of Christ, Rom. i. 1. He calls every Christian so, 1 Cor. vii. 22. Sinners are called bond-servants of sin, Rom. vi. 16. Christians are forbidden to be bond-servants of men, because they have been bought by Christ, 1 Cor. vii. 23. Settled, Col. i. 23, firmly seated. Shambles, meat-market. Shew-bread, Matt. xii. 4, bread set before God. Shrines, temples. Sleight, subtle arts. Sojourn, to dwell without fixed abode. Soothsaying, pretence to foretell events. Sorcerer, one who uses arts of magic to deceive. Spirits, 1 John iv. 1, men who said that the Holy Spirit spoke by them. Stature, size of body. Strait, narrow.

Straitened, to suffer from narrowness. Straitest sect, Acts xxvi. 5. strictest sect. Straitly, strictly (charge). Matt. ix. 30 ; Acts v. 28. Subvert, Titus i. 11, upset. Subverted, Titus iii. 11, quite turned away. Succour, help. Succourer, helper. Superscription, words written above. Superstitious, Acts xvii. 22, devoted to the worship of demon gods. Sustenance, Acts vii. 11. food. Synagogue, a place of meeting, Matt. xii. 9, for Jews ; James ii. 2, for Christians.

Tabernacle, Heb. viii. 5, tent-dwelling; Heb. xi. 9, tents. Tempt, the Greek word sometimes means to put to test, as in Matt. iv. 7, thou shalt not test, (from distrust) ; Luke viii. 13, in time of trial. Terrestrial, earthly. Testament, always covenant, even in Heb. ix. 16, 17. Testator, Heb. ix. 16, the sacrifice which confirmed a covenant. Tithes, tenths. To wit, we do you ; 2 Cor. viii. 1, we make known to you. Traditions, commands delivered ; 2 Thes. iii. 6, by God ; Col. ii. 8, by men. Travail, to be in child-birth, John xvi. 21 ; to be in pain as of child-birth, Gal. iv. 19. Twain, two. Types, margin of 1 Cor. x. 11, picture-lessons.

Unbeliever, Luke xii. 46 ; 2 Cor. vi. 14, one without trust. Unbelieving, 1 Cor. vii. 14, 15, who does not trust. Unbelief, want of trust.

Vagabond Jews, Acts xix. 13, Jews who went about. Variance, strife. Vengeance, Luke xxi. 22 ; Rom. xii. 19, just sentence. Vials, Rev. v. 8, xvi. 2, bowls. Victuals, Matt. xiv. 15, food. Vocation, Eph. iv. 1, call.

Washed, often for bathed. Acts xxii. 16, be immersed, and bathe away thy sins. 1 Cor. vi. 11, ye have been bathed to cleanness. Heb. x. 22, bathed as to the body in clean water. Wax, to become, in Matt. xxiv. 12, to become (cool). In 2 Tim. iii. 13, to go on becoming (worse). Whit, every, entirely. Not a whit, 2 Cor. xi. 5, in nothing. Wist, knew. Wit, we do you to ; we make known to you, 2 Cor. viii. 1. Witness, a witness-bearer. I wot, I know.

CONDEMNED READINGS.

XIII. THE PESHITO-SYRIAC TEXT, AS A FAITHFUL WITNESS, CONDEMNS THE FOLLOWING CHANGES, WHICH, IN THE REVISED ENGLISH VERSION OF 1881, WERE FOUNDED ON DEVIATIONS FROM THE RECEIVED GREEK TEXT.

We need to remember that the testimony of exact copies, differs entirely, in kind and worth, from the testimony of critics ; and of readings selected from conflicting copies. The testimony of an exact copy is *a decisive proof* of what the words of the pages copied were. The faith of the first Christians rested on words proved by miracle to be "words taught by the Holy Spirit," and not "by the wisdom of man." (1 Cor. ii. 13.) Exact copies tell us what those words were, and enable us to rest, as the first Christians did, on words proved by miracle to be those of God. But if we have to trust to readings selected by "human wisdom" from corrupt copies, our faith, instead of resting on words proved to be those of God, is compelled to rest on words which "human wisdom" selects for us as likely to be God's words. We have then to rest, not on words proved by miracle to be those of God, but on THE OPINIONS OF "HUMAN WISDOM" as to what words are his, and what are not. This "wisdom" may be blind to spiritual things, may be warped by prepossessions or by private purposes, may be guided by conjectures or fictions, and may be marred by pride, self-sufficiency, or perversity. As the copies of the Peshito in Coordistan, in India, and in Mesopotamia, were made there from copies possessed in the first days of Christianity, and yet are substantially agreed; they are proved by this agreement to have been exactly copied from the earliest times, and to contain a text which may be appealed to as a standard, and test of correctness.

This list of CONDEMNED CHANGES does not include those of little connecting words, except where the change of these has an important influence on the meaning of a sentence; nor of other little changes which do not much affect the sense.

In the list which follows after this, the principal changes, so far as founded on the new Greek text of the Revisers, which are IN AGREEMENT WITH THE PESHITO-SYRIAC, are given.

In these two lists the reader has THE COMPLETE TESTIMONY OF THE PESHITO on all the more important changes in the Revised English Version, which are founded on a new Greek Text.

The differences which exist between the Peshito and the Received Greek text, are shown by the translations of them given in the body of the work.

If the reader duly considers *the immense number* of the condemned changes in this list, he will see how much reason the late Dean Burgon had for saying that "the Revisers . . . . have rejected the words of inspiration in every page." (R.R. p. vii.) If he thinks fit to observe how important *the subjects* are to which many of the mutilations and rival readings refer, including even the underived Deity of the Redeemer, he will see what reason Dean Burgon had for saying that the issue of this Revised Version is one of "the most calamitous" events of the age. (p. xi.)

EXPLANATIONS : Omn, and Adn, mean that the words named are an omission from, or an addition to, the Received Greek Text. When preceded by M., the omission or addition is one suggested in the margin. Words substituted for others are followed by "for" or "instead of." The words put in circular brackets do not form part of the changes, but are added to show the position and connection of the words omitted or added; for instance, Omn. your (fathers), means that the omitted word, your, stands before fathers.

Square brackets [ ] mean that the words enclosed in them are implied, but not expressed in the originals.

The Received Greek Text chiefly used in making this list is Dr. Scrivener's "New Testament in Greek, with the variations in the Revised Version of 1881." The title states that the Greek is, " according to the text followed in the Authorised Version." The Oxford "Greek Testament, with the readings adopted by the Revisers," has also been used.

The Syriac editions which have been used, include that of Walton's Polyglot, 1653-7; that of Guthier, 1663; the Maronite of 1703; Schaaf's of 1709, and of 1717; Lee's of 1816; and that of Ooroomiah, in the Nestorian letters of the Coordistan text, 1852, reprinted in 1878.

MATTHEW i. 7, 8. M. Asaph, for, Asa, twice.　　10. M. Amos, for, Amon, twice.　　25. a son, for, her first-born son.

Ch. iii. 8. fruit, for, fruits.　　16. M. omn. to him.

Ch. v. 22. Omn. without a cause.　　30. go, for, be cast (into hell.)　　44. Omn. Bless those who curse you, do good to those who hate you; . . . who despitefully use you, and.　　47. the Gentiles, for, the tax-collectors.　　48. heavenly, for, who is in heaven.

Ch. vi. 1. righteousness, for, alms.　　4. Omn. he . . . . openly. 5. ye pray, ye; for, thou prayest, thou.　　6. Omn. openly.　　13. Omn. For thine is the kingdom, and the power, and the glory, for ever.　　21. thy, for, your, twice.　　33. the kingdom, for, the kingdom of God.

Ch. vii. 13. M. omn. is the gate.

Ch. viii. 9. Adn. set (under.)　　10. M. in no one, for, not even. 15. to him, for, to them.　　25. they came, for, his disciples came. Save, for, save us.　　31. send us, for, permit us to go away.

Ch. ix. 2. 5. forgiven, for, forgiven to thee, twice.　　12. said, for, said to them.　　14. M. fast, for, fast oft.　　24. said, for said to them.　　36. were distressed, for, were wearied.

Ch. x. 3. and Thaddæus, for, and Lebbæus, who is surnamed Thaddæus.

Ch. xi. 9. Why went ye out? to see a prophet? for, what went ye out to see? a prophet?　　15. M. omn. to hear.　　17. Omn. to you (after mourned.)　　23. Shalt thou be exalted to heaven? thou shalt go down to Hades; for, thou which hast been exalted to heaven, shalt be brought down to Hades.

Ch. xii. 4. M. they ate, for, he ate.　　6. a thing, for. One (greater).　　15. many people, for, many multitudes.　　22. the dumb man, for, the blind and dumb man.　　31. Omn. to men (at end of verse.)　　47. M. omn. And one said to him, Behold, thy mother and thy brothers stand without, seeking to speak to thee.

Ch. xiii. 9. Omn. to hear.   22. the world, for this world.   34. nothing, for, not.   35. M. omn. of the world.   37. said, for, said to them.   40. the world, for, this world.   43. Omn. to hear.   44. Omn. Again.   51. Omn. Jesus said to them. Omn. Lord.   52. to the kingdom, instead of, for the kingdom. 55. Joseph, for, Joses.

Ch. xiv. 15. the disciples, for, his disciples. This substitution occurs frequently. It does so in verse 22 ; in xv. 12 ; 33 ; 36 ; xvi. 5 ; 20 ; xix. 10 ; xxvi. 8 ; 45.   25. he, for, Jesus. This change occurs frequently ; but as the meaning is not altered, the change is not always noticed in this list.   29. M. and came, for, to come.   30. saw the wind, for, saw the wind strong.   33. Omn. came and.   34. to, for, of (Gennesaret.)

Ch. xv. 2. the hands, for, their hands.   4. the, for, thy (father.) 6. Omn. or his mother.   14. Omn. of the blind.   15. the, for this (parable.)   31, 35. multitude, for multitudes ; twice.

Ch. xvi. 2, 3. M. omn. When it is evening, ye say, It will be fair weather, for the heaven is red. And in the morning, It will be foul weather to-day, for the heaven is red and gloomy. Ye hypocrites, ye know how to distinguish the face of the heaven, but the signs of the times ye cannot.   3. Omn. ye hypocrites. 4. Omn. the prophet.   8. Omn. to them.   ye have, for, ye have brought.   11. But beware ye, for, that ye should beware. 13. that the Son of man is, for, that I, the Son of man, am.

Ch. xvii. 4. I will make, for, let us make.   11. Omn. to them. Omn. first.   20. little trust, for, want of trust.   21. Omn. But this kind goes not out except by prayer and fasting.   26. And when he said, for, Peter said to him.

Ch. xviii. 2. Omn. Jesus.   11. Omn. For the Son of man came to save that which had perished.   14. M. my, for, your (Father.)   15. M. omn. against thee.   28. pay, if thou owest anything, for, pay me what thou owest.   29. Omn. at his feet. Omn. all.   34. Omn. to him.   35. Omn. his trespasses.

Ch. xix. 3. Omn. for a man.   4. Omn. to them.   M. created, for, made.   9. M. causes her to commit adultery, for, and shall marry another, commits adultery.   M. omn. and he who marries her who is put away, commits adultery.   16. Teacher, for, Good Teacher.   17. Why dost thou ask me about what is good ? one is the Good, for. Why dost thou call me good ? no person is good but one,—God.   20. Omn. from my youth.   29. Omn. or wife.   Many times more, for, a hundred times more.

Ch. xx. 6. Omn. hour.   Omn. idle.   7. Omn. and whatever is right, ye shall receive.   16. Omn. For many are called, but few are chosen.   17. and in the way, for, in the way, and. 19. he shall be raised up, for, he shall rise again.   22. Omn. and to be immersed in the immersion in which I am to be immersed ?   23. Omn. and in the immersion in which I am to be immersed shall ye be immersed.   34. Omn. their eyes.

Ch. xxi. 4. Omn. all.   12. M. Omn. of God.   13. ye make it, for, ye have made it a den of thieves.   31. Omn. to him. 33. A man, for, a certain man.   44. M. omn. And he who falls on this stone, will be broken, but on whom it shall fall, him it will scatter [as dust].
Ch. xxii. 7. Omn. when he heard of it.   30. Omn. of God. 39. which is like, is this, for, is like to it.
Ch. xxiii. 3. say, for, bid observe.   5. Omn. of their garments. 8. Teacher, for, Chief.   9. the heavenly, for, who is in heaven.   14. Omn. Woe to you, Scribes and Pharisees, hypocrites, for ye devour widows' houses, and for a pretence make long prayers; therefore ye shall receive greater condemnation. (The Syriac places this verse before verse 13.)   17. has made holy, for makes holy (the gold.)   19. Omn. fools and.   23. to have left, for, to leave.   26. of it, for, of them.   38. M. omn. desolate.
Ch. xxiv. 2. he answered and said, for, he said.   6. Omn. all. 7. Omn. and pestilences.   36. Adn. nor the Son.   38. Adn. in those (days.)   42. what day, for, what hour.   45. the Lord, for, his Lord.   48. Omn. to come.
Ch. xxv. 6. Omn. is coming.   15. went. Straightway he, for, straightway went. He.   18. the earth, for, in the earth.   20, 22. Omn. beside them, twice.   31. Omn. holy.
Ch. xxvi. 3. Omn. and the scribes.   17. said, for, said to him. 22. each one, for, each of them.   28. covenant, for, new covenant.   33. if, for, even if.   42. this, for, this cup.   44. Adn. (same words) again.   55. Omn. with you.   59. Omn. and the elders.   63. Omn. answered and.   65. the blasphemy, for, his blasphemy.   75. said, for, said to him.
Ch. xxvii. 2. delivered, for, delivered him.   4. M. righteous, for, innocent.   9. The Revisers retain Jeremiah, which word is not in the Syriac.   23. Omn. Governor, some Syr. copies, Pilate. 24. M. this blood, for, the blood of this righteous person.   28. M. clothed him, for, stripped him.   34. wine, for, vinegar. 42. He is, for, if he is.   49. M. Adn. And another took a spear, and pierced his side, and there came out water and blood.   58. it, for, the body (to be given up.)   64. Omn. by night.
Ch. xxviii. 2. Omn. from the door.   6. M. omn. the Lord. 17. they worshipped, for, they worshipped him.   20. Omn. Amen.
MARK. Ch. i. 1. M. omn. the Son of God.   4. John came, who was immersing, for, John was immersing.   13. was, for, was there.   14. Omn. of the kingdom.   16. passing along, for, walking.   The brother of Simon, for, his brother.   Casting, for, casting a net.   18. the nets, for, their nets.   23. Adn. immediately (there was.)   27. A new teaching, for, What is this new teaching? for.   28. Adn. everywhere.   29. M. he, for, they (most Syr. copies, they.)   31. Omn. immediately.   34. M. adn. to be the Anointed.   38. Adn. elsewhere.   39. came, for,

was (proclaiming.)   40. M. omn. kneeling down to him.   Syriac, fell at his feet.   41. Omn. Jesus.

Ch. ii. 4. M. bring him, for, come near.   5. forgiven, for, forgiven to thee.   7. speak thus? he blasphemes; for, thus speak blasphemies?   9. Omn. to thee.   12. arose and immediately, for, immediately arose, and.   15. that he was, for, that while he was (lying at table.)   16. the scribes of the Pharisees, for, the scribes and the Pharisees.   He eats, for, How is it that he eats?   M. omn. and drinks.   18. the Pharisees, for, the (disciples) of the Pharisees.   the disciples of, for, those of (the Pharisees).   21. the new filling up of the old takes away from it, for, the new filling up of it takes away from the old.   22. will burst, for, doth burst (the skins.)   the wine perishes, and the skins, for, the wine is spilled, and the skins perish.   Omn. must be put.

Ch. iii. 7. followed, for, followed him.   8. were hearing, for, had heard.   14. M. adn. whom he also named apostles.   15. Omn. to heal diseases, and.   16. M. adn. and he made the twelve.   19. he came, for, they came.   25. will not be able, for, is not able.   29. eternal sin, for, eternal condemnation.   Syr. condemnation which is for ever.

Ch. iv. 10. the parables, for, the parable.   11. is given the mystery, for, is given to know the mystery.   12. it be forgiven, for, their sins be forgiven.   15. in them, for, in their hearts.   18. and others, for, and these.   19. the world, for, this world.   22. nothing hid but that it might be made manifest, for, nothing hid which shall not be made manifest.   24. Omn. who hear.   28. Omn. for.   30. how, for, to what.   with what shall we put it in comparison? for, by what comparison shall we compare it.   31. though it is least, for, is the least.   34. to his own disciples, for, to his disciples.   40. why are ye fearful? have ye not yet trust? for, why are ye so fearful? how is it that ye have not trust?

Ch. v. 1. Gerasenes, for, Gadarenes.   3. No longer with a chain, for, with chains.   12. Omn. all the demons.   Syriac has, those demons.   14. they came, for, they went out.   18. when he was entering, for, when he had entered.   23. beseeches, for, besought.   that she may be healed.   Syr., she will be healed. that she may live, for, she will live.   25. Omn. a certain.   27. Adn. the things (concerning Jesus.)   40. Omn. was lying.   42. Adn. immediately (they were astonished.)

Ch. vi. 1. comes, for, came.   2. M. the many, for, many. and such, for, that such.   11. whatsoever place, for, whosoever. Omn. Verily I say to you, it shall be more tolerable for Sodom and Gomorrah in the day of judgment, than for that city.   14. M. they were, for, he was (saying.)   15. Omn. is (a prophet.)   16. Omn. is (John), he . . . from among the dead.   20. was perplexed, for, was doing.   22. M. his daughter Herodias, for, the daughter of Herodias herself.   24. who immerses, for, the Immerser.   33.

Omn. the multitudes, Syr. many persons.   34. Omn. Jesus.
36. buy something to eat, for, buy bread, for they have nothing to
eat.   48. Omn. and (about.)   51. Omn. and wondered.   52.
but, instead of, for (their heart.)   53. to the land, they came to,
for, they came to the land of (Gennesaret.)
    Ch. vii. 2. Omn. they found fault.   4. M. sprinkle themselves,
for, immerse themselves. Omn. of beds.   5. defiled, for, un-
washed.   8. Omn. immersions of cups and pots ; and many things
which are like these.   12. Omn. And (ye suffer.)   14. again,
for, all (the multitude.)   15. from the man, for, from him.
Omn. those things.   16. Omn. He who has ears to hear, let him
hear.   17. Omn. concerning.   24. M. omn. and Sidon.
31. he came through Sidon to the sea, for, and of Sidon, he came
to the sea.   35. Omn. immediately.
    Ch. viii. 1. Adn. again.   9. Omn. those who ate.   13. Omn.
into the boat.   16. M. they have not, for, we have not.   17.
hardened, for, still hardened.   21. Omn. how is it.   22. they
come, for, he comes.   23. if thou seest, for, if he saw.   24.
for I behold them as trees, instead of, as trees.   25. he looked,
for, he made him look up. The Syriac has neither.   26. Omn.
nor tell it to any one in the village.   29. asked them, for Syriac,
Jesus says to them.   34. if any one, for, whoever.   36. to gain,
and to lose, for, if he shall gain, and lose.   37. for what, instead
of, or what.
    Ch. ix. 3. Omn. as snow.   3. Adn. so.   6. answer, for,
say.   7. Omn. saying.   14. when they came, they saw, for,
when he came, he saw.   16. and he asked them, for, he asked
the scribes.   17. answered him, for, answered and said.   23.
if thou canst! for, if thou canst trust.   Omn. with tears.   26.
torn, for, torn him.   29. Omn. and with fasting.   31. after
three days, for, on the third day.   33. Omn. among yourselves.
42. M. who trust, for, who trust in me.   43. shall make, for,
makes (thee stumble).   44. Omn. where their worm dies not, and the
(Syriac their) fire is not quenched.   46. Omn. where their worm
dies not, and the (Syriac their) fire is not quenched.   47. into
hell, for, into the hell of fire.   49. Omn. and every slain offering
shall be salted with salt.
    Ch. x. 5. Omn. answered and.   6. he made them, for, God
made them.   7. M. omn. and shall be joined to his wife.   12.
if she, having put away her husband, shall marry, for, if a woman
shall put away her husband, and shall marry.   13. them, for,
those who brought them.   20. Omn. answered and.   21. Omn.
take up thy cross.   24. M. omn. for those who trust in riches.
26. to him, for, among themselves.   29. Omn. answered and.
Omn. or wife.   32. those who, for, they (followed.)   34.
after three days, for, on the third day.   35. ask of thee, for, ask.
43. is, for, shall be.   44. among you, for, of you.   46. a blind

beggar, for, blind man.   Omn. begging.   49. said, call him, for, commanded him to be called.   50. sprang up, for, arose.

Ch. xi. 2. Adn. never.   3. he sends him again, for, he will send him.   6. said, for, commanded.   7. bring, for, brought. 8. do cast, for, did cast.   fields, for, trees.   Omn. and strowed them in the way.   9. Omn. saying.   11. Omn. Jesus.   15. Omn. Jesus.   18. for, instead of, because.   23. Omn. whatever he shall say.   24. have received, for, are to receive.   26. Omn. But if ye do not forgive, neither will your Father who is in heaven forgive your trespasses.   28. they said, for, they say. or, for, and (who.)   29. Omn. I also.

Ch. xii. 4. Omn. they stoned him.   Dishonoured him, for, sent him away dishonoured.   5. Omn. again.   17. marvelled greatly, for, marvelled.   19. child, for, children.   21. without leaving, for, nor did he leave.   22. And . . . did not leave, for, and . . . had her, and did not leave.   23. Omn. therefore. 25. Omn. (angels) who are.   27. Omn. ye therefore.   29. (Jesus) answered, for Syr. said to him.   Omn. of all the commands.   30, 31. Omn. this is the first command, and.   31. Omn. which is like it.   33. Omn. with all the soul.   Much more, for, more.   36. M. beneath, for, the footstool beneath. 37. Omn. therefore.   41. Omn. Jesus.

Ch. xiii. 8. there shall be, for, and there shall be.   Omn. and tumults.   11. Omn. neither premeditate.   14. Omn. which was spoken by Daniel the prophet.   18. Omn. your flight.   22. the chosen, for, even the chosen.   27. the, for, his (angels.) 32. or, for, and (that hour.)   33. M. omn. and pray.   34. to each, for, and to each.

Ch. xiv. 4. Omn. and saying.   5. This ointment, for, this. 9. the gospel, for Syriac, this my gospel.   14. my, for, the (guestchamber.)   19. Omn. And they.   24. covenant, for, new covenant.   27. Omn. on account of me this night.   40. he came again, for Syriac, he returned again, and came.   45. Omn. Rabbi, once.   65. received him, for, struck him.   68. I neither know nor understand, for Syriac, I know not.   M. what dost thou say? for, what thou sayest.   M. omn. and the cock crew.   70. Omn. and thy speech is like (that of Galilee.)

Ch. xv. 4. they accuse thee of, for, they witness against thee. 8. went up, for, called out.   12. Omn. do you wish.   23. Omn. to drink.   24. they crucify him, and divide, for, when they had crucified him, they divided.   28. Omn. And the Scripture was fulfilled which says, And he was numbered with the lawless. 31. M. can he not save? for, he cannot save (himself.)   34. Omn. saying (Eloi.)   39. Omn. (that) having cried out.   45. corpse, for, body.

Ch. xvi. 9-20. The Revisers state in the Margin that "the two oldest Greek manuscripts, and some other authorities, omit" these twelve verses. The bad character of those two oldest copies is shown by the record which is here given of mutilations which are chiefly derived from them. Dean Burgon says, " With the exception of those two manuscripts, there is *not one* codex in existence, uncial or cursive, (and we are acquainted with at least eighteen other uncials, and about six hundred cursive copies of this Gospel) which leaves out the last twelve verses of Mark." (Book on these verses, 1871. p. 71.)   17. Omn. new (before tongues.)

LUKE, Ch. i. 17. M. come to, for, go before.   28. Omn. the angel.   Omn. thou art blessed among women.   29. Omn. when she saw [him.]   the, for, his (saying.)   35. Omn. of thee, (after, to be begotten.)   42. outcry, for, voice.   45. M. has believed that, for, has trusted, because.   61. of, for, among (thy kindred.)   66. for, instead of, and (the hand.)

Ch. ii. 9. Omn. behold.   14. peace among men of good-will, for, (on earth) peace; [God's] good pleasure among men. (Syriac, and good hope for men.)   21. him, for, the child.   33. his father, for, Joseph.   37. even for, for, of about.   38. God, for, the Lord.   40. Omn. in spirit.   43. his parents, for, Joseph and his mother.   51. Omn. these (sayings.)

Ch. iii. 4. Omn. who said.   10, 12, 14. what must, for, what shall we do, three times.   17. to clean, . . . to gather, Syriac, is cleaning, . . . is gathering.   19. Omn. Philip.   22. in bodily form as, Syriac, in the likeness of the body of a dove. Omn. which said.

Ch. iv. 2. Omn. afterwards.   4. Omn. and said.   Omn. but upon every word of God.   5. Omn. the devil, (Syriac Satan) . . . into a high mountain.   9. Omn. the, (before Son of God. The Syriac very rarely expresses *the*.   The Greek, without *the*, may mean either, a son, or, the Son.)   18. Omn. to heal the heart-broken.   34. Omn. saying.   41. Omn. the Anointed. 44. M. of Judea, for, of Galilee.

Ch. v. 1. and heard, for, to hear.   5. (Simon) said, for, said to him.   5, 6. nets, for, net.   7. Omn. who were.   17. to heal him, for, to heal them.   20. said, for, Syriac, said to the para-lytic.   33. Omn. why ?   34. Jesus, for, he.   36. will cut, for, cuts.   will not agree, for, agrees not.   38. Omn. and both are preserved.   39. Omn. immediately.

Ch. vi. 2. said, for, said to them.   9. I ask, for, I will ask. 10. he did, for, he did so.   Syriac, he stretched it out.   Omn. as the other.   25. Adn. now (after full.)   25, 26. woe, for, woe to you, twice.   36. Omn. therefore.   43. nor again, for, nor. 45. the evil one, for, the evil man.   Out of the evil, for, out of the evil treasure of his heart.   48. because it had been well built, for, because it had been founded upon the rock.

Ch. vii. 10. Omn. who had been ill.   11. soon after, for, next

day.   19. to the Lord, for, to Jesus.   22. Omn. Jesus.   28.
Omn. a prophet.   Omn. the Immerser.   32. Omn. to you (after
mourned.)   39. M. the, for, a (prophet.)
     Ch. viii. 12. have heard, for, hear.   21. do, for, do it.   24.
he awoke, for, he arose.   26, 37. Gerasenes; M. Gergesenes, or
Gadarenes, for, Gadarenes.   27. Omn. him (after met.)   For a
long time had worn, for, had had demons for a long time, and had
worn.   38. Omn. Jesus.   43. M. omn. had spent all her
living on physicians, and.   45. M. omn. and those with him.
Omn. and sayest thou, Who touched me?   48. Omn. be of good
comfort.   49. saying, for, saying to him.   50. answered him,
for, said.   54. Omn. put them all out.
     Ch. ix. 2. M. omn. the sick.   5. the dust, for, also the dust.
7. Omn. by him.   10. to the city called, for, to a desert place of
the city called. (The Syriac has not called.)   14. about fifty, for,
fifty.   34. when they, for, when those (entered. The Syriac has,
when they saw Moses and Elijah enter.)   35. my chosen, for, my
beloved (Son.)   43. Omn. Jesus.   48. is, for, shall be (great.)
54. Omn. as also Elijah did.   55, 56. Omn. And said, ye know
not of what spirit ye are. For the Son of man has not come to
destroy the lives of men, but to save. (Syriac, to destroy lives, but
to give life.)   57. Omn. O Lord.   60. Omn. Jesus.
     Ch. x. i. 17. M. seventy-two, for, seventy, twice.   5. M. enter
first, for, first say.   11. has come near, for, has come near to you.
15. shalt thou be exalted to heaven? for, which hast been exalted
to heaven.   19. I have given, for, I give.   21. Omn. Jesus.
32. Omn. being (at the place.)   33. saw, for, saw him.   36.
Omn. therefore.   38. Omn. it came to pass.   40. was leaving
me, for, has left me.   41. the Lord, for, Jesus.   41, 42. M.
omn. thou art anxious and . . . about many things.
     Ch. xi. 2. Omn. Our (Father) who art in heaven.   Omn. Thy
will be done, as in heaven, also on earth.   4. Omn. but deliver
us from evil.   11. M. omn. a loaf, will he give him a stone? and
if.   14. Omn. and it was.   29. Omn. the prophet.   34.
Omn. therefore.   44. Omn. Scribes and Pharisees, hypocrites.
48. ye are witnesses, for, ye bear witness.   ye build, for, ye
build their tombs.   53. when he had come out thence, for, while
he said (Syriac, when he had said) these things to them.   54.
Omn. and seeking.   Omn. that they might accuse him.
     Ch. xii. 7. Fear not, for, fear not therefore.   18. my corn, for,
my increase.   22. the life, for, your life.   25. a cubit, for, one
cubit.   31. his, for, God's (kingdom.)   these things, for, all
these things,   38. Omn. servants.   40. Omn. therefore.   41.
said, for, said to him.   56. ye know not how to discern, for, ye
do not discern.
     Ch. xiii. 2. Omn. Jesus.   These, for, such things.   9. bear
fruit afterwards, for, if not. afterwards.   11. Omn. there was (a

woman.) 15. ye hypocrites, for, thou hypocrite. 18. therefore, for, and (he said.) 19. a tree, for, a great tree. 24. M. shall
not be able when, for, shall not be able. When, etc. 25. Omn.
Lord, once. 27. I know not whence, for, I know you not,
whence. 31. (In that) hour, for, day. 35. (Your house is)
left, for, left desolate.

Ch. xiv. 6. Omn. him (to these things.) 17. Omn. all things.
21. the servant, for, that servant. 22. that which, for, as. 27.
Whosoever, for, And whosoever. 34. Adn. therefore.

Ch. xv. 16. to be filled with, for, to fill his belly with. 19, 21.
I am, for, and I am; twice. 21. M. Adn. make me as one of
thy hired servants. 22. bring forth quickly, for, bring forth.

Ch. xvi. 1. the, for, his (disciples.) 12. M. our own, for, your
own. 18. Omn. everyone. 20. Omn. there was. 21. Omn.
the crumbs. 26. in, for, beside (all these things.) 29.
(Abraham) said, for, said to him.

Ch. xvii. 2. a millstone, for, an ass-millstone. 4. Omn. a day
(turn.) 6. if ye have, for, if ye had. 7. (come) immediately,
for, (will say) immediately. 9. Omn. that (servant.) commanded? for, commanded him? I think not. 10. we have done,
for, because we have done. 21. or there, for, or (Syriac, and)
behold there. 23. Behold there, behold here, for, behold here,
and behold there. 24. M. omn. in his day. 33. Omn. it,
Syriac, his life, (shall preserve it.) 36. Omn. Two shall be in the
field; the one shall be taken, and the other left.

Ch. xviii. 1. Omn. also (a parable.) 13. his breast, for, upon
his breast. 24. Omn. that he was very sorrowful. 28. our
own things, for, all things. 41. Omn. saying.

Ch. xix. 5. Omn. saw him, and. 15. they had gained, for,
each had gained. 20. the other, for, another. 26. I say, Syriac,
He said to them, I say. 29. the, for, his (disciples.) 31. say,
for, say to him. 40. said, for, said to them. 42. Syriac, the
things which are for thy peace, at least in this thy day. The R. E.
V. in this day, even thou, the things which belong unto peace.
45. who sold, for, who sold in it, and bought. 46. shall be, for,
is (a house of prayer.)

Ch. xx. 2. spoke, saying to him, for Syriac, said to him. 9.
a man, for, a certain man. 13. Omn. when they see. 14.
Omn. come. 23. Omn. why tempt ye me? 26. of a word,
for, of a word from him. 28. be, for, die (childless.) 30. Omn.
took the woman, and died childless.

Ch. xxi. 2. Omn. also. 4. Omn. of God. 6. Adn. here
(one stone.) 34, 35. suddenly as a snare; instead of, suddenly:
for as a snare. 36. But, for, therefore. may be able, for, may
be counted worthy.

Ch. xxii. 14. the Apostles, for, the twelve Apostles. 16. not,
for, not any more. 18. Adn. from now. 19. M. omn. which

is given on behalf of you; this do ye in remembrance of me. 20. M. Omn. in like manner also the cup after supper saying, this cup is (Syriac, this is the cup of) the new covenant in my blood, which is to be poured out on behalf of you.   22. For, instead of, And (the Son.)   30. ye shall sit, for, that ye may sit.   31. Omn. And the Lord (Syriac, Jesus) said.   37. this, for, also this.   39 and 45. the, for, his (disciples), twice.   43, 44. M. omn. And there appeared to him an angel from heaven, strengthening him. And being in an agony, (Syriac, in fear,) he prayed more earnestly, and his sweat became as drops of blood falling on the ground.   49. said, for, said to him.   61. Adn. to-day.   64. Omn. they struck him on the face, and.   68. answer, for, answer me, nor let me go.

xxiii. 6. Omn. of Galilee.   8. Omn. many things.   15. he sent him back to us, for, I sent you (Syriac, him,) to him.   17. Omn. For it was necessary for him to release to them one at the feast.   23. Omn. and of the chief priests.   25. released, for, released to them.   34. M. omn. And Jesus said, Father, forgive them, for they know not what they do.   38. Omn. written in Greek, and Latin, and Hebrew.   39. Art not thou the Anointed? for, If thou art the Anointed.   42. Omn. Lord.   into, for, in (thy kingdom.)   43. He, for, Jesus (said.)   44. now about, for, about.   45. (the sun) was eclipsed, for was darkened.

Ch. xxiv. 1. Omn. and some with them.   6. M. omn. he is not here, but is risen.   9. M. omn. from the tomb.   12. M. Omn. and Peter rose up, and ran to the tomb, and stooping down, he saw the linen clothes laid by themselves, and departed, wondering in himself at what had happened.   17. and they stood still, looking sad, for, and are sad.   36. he, for, Jesus.   M. omn. and said to them, Peace be unto you.   38. your heart, for, your hearts.   40. M. omn. And when he had said this, he showed them his hands and his feet.   42. Omn. and part of a honey-comb. 44. my words, for, the words.   46. Omn. and thus it was right that. 47, 48. M. ye, beginning at Jerusalem, are witness-bearers, for, beginning at Jerusalem. And ye are witness-bearers.   49. Omn. Jerusalem.   51. M. omn. and was carried up into heaven. 52. M. Omn. they worshipped him.   53. Omn. praising and. Omn. Amen.

JOHN i. 3, 4. M. without him was nothing made. That which has been made in him was life; instead of, without him was nothing made which has been made. In him was life.   15. M. this was he who said, for, this was he of whom I said.   18. M. an only-begotten God, for, the only-begotten Son :—Syriac, that only God.   27. Omn. He it is .... who was before I [was].   29. Omn. John,   30. on behalf of whom, for, about whom.   42. John, for, Jona.   43. Omn. Jesus.   Adn. Jesus (said to him.)   49. Omn. and said to him.   51. Omn. from now.

Ch. ii. 10. Omn. then.   12. Omn. his (brothers.)   17. will eat, for, has eaten (me up.)
Ch. iii. 2. him, for, Jesus.   13. M. omn. who is in heaven.   15. Omn. might not perish.   17. the Son, for, his Son.   31. M. omn. is above all.   32. Omn. And (what.)   34. Omn. God (gives.)
Ch. iv. 6. about the sixth, for, Syriac, the sixth.   9. M. omn. For Jews have no dealings with Samaritans.   15. come through, for, come.   35, 36. M. already he who reaps, for, already white to harvest, and he who reaps.   42. Omn. the Anointed.   43. Omn. and went away.   46. Omn. Jesus.   47. Omn. (intreated) him.   51. Omn. and told him.   51. his son, for, thy son.
Ch. v. i. M. the feast, for, a feast.   2. M. Bethsaida, or Bethzatha, for, Bethesda.   3. Omn. great.   3, 4. Omn. waiting for the stirring up of the water. For a messenger from time to time went down into the bathing-pool, and stirred up the water; and he who first went down after the stirring up of the water, was cured of whatever disease he had.   12. Omn. thy bed.   16. Omn. and sought to kill him.   27. Omn. also.
Ch. vi. 7. Omn. (each) of them.   10. about, Syriac, (five thousand.)   14. M. signs, for, sign.   14. Omn. Jesus.   17. had not yet, for, had not (come to them.)   22. Omn. that into which his disciples had entered.   23. but there came boats, for, but there came other boats.   42. how does he now say? for, how then does this [man] say?   45. Omn. therefore.   47. Omn. in me.   51. Omn. which I will give.   55. true, for, truly, twice.   58. Omn. your (fathers) . . . . the manna.   65. the Father, for, my father.   69. the Holy One of God, for, the Anointed, the Son of the living God.
Ch. vii. 4. M. he seeks that it may be, for, he himself seeks to be.   8. Omn. this (feast.)   M. I do not, for, I do not yet; Syriac, now.   15. Therefore, for, and (the Jews.)   16. Adn. Therefore (Jesus.)   20. Omn. and said.   21, 22. M. ye all marvel because of this. Moses gave; for, ye all marvel. Because of this, Moses gave.   26. Omn. truly (the Anointed?)   29. I, for, but I (know him.)   31. Omn. than these.   39. had trusted, for, were trusting.   40. Omn. many.   40. these words, for, his words.   41. but some, for, but others.   46. Omn. as this man does.   50. Omn. by night.   50. Adn. before.   52. M. see; because, for, see that (no prophet.)   53. (The words, And each went to his house, are not in the Peshito.)
Ch. viii. 1—11. (These verses are not in the Peshito.)   21. Omn. Jesus.   28. Omn. to them.   28. the Father, for, my Father.   29. Omn. Syriac, my Father.   38. the Father, for, my Father.   38. ye have heard, for, ye have seen.   38. Omn. your (father.)   39. if ye are, for, if ye were (the children of Abraham); M. do ye, for, ye would do (the works of Abraham.)   59. Omn. He passed through the midst of them, and went away.

Ch. ix. 4. We must, for, I must.   6. Omn. of the blind man.
10. Adn. (How) then?   11. Omn. and said, Syriac, to them.
11. Omn. the pool, Syriac, the waters.   14. the day on which,
for, when.   25. Omn. and said, Syriac, to them.   26. Omn.
again.   35. said, for, said to him.   35. M. Son of man?
instead of, Son of God?   41. Omn. therefore (your sin.)
Ch. x. 4. all his own, for, his own sheep.   12. scatters, for,
scatters the sheep.   13. Omn. the hireling flees.   14. mine
know me, for, I am known by mine.   18. M. has taken it away, for,
takes it away.   26. Omn. as I said to you.   29. M. that which
my Father has given me, is greater than all things; for, my Father
who has given them to me, is greater than all.   29. the Father's
hand, for, my Father's hand.   32. the Father, for, my Father.
33. answered, for, said.   38. (that ye may) know and know, for,
know and believe.
Ch. xi. 12, 54. the, for, his (disciples); twice.   19. Omn. their
(brother.)   22. And now, for, but even now.   28. (said) this,
for, these things.   M. called Mary, ... saying secretly, for,
called Mary.1... secretly, saying.   30. Adn. still (in the place.)
50. (expedient) for you, instead of, for us.
Ch. xii. 7. Suffer her to keep it for the day of my burial, for, Let
her alone, she has kept it for the day of my burial.   22. (Andrew
and Philip) come and tell, for, tell (Jesus)   25. loses, for, shall
lose (his life.)   35. among you, for, with you.   40. I will heal,
for, I should heal (them.)   41. (said Isaiah) because, for, when
(he saw.)
Ch. xiii. 3. Omn. Jesus.   10. M. Omn. his feet.   18. (He
who eats) my bread, for, bread with me.   24. (Peter beckoned
to him,) and said to him, for, that he should ask who it would be.
25. and he thus fell upon; for, and he, (Syriac, that disciple) fell
upon (the bosom of Jesus.)   26. Adn. he took it, and (gave it
to Judas.)   32. Omn. if God has been glorified in him.
Ch. xiv. 4. (whither I go,) ye know the way, for, ye know, and
the way ye know.   5. How do we know? for, and how can we know?
10. (the Father) does his works, for, does the (Syriac, these) works.
12, 28. the Father, for, my Father, twice.   15, ye will keep, for,
keep ye.
Ch. xv. 7. ask ye, for, ye shall ask.   8. M. that ye may be, for,
so shall ye be.   14. the things which, for, whatsoever things.
Ch. xvi. 10. the Father, for, my Father.   15. takes, for, shall
take.   16. Omn. because I go to the Father.   23. If ye shall
ask anything of the Father, he will give it you in my name; for,
whatsoever he shall ask of the (Syriac, my,) Father in my name,
he will give it you.   29. (his disciples) say, for, say to him.
32. Omn. now.   33. ye have, for, ye will have.
Ch. xvii. 1. that the Son, for, that thy Son.   11. (keep those
in thy name), [the name] which thou hast given me; for, those

whom (Syriac, that which) thou hast given me. 12. (while I was with them) omn. in the world, (I kept them in thy name), which [name] thou hast given me ; for, those whom thou hast given me (I have kept.) 17. the truth, for, thy truth. 21. (that they also may be) in us ; for, one in us. 24. (Father, I wish that) that which, for, those whom (thou hast given me), etc.

Ch. xviii. 40. they, for, they all cried out.

Ch. xix. 3. Adn. and they came to him. 7. (according to) the law, for, our law. 13. these words, for, this saying. 16. Omn. and led him away. 17. bearing the cross on himself, for, bearing his cross. 29. so they put a sponge, full of vinegar, on hyssop, for, and they filled a sponge with vinegar, and put it on hyssop. 38. (and took) his body, for, the body of Jesus. 39. (who came) to him, for, to Jesus. M. a wrapping, for, a mixture (of myrrh and aloes.)

Ch. xx. 17. the, for, my (Father.) 29. M. hast thou believed ? for, thou hast believed. 30. the, for, his (disciples.)

Ch. xxi. 14. the, for, his (disciples.) 15, 16, 17. son of John, for, son of Jonas, thrice.

ACTS i. 4. While he ate, for, while he ate with them. 8. my, for, to me (witness-bearers.) 15. of the brothers, for, of the disciples. 16. the Scripture, for, that Scripture. 17. among us, for, with us. 19. in their language, for, Syriac, in the language of the place. 23. Barsabbas, for, Barsabas. 25. the place, for, the lot (of this service.)

Ch. ii. 7. Omn. one to another. 23. ye, by the hand of the lawless, have crucified, for, Syriac, ye have delivered into the hands of the wicked, and have crucified. 33. which ye see, for, Syriac, which, behold, ye see. 38. (Peter) to them, for, said to them. (for the pardon) of your, for, of (sins.) 41. those who received, for, those who readily received. 42. in the breaking of bread, for, Syriac, in the breaking of the Eucharist.

Ch. iii. 1. Omn. together. 6. Omn. rise up and. 13. denied, for, denied him. 22. Omn. For (Moses.) the Lord God, for, Syriac, the Lord. 25. (with) your, for, our (fathers.)

Ch. iv. 1. M. the chief priests, for, the priests. 5. Adn. to, Syriac, in Jerusalem. 8. Omn. of Israel. 18. commanded, for, commanded them. 24. Omn. thou art God. 25. M. The Greek text in this clause is somewhat uncertain. Text ; who, by the Holy Spirit, [by] the mouth of our father David, thy servant, didst say ; for, Syriac, And thou art he who, by means of the Holy Spirit, by the mouth of thy servant David, hast said. 33. M. of the Lord Jesus the Anointed ; for, Syriac, of Jesus the Anointed.

Ch. v. 9. (Peter) to her, for, said to her. 28. we strictly commanded, for, did we not strictly command (you) ? 32. M. and God has given the Holy Spirit, for, and [so is] the Holy Spirit, whom God has given. 33. wished, for, took counsel. 34. the men,

for, the apostles.   37. (drew away) people, for, many people.
39. ye will not be able, for, ye cannot.   overthrow them, for, overthrow it.
    Ch. vi. 3. M. but, for, therefore.   of the Spirit, for, Syriac, the
Spirit of the Lord.
    Ch. vii. 16. of Hamor, in Shechem, for, Syriac, of Hamor.   17.
(which God) had made, for, had made by oath.   30. an angel, for,
an angel of the Lord.   31. (the voice of the Lord came), omn., to
him.   35. with the hand, for, by the hands.   36. in Egypt,
for, in the land of Egypt.   37. (shall) God, for, the Lord God.
Omn. him shall ye hear.   51. in hearts, for, in their heart.
    Ch. viii. 8. much, for, great (joy.)   10. (the power) called
great, for, the great (power.)   18. M. the Spirit, for, the Holy
Spirit.   22. (intreat) the Lord, for, God.
    Ch. ix. 5. Omn. the Lord said.   12. has seen, for, has seen in
a vision.   12. hands, for, hand.   25. his disciples, for, the
disciples (took him . . . . by night.)   29. of the Lord, for, of
Jesus.   38. Delay not to come to us, for, that he would not delay
to come to them.
    Ch. x. 1. Omn. there was.   5. a certain Simon, for, Simon.
10. (a trance) came, for, fell (upon him.)   11. Omn. bound, and.
16. Adn. immediately (the vessel.)   17. by, for, from (Cornelius.)
24. M. he, for, they (entered.)   30. Omn. I was fasting.   32.
Omn. who will come and speak to thee.   33. by the Lord, for,
by God.   36. M. he sent the word, for, the word which he sent.
    Ch. xi. 9. Omn. me (a second time.)   11. we were, for, I was.
13. saying, for, saying to him.   28. Claudius, for, Claudius
Cæsar.
    Ch. xii. 5. earnestly, for, earnest (prayer.)   5. for, instead of,
on behalf of.   9. followed, for, followed him.   25. M. to,
instead of, from (Jerusalem.)
    Ch. xiii. 19. Omn. to them.   20. he made them inherit for
about four hundred and fifty years, instead of, he gave them judges
for about, etc.   23. has brought to, for, has raised up for.   25.
what, for, whom (think ye)?   26. to us, for, to you.   33. to
our children, for, to us, their children.   40. Omn. upon you
(what was spoken.)   44. M. (the word) of the Lord, for, of God.
    Ch. xiv. 28. Omn. there (they abode.)
    Ch. xv. 8. Omn. to them (the Holy Spirit.)   11. the Lord
Jesus, for, the Lord Jesus the Anointed.   17, 18. who makes
these things known from eternity, for, who does all these things.
Known from eternity are the works of God.   23. Omn. (they
wrote) these things; Syriac, thus.   24. M. omn. who went out
(from us.)   24. Omn. saying that ye should be circumcised, and
keep the law.   29. things strangled, for, what is strangled.
30. came down, for, came.   33. to those who had sent them
forth, for, to the apostles.   34. This verse is not in the Peshito :—

But it was the wish of Silas to remain there.   40. of the Lord, for, of God.
    Ch. xvi. 1. Omn. a certain (Jewess.)   10. God, for, the Lord.
13. out of the gate, for, Syriac, out of the gate of the city.   13.
where we supposed there was, for, Syriac, because (a house of prayer)
was seen there.   31. Omn. the Anointed.   32. M. of God,
for, of the Lord.   34. the house, for, his house.   36. the words,
for, these words.
    Ch. xvii. 18. (because he told) omn. them.   23. that which,
for, him whom (ye ignorantly worship.)   23. this thing, for, him
(I declare to you.)   26. (has made) of one, for, of one blood.
30. M. announces to men that all should repent, for, commands
men all to repent.
    Ch. xviii. 1. Omn. Paul.   3. they worked, for, he worked
with them.   15. Omn. for, (I do not wish.)   20. Omn. with
them.   21. Omn. I certainly ought to keep the feast which is
coming in Jerusalem.
    Ch. xix. 2. Omn. they said.   3. Omn. (he said) to them.   4.
in Jesus, for, in Jesus the Anointed.   9. of Tyrannus, for, Syriac,
of a man whose name was Tyrannus.   12. were carried away,
for, were brought.   13. I, for, we (charge you on oath.)   16.
(overcame) them both, for, them.   29. the city, for, the whole
city.
    Ch. xx. 1. sent for, instead of, called to him.   4. M. omn. as
far as Asia.   4. (Sopater,) Adn. son of Pyrrhus.   5. M. came
to us, for, went in advance.   15. Omn. and stayed in Trogyl-
lium.   21. M. Omn. the Anointed.   24. But I make life of no
account [as] dear to me, for, Syriac, But my life is not esteemed
by me to be anything, ([unless it be] so that.)   25. the kingdom,
for, the kingdom of God.   28. Omn. therefore.   28. M. (the
assembly) of the Lord, for, as in most Syriac copies, of the Anointed.
These copies include the editions of Walton, Gutbier, the Maronites,
Schaaf, and that of Ooroomiah. Lee has God, but he does not
state on what authority. He says that other copies have, the
Anointed.   29. Omn. For (I know.)   32. M. to the Lord, for,
to God.   32. to give, for, to give you.
    Ch. xxi. 20. among the Jews, for, Syriac, in Judea.   22.
certainly they will hear, for, Syriac, because therefore they have
heard.   24. so that they will shave, for, that they may shave.
and all will know, for, that all may know.   25. M. we have sent,
for, we have written.
    Ch. xxii. 20. Omn. to his being killed.   30. (he commanded)
the council to come together, for, Syriac, the assembly of their
chief men to come.
    Ch. xxiii. 9. Omn. let us not fight against God ; the Syriac has
instead, what is there in this ?   12. the Jews, for, some of the Jews.
20. (as if) thou wast, for, they were (wishing to learn.)   28. M.

omn. I brought him down to their council.   30. Omn. by the Jews.   30. Omn. Farewell.

Ch. xxiv. 1. with some elders, for, with elders.   5. tumults, for, tumult.   6—8. Omn. and wished to judge him according to our law, but Lysias, the commander of a thousand men, came, and with great violence took him out of our hands, Syriac, and sent him to thee; he also commanded his accusers to come to thee. 15. (resurrection) omn. of the dead.   20. (they found) omn. in me.   23. that he, for, that Paul (be guarded.)   24. in the Anointed Jesus, for, in the Anointed.

Ch. xxv. 13. having saluted, for, to salute (Festus.)   16. omn. to destruction.   22. (Agrippa) omn. said.

Ch. xxvi. 3. Omn. I know.   3. I beseech, for, I beseech thee. 7. O king, for, O king Agrippa.   16. (one who bears witness) of the things thou hast seen respecting me, and of those [in which] I will appear to thee; for, of this, that thou hast seen me, and of [when] thou in the future wilt see me.   28. Omn. (Agrippa) said.   28. By little, thou art persuading to make me a Christian; for, in a little degree, thou art persuading me to become a Christian.   29. Omn. (Paul) said.

Ch. xxvii. 14. Euraquilo, for, Euroclydon.   19. they, for we (cast out.)   37. M. Adn. (we were) about.   39. M. to save, for, to drive (the ship.)   41. (by the violence) omn. of the waves.

Ch. xxviii. 1. M. Melitene, for, Melita; Syriac, Militi.   13. M. we took away [something] all round, for, we made a circuit. The change of one letter in a Greek word makes the difference of meaning, and is, no doubt, a writer's blunder.   15. they came, for, they came out (to meet us.)   17. he, for, Paul (called together.) 30. he, for, Paul.

ROMANS i. 8. (I thank my God) concerning, for, on behalf of (all of you.)   29. Omn. fornication.   31. Omn. implacable.

Ch. ii. 2. M. For, instead of, And (we know.)   16. (when God) M. judges, for, will judge.

Ch. iii. 7. But, instead of, For (if the truth.)   22. (righteousness unto all) omn. and upon all.   28. M. For, instead of, Therefore (we reckon.)   30. if indeed, for, because (it is one God.)

Ch. iv. 1. (that Abraham) M. Omn. found.   11. (to them) omn. also.   15. but, instead of, for (where.)

Ch. v. 1. (being declared just) let us have, for, we have, Syriac, we shall have (peace.)   2. (have had entrance) M. omn. through trust.   17. Omn. and of the gift.

Ch. vi. 1. let us continue? for, shall we continue?   11. Omn. our Lord.   15. let us sin? for, shall we sin?

Ch. vii. 18. Omn. I find not.   23. under, for, to (the law of sin.)

Ch. viii. 1. Omn. who walk not after the flesh. (The Syriac has not, but after the Spirit.)   26. (the Spirit pleads) omn. on our behalf.   34. (It is the Anointed) adn. Jesus (who died.)   (who was raised) adn. from among the dead.   35. (from the love) M of God, for, of the Anointed.

Ch. ix. 5. In deference to "some modern interpreters," the M. puts a full stop after "flesh;" and in deference to others, a full stop after "over all;" in both cases destroying the statement that Jesus is God. The Syriac is like the Greek when read as one sentence. It is,—and from them appeared the Anointed in the flesh, who is God, who is over all; to whom be praises and blessings for ever and ever. Amen.   31. (has not attained to the law) omn. of righteousness.   32. (by the works) omn. of the law.   Omn. for (they stumbled.)

Ch. x. 3. their own, for, their own righteousness.   5. (Moses writes,) that the man who does the righteousness of the law shall live by it ; for, as to the righteousness which is by the law, that the man who shall do those things shall live by them.   9. M. profess the word with thy mouth that Jesus is Lord, for, profess with thy mouth the Lord Jesus.   15. Omn. of those who tell good tidings of peace.   17. (the word) of the Anointed, for, of God.

Ch. xi. 2. Omn. saying.   6. Omn. but if it be of works, it is not of merciful favour ; else, work is not work.   13. Adn. therefore (so far as I am.)   22. (but toward thee) the goodness of God, for, goodness.   30. (for as ye) omn. also.   31. (that they also may obtain mercy) adn. now.

Ch. xii. 2. Omn. of your (minds.)   11. M. (serve ye) the opportunity, for, the Lord.

Ch. xiii. 1. by, for, from (God.)   those, for, the authorities (which are).   7. (Render) omn. therefore.   11. for you, instead of, for us (to awake.)

Ch. xiv. 6. Omn. and he who regards not the day, to the Lord he regards it not.   9. (the Anointed) omn. also.   Omn. and rose.   10. (the judgment-seat) of God, for, of the Anointed. 18. (he who) in this, for, in these things.   19. M. we pursue, for, let us pursue.   21. stumbles, for, is made to stumble.

Ch. xv. 8. that the Anointed, for, that Jesus the Anointed.   15. Omn. my brothers.   19. of the Holy Spirit, for, of the Spirit of God. 24. (into Spain) I hope, while on my way, to see you ; for, I hope to come and see you.   29. Omn. of the good tidings (of the Anointed.)

Ch. xvi. 3. Prisca, for, Priscilla.   5. of Asia, for, of Achaia. 8. Ampliatus, for, Amplias.   18. (serve not) the Anointed, for, Jesus the Anointed.   20. M. Omn. The merciful favour of our Lord Jesus the Anointed be with you.   24. Omn. in central text, The merciful favour of our Lord Jesus the Anointed be with you all. Amen.   In the Syriac this verse comes last in the letter.   The central text of the R. E. V. has like words in verse 20.   It omits verse 24.

1 CORINTHIANS i. 4. M. (I thank) God, for, my God.   13. M.
(the Anointed) has been, for, has he been ? (divided.)   14. M.
I give thanks, for, I thank God.   15. that ye were immersed, for,
that I have immersed (into my name.)   20. (the wisdom) of the,
for, of this (world)?   29. (that no flesh might glory) before God,
for, before him.

Ch. ii. 9. whatsoever things, for, the things.   10. M. For,
instead of, But (God has revealed them.)   by the, for, by his
(Spirit.)

Ch. iii. 3. Omn. and divisions.   4. (are ye not) men, for fleshly?
5. What, for, who (is Paul)? what, for, who (is Apollos) ?   They
are, for, (who) but (servants) ?   12. on the, for, on this (foundation.)

Ch. iv. 6. Omn. to think [of men] (more highly than is written.)

Ch. v. 1. Omn. is (not) named.   M. verse 2, a question.   4.
Omn. the Anointed, twice.   5. M. omn. Jesus.   7. Omn. on
our behalf.   10. not, for, but not.   12. Do not ye judge? for,
Syriac, Judge ye.   13. does not God judge ? for, God judges.

Ch. vi. 4. the verse made a question.   20. Omn. and in your
spirit, which are God's.

Ch. vii. 1. Omn. (have written) to me.   3. what is due, for,
due affection.   5. Omn. to fasting and.   be together, for, come
together.   Syriac, return to the same will.   7. But, instead of,
For (I wish.)   14. (in respect of the) brother, for, husband.
15. M. (has called) you, for, us (in peace.)   31. the, for, this
(world.)   34. Adn. also (a difference.)   37. will do, for, does
(well.)   38. will do, for, does (better.)   39. (a wife is bound)
omn. by law.   39. the, for, her (husband.)

Ch. viii. 2. Omn. nothing.   4. Omn. other (God.)   7. from
customary [worship], for, from conscientious [reverence] (of the
image.)   8. will not, for, does not (give access to God.).   Omn.
for (neither if we eat.)

Ch. ix. 1. Omn. the Anointed.   7. its fruit, for, of its fruit.
13. Adn. the things (from the temple.)   15. (than that my
glorying) no one shall make void, for, anyone should make void.
18. (the good tidings) omn. of the Anointed.   20. (as under the
law,) adn. not being myself under the law.   22. Omn. as (weak.)
23. all things, for, this (I do.)

Ch. x. 9. the Lord, for, the Anointed.   as, for, as also.   11.
Omn. all (these things.)   by way of picture, for, as picture
lessons.   19. that a sacrifice to an image is anything, or that an
image is anything, instead of, that an image, etc., or a sacrifice to
an image, etc.   23. (all things are lawful) omn. for me, twice.

Ch. xi. 2. Omn. my brothers.   24. Omn. Take ye, eat.   Omn.
(my body) broken (on behalf of you.)   26. Omn. this (cup.)
27. the bread, Syriac, of the bread of the Lord.   29. Omn.
unworthily.   (the body) omn. of the Lord.

Ch. xii. 1. Adn. when.   3. Jesus is, for, that Jesus is (anathema.) Jesus is, for, that Jesus is (Lord.)   6. Omn. it is (the same God.) 9. by one, for, by the same (Spirit.)   26. (or if) a member, for, one member (is glorified.)   31. But desire the greater gifts, for, Syriac, But if ye desire great gifts, (I again will show you.) Ch. xiii. 3. M. (if I give my body) that I may glory, for, that I may be burned, Syriac, that it may be burned.   10. Omn. then. 11. when, for, but when (I became a man.) Ch. xiv. 5. and, instead of, for (greater is.)   21. by the lips of strangers, for, by strange lips, Syriac, in another tongue.   26. each, for, each of you; Syriac, he who of you (has a Psalm, let him speak.)   34. Let the, for, your (women be silent.)   let them be submissive, for, [it is required] that they be submissive.   35. (it is shameful for) a woman, instead of women (to speak in the assembly.)   37. (are) the command, for, the commands (of the Lord.)   38. M. if anyone knows not, he is not known; for, if anyone is ignorant, let him be ignorant. Ch. xv. 2. M. by which ye are saved, if ye hold fast the words of the good tidings which I told you; for, Syriac, in which ye have life [-bliss], by means of the words which I told you; if (some copies have not if) ye keep them in memory, (unless ye have trusted in a vain way.)   14. M. our, for, your (trust is useless also.) 20. Omn. and has become (the first-fruit.)   29. (why are they immersed on behalf) of them, for, of dead bodies?   32. (The joining of) if the dead are not raised, with, let us eat and drink. 44. If, instead of, For (there is a natural body.)   (a spiritual) one, for, body.   47. (the second man is) from heaven, for, the Lord from heaven.   49. M. let us bear, for, we shall bear (the likeness of him who is from heaven.)   54. M. Omn. this destructible shall put on indestructibility.   55. O death, where is thy victory? O death where is thy sting? for, O death, where is thy sting? O Hades, (Syriac, Shiul) where is thy victory? Ch. xvi. 19. Prisca, for, Priscilla.   22. (If anyone loves not) the Lord, instead of, the Lord Jesus the Anointed.

2 CORINTHIANS i. 6. (and salvation; or if we are comforted, it is for the comforting of you,) which works in the patient endurance of; instead of, and that there may be in you an endeavour to bear patiently (those sufferings which we also suffer.   And our hope.) 8. Omn. to us (in Asia.)   10. (a death), and will deliver.   The Syriac has it not; nor, and does deliver.   12. with holiness and sincerity, for, with simplicity and sincerity.   15. M. a second joy, for, a second favour-gift.   17. desired, for, purposed (this.) 18. (our word to you) is not, for, was not.   20. (are yes); therefore also by means of him is the Amen to God, for glory, by means of us; instead of, for this reason, by means of him, we give Amen, to the glory of God. Ch. ii. 1. M. For, instead of, But.   3. (I have written) omn. to

you.   9. (the testing of you,) M. by which, for, whether (ye are obedient.)   10. for what I have forgiven, if I have forgiven anything; instead of, for that which I also have forgiven to him whom I have forgiven, (it is on your account I have forgiven it.)

Ch. iii. 1. Omn. or of a recommendation (from you.) Syriac, or that you should write and recommend us.   3. in tables [which are] hearts of flesh, for, in tables of the heart, of flesh.

Ch. iv. 4. (might not shine) omn. upon them.   6. M. who said, Light shall shine, for, who commanded the light to shine (out of darkness.)   14. M. Jesus, for, our Lord Jesus.   with, for, by means of (Jesus.)   16. our, for, the (inner man.)

Ch. v. 17, 18. behold [things] have become new.   And all things [are] of God ; instead of, and all things have been made new by God.   21. Omn. For.

Ch. vi. 15. M. Beliar, Syriac, Satan.   16. we, for, ye (are.)

Ch. vii. 8. M. omn. for.   12. but that your earnest care for us might be made manifest to you; instead of, but that your earnest care on account of us, might be made known before God.

Ch. viii. 4. respecting [their] free gift, and [their] sharing in ; for, that they might have part in the free gift of (service to the saints.)   19. (for the glory) of the Lord, for, of God himself, (and [to show] our goodwill.)

Ch. ix. 4. (lest we be put to shame) by this confidence ; for, by that glorying with which we have gloried.   5. (your bounty) before promised, for, of which ye have been reminded beforehand.

Ch. x. 8. (which the Lord has given) omn. to us ; Syriac, to me. 13. as a measure to reach, for, that we should come (even as far as to you.)

Ch. xi. 1. (you would bear with me) in a little foolishness, instead of, a little, that I might speak foolishly.   3. Omn. so (your minds.)   3. (from [their] simplicity, adn. and [their] purity.   4. ye do well to bear with [him], for, ye would rightly obey him.   6. we have made [it] manifest, for, we have been made manifest.   31. of the Lord Jesus, for, of our Lord Jesus, the Anointed.

Ch. xii. 7. Adn. because (that I might not.)   9. Omn. my (strength.)   11. Omn. in my glorying.   14. (I will not burden) omn. you.   15. If I love you very much, am I loved the less ? for, even if, while I love you very much, ye love me the less.   19. ye, from of old, suppose that we ; for, do ye again suppose that we (are excusing ourselves to you ?)

Ch. xiii. 2. (now while absent) omn. I write.   4. For, instead of, For though (he was crucified in weakness.)   4. (but) we shall live, for, we live (with him by the power of God which is in you.) 7. (And) we, for, I (pray.)   14. Omn. Amen.

GALATIANS i. 3. M. our Father, and the Lord, for, the Father, and our Lord.   8. (other good tidings) M. omn. to you.   10. If. instead of, For if (I still pleased men.)

Ch. ii. 16. But knowing, for, because we know.
Ch. iii. 17. Omn. in the Anointed.   29. Omn. and (inheritors.)
Ch. iv. 6. into our, for, into your (hearts.)   7. (an heir) by
means of God, for, an heir of God, by means of Jesus the Anointed.
14. the trial of you, for, the (trial which was in my flesh.)   25.
M. And Sinai is a mountain in Arabia, instead of, for Hagar is
mount Sinai, which is in Arabia.   28. M. ye, for, we (are children
of promise.)
Ch. v. 1. With freedom the Anointed has set us free. Stand therefore; instead of, stand therefore in the freedom with which the
Anointed has made us free.   17. for, instead of, and (these are
opposed.)   21. Omn. murders.   respecting which I forewarn
you, as I have forewarned you; for, as I have said to you before, I
also say now.   24. (those who are of) the Anointed, Jesus; for,
of the Anointed.
Ch. vi. 17. (the marks) of Jesus, for, of our Lord Jesus the
Anointed.

EPHESIANS i. 1. M. Omn. in Ephesus.   10. (things) upon,
for, in (the heavens.)   15. Omn. your love (toward all the holy
ones.)   16. Omn. of you (in my prayers.)
Ch. ii. 5. (has raised us to life with), M. [and] in, (the Anointed.)
21. (Revised Version), each several building, for, all the building.
Ch. iii. 6. (and be fellow-sharers of the promise) in the Anointed,
Jesus, for, which has been given in him.   8. (to tell the good
tidings) to, instead of, among (the Gentiles.)   9. M. to bring to
light, for, to make all men see.   14. Omn. of our Lord Jesus
the Anointed.   21. (to him be glory in the assembly,) and in,
for, by (Jesus, the Anointed.)
Ch. iv. 6. in all, for, in us all.   9. (he descended) omn. first.
17. as the Gentiles, for, as the rest of the Gentiles.   24. M. (and
that ye put on the new man) who is after God, for, who has been
created by God.
Ch. v. 2. (the Anointed loved) you, for, us.   M. (and gave
himself up on behalf of) you, for, us.   5. ye, knowing, know,
for, ye know.   22. (ye wives) omn. submit yourselves.   27.
(that he might present) omn. it, Syriac, the assembly.   30. Omn.
(members) of his flesh and of his bones.
Ch. vi. 10. Omn. my brothers.   12. of this darkness, for, of
the darkness of this world. Syriac, of this dark world.

PHILIPPIANS i. 11. fruit, for, fruits.   22. M. But if to live in
the flesh [be my lot], this is the fruit of my work; and what shall
I choose? instead of, But if also, in this life of flesh, I have fruits
of my labours, I know not what I shall choose for myself.
Ch. ii. 2. of the same, for, of one (mind.)
Ch. iii. 3. who worship by the Spirit of God, for, who worship
God by the Spirit, or in spirit.   12. M. that I may seize, seeing
that I also have been seized; for, that I may seize that [prize]

because of which I have been seized by (Jesus the Anointed.)   13.
I do not yet, for, I do not (count myself.)   16. let us walk by the
same [rule], for, let us go on to completion in one course, (and with
one consent.)   21. Omn. that it may be made (like his glorious
body.)
   Ch. iv. 3. yes, I also, for, I also (intreat thee.)   13. by him,
for, by the Anointed, (who gives strength to me.)   23. (The
merciful favour) of the Lord, for, of our Lord.   (be with) your
spirit, for, you all.   Omn. Amen.

   COLOSSIANS i. 7. (on behalf) of us, for, of you.   28. in the
Anointed, for, in Jesus the Anointed.
   Ch. ii. 2. The M. of the R. E. Version says that the Greek copies
" vary much " in the latter part of this verse.   Its text has,—(unto
all riches of the full assurance) of understanding, that they may
know the mystery of God, [even] Christ, in whom.   The Syriac
means,—and to the understanding of the knowledge of the
[revealed] secret of God the Father, and [to the understanding] of
the Anointed, in whom.   7. abounding in thanksgiving, for,
abounding in it, (faith), with thanksgiving.   11. (by putting off)
the body of the flesh ; Syriac, the flesh of sins.   18. (searching
into things which) he has seen, for, he has not seen.
   Ch. iii. 4. M. your, for, our (life.)   5. Omn. your (members.)
6. M. Omn. upon the sons of disobedience.   13. The Lord, for,
the Anointed (has forgiven you.)   16. M. (the word of) the Lord,
or God, for, the Anointed.   20. in, for, before (our Lord.)
   Ch. iv. 8. that ye may know our affairs, for, that he may know
your affairs.   12. of the Anointed, Jesus, for, of the Anointed.
and fully assured, for, and completed.   13. much toil, for, much
zeal.   15. (the assembly) in their, M. her, for his (house.)   18.
Omn. Amen.

   1 THESSALONIANS i. 2. (making mention) omn. of you.   5. to
you, for, among you.   ii. 7. M. babes, instead of, gentle.
15. the prophets, for, their own prophets.   iii. 2. (Timothy, our
brother), and, M. God's fellow-worker, for, the servant of God,
and our helper.   on behalf of, for, concerning (your trust.)   11
and 13. Omn. the Anointed, twice.   iv. 1. Adn. as also ye do
walk.   8. (God) gives, for, has given (his Holy Spirit.)   13.
We, for, I (wish.)   v. 4. M. as thieves, for, as a thief.   27.
Omn. (the) holy (brothers.)   28. Omn. Amen.

   2 THESSALONIANS i. 2. Omn. our (Father.)   8. Omn. the
Anointed.   10. (in all) who have trusted, Syriac, his faithful.
12. Omn. the Anointed.   ii. 3. M. (the man) of lawlessness, for,
of sin.   4. Omn. as God.   8. will take away, for, will con-
sume.   11. sends, for, will send.   13. M. (God has chosen
you) as a first-fruit, instead of, from the beginning.   iii. 4. (the
things which we command) omn. you.   6. (the delivered command

which) Text, they; M. ye; Syriac, he (received from us.) 12. (we command) by the, for, our (Lord Jesus the Anointed.) 18. Omn. Amen.

1 TIMOTHY i. 2. the, for, our (Father.) 4. (rather than) the steward-ship, for, the building up, (Syriac, of trust in God.) 12. M. who strengthens, for, has strengthened (me.) ii. 3. Omn. For (this.) 9. So, for, So also. iv. 10. we strive, for, we suffer reproach. v. 16. Omn. (If any) trusting brother or. 21. of the Anointed Jesus, for, of our Lord Jesus the Anointed. vi. 5. in Syriac, ver. 6. Omn. from such withdraw thyself; Syriac, but thou go far from these. 7. Omn. it is evident; Syriac, it is known. 17. but on God, instead of, on the living God. 21. with you, (plural), for, with thee. Omn. Amen.

2 TIMOTHY i. 3, 4. night and day longing to see thee, for, in my prayers by night and by day. 11. a teacher, for, a teacher of the Gentiles. ii. 3. suffer evil with [me], for, suffer evil. 14. M. (before) God, for, our Lord. 26. R. E. Version, having been taken captive by the Lord's servant, (M. by the devil) unto the will of God; Syriac, (may depart from the snare of Satan) who have been captured at his will. iii. 14. (of what) persons, for, person. 16. R. E. V., Every scripture inspired of God [is] also profitable; Syriac, For every writing which has been written by the Spirit, is profitable (for teaching, etc.) iv. 1. the Anointed, Jesus, for, our Lord Jesus the Anointed. and by his appearing and his kingdom, for, Syriac, at the revealing of His kingdom. 22. The Lord, for, our Lord Jesus the Anointed. Omn. Amen.

TITUS i. 4. from the Anointed Jesus, for, from our Lord Jesus the Anointed. ii. 11. which saves, Syriac, which saves all, (has been revealed to all men.) iii. 15. Omn. Amen.

PHILEMON 2. to Apphia, our sister, for, our beloved. 5. M. (hearing) of thy love and trust which thou hast in the Lord Jesus, and in all the holy ones; for, Syriac, of thy trust, and of the love thou hast for our Lord Jesus, and for all the holy ones. 6. M. (in the knowledge of) every good thing which is in us unto the Anointed, for, Syriac, of all the good things which ye have in Jesus the Anointed. 7. I had, for, we have (great joy.) 12. whom himself I have sent back to thee; for, Syriac, I have sent him to thee; and do thou so receive him (as my own son.) 25. M. of the Lord, for, of our Lord. M. Omn. Amen.

HEBREWS i. 2. at the end of these days, for, in these last days. 3. Omn. by himself, of sins. The Maronite, Lee's, and the Ooroomiah editions have, our sins. Walton, Gutbier, and Schaaf, have not, our. 6. And when he again brings in, for, And again, when he brings in. S. M. Aleph and B, "the two oldest Greek manu-

scripts read, his," instead of, thy (kingdom.)   12. (as a mantle
shalt thou roll them up) adn. as a garment.
Ch. ii. 7. M. Omn. Thou didst set him over the works of thy
hands.
Ch. iii. 1. Jesus, for, Jesus the Anointed.   9. (tested) omn.
me.   by proving, for, put [me] to proof.   10. this, for, that
(generation.)
Ch. iv. 2. (because those who heard) were not united by trust
with those who heard ; for, because it [the word] was not united
with trust in those who heard it.
Ch. v. 4. but [takes it] when called, for, but he who is called.
Ch. vii. 14. (concerning) priests, instead of, priesthood.   17.
It is testified, for, he testifies.   21. Omn. after the order of
Melchizedec.   22. (by so much) adn. also.
Ch. viii. 4. (because there are) omn. priests.   5. thou shalt
make, for, that thou make.   11. (from the least) omn. of them.
Ch. ix. 17. not a question; while that which makes it lives.
Ch. x. 9. Omn. O God.   16. mind, for, minds.   34. Omn.
in heaven.   38. my, for, the (righteous man.)
Ch. xi. 3. what is seen, for, the things seen.   4. M. "The Greek
text in this clause is somewhat uncertain." Syriac, and God bore
witness respecting his gift-offering.   8. to a place, Syriac, to that
place.   11. Omn. she gave birth.   20. Adn. even (concerning
things to come.)
Ch. xii. 7. It is with view to chastening that ye endure, for,
Syriac, patiently bear chastening, because, (as with sons, etc.)
15. the many, for, many (be defiled.)   24. than Abel, for, than
that of Abel.
Ch. xiii. 18. we are persuaded, for, we trust.   21. (in every
good) thing, for, work.
JAMES i. 12. Omn. Syriac, God (has promised.)   19. Ye know,
for, And ye, (my beloved brothers.)
Ch. ii. 1. The M. makes the verse a question. It is an exhortation, in the Syriac.   3. (And say) omn. to him.   (or sit)
omn. here.   5. (the poor) in, for, of (the world.)   18.
Omn. my (trust.)   20. (trust without works is) fruitless, for,
dead.
Ch. iii. 3. But if, instead of, For, behold.   5. (Behold, how
large a wood,) how large, for, a little (fire sets ablaze.)   6. The
R. E. V. gives in its text and margin, three different Greek readings
of this verse. Dr. Murdock translates the Syriac thus :—Now the
tongue is a fire, and the world of sin is like a forest. And this
tongue, which is one among our members, marreth our whole body;
and it inflames the series of our generations, which roll on like a
wheel ; and it is itself on fire.   8. a restless, for, an uncontroll-
able (evil.)
Ch. iv. 4. Ye adulteresses, for, ye adulterers.   5. (that the spirit

which) he has made to dwell, for, dwells (in us, is prone to envy ?)
13. a year, for, one year.   14. What is your life ?   For ye are a
vapour ; instead of, For what is our life but a vapour ?
Ch. v. 5. Omn. as (in a day.)   16. your sins, for, your faults.
20. M. know ye, for, let him know.

1 PETER i. 12. for you, instead of, for us (they were setting forth
those things.)   16. Ye shall be, for, Be ye (holy.)   22. out of
the heart, for, out of a pure heart.   23. (by means of the living
word of God, which continues) omn. for ever.

Ch. ii. 7. (to those who) do not trust, for, do not obey.   21.
(the Anointed suffered on behalf of) you, for, us ; (and left) you,
for, us (an example.)

Ch. iii. 15. Adn. but (with meekness.)   16. ye are spoken
against, for, they speak against you, as against bad men.

Ch. iv. 19. to a faithful Creator, instead of, [to him] as to a
faithful Creator.

Ch. v. 2. M. Omn. exercising the oversight.   Syriac, take the
care of it spiritually.   (willingly) adn. according to God.   8.
Omn. because (your adversary.)   10. (who has called) you, for,
us.   (by means of) the Anointed, for, Jesus the Anointed.   11.
(to him) omn. be glory and.   14. Omn. Amen.

1 JOHN i. 4. (we write) omn. to you.

Ch. ii. 20. M. and ye all know, for, and ye know every man.
25. M. (which he has promised) you, for, us.   28. that if, for,
that when (he shall be revealed.)

Ch. iii. 2. we know that if, for, but we know that when.   5.
(to take) sins, for, our sins.   13. brothers, for, my brothers.   14.
(that loveth not) omn. his brother.   16. (the love) omn. of God.
Syriac, his love for us.   18. Little children, for, my little children.
19. By this we shall know, for, And by this we know.   19, 20.
shall assure our heart before him, whereinsoever our heart may
condemn us ; for, shall assure our heart.   And if our heart condemns us, etc.   21. (if) the, for, our (heart.)

Ch. iv. 3. M. who denies, for, who does not confess.   Jesus, for,
that Jesus the Anointed has come in the flesh.   16. not in Syriac,
and God continues in him.   19. (Let us love) omn. him.   Syriac,
let us love God.   20. cannot love God, for, how can he love God
(who is not seen) ?

Ch. v. 9. (this is the witness borne by God) because, for, which
(he has borne.)   10. (has the witness) in him, for, in himself.
18. (keeps) him, for, himself.

SOME OF THE ABOVE CHANGES, all of which are the result of a
selection from the multitude of Greek readings, of those which the
Revisers themselves thought most likely to be correct, IMPAIR OR
ALTER GOD'S TESTIMONY ON POINTS OF GREAT IMPORTANCE.   It
may be acceptable to the reader, if a few passages be named which

will be found, on examination, to do this. It will be sufficient to name them, the nature of the change, and whether made in the text, or in the margin, being shown in the above list.

A.—The Angels' song, Luke ii. 14. The appearing of Jesus after his resurrection, Luke xxiv. 36, 40, 42. The ascension of Jesus to heaven, Mark xvi. 19; Luke xxiv. 51. Atonement; no attempt is made to show that Jesus made the real atonement which was made in shadow by the old sacrifices. See also Luke xxii. 19, 20; John vi. 51; Hebrews i. 3.

B.—Baptism, Matt. xx. 22, 23; Mark vii. 4, 8; xvi. 16. The bloody sweat of the Redeemer, and the visit of the angel in Gethsemane, Luke xxii. 43, 44.

C.—Christians, as members of the flesh and bones of Jesus, Eph. v. 30. The chosen of God, Matt. xx. 16; Luke xvii. 36; given to Jesus, John xvii. 11, 12, 24; from the beginning, 2 Thess. ii. 13. The Covenant, the New, Matt. xxvi. 28; Mark xiv. 24; Luke xxii. 20. The Cross, the first words of Jesus when nailed to it, Luke xxiii. 34. The inscription on it, Luke xxiii. 38.

D.—The Deity of the Redeemer.—Substitution of, a thing, for, One greater than the temple, Matt. xii. 6. Worship paid him, Matt. xxviii. 17; Mark i. 40; Luke xxiv. 52. The Son of God, Mark i. 1. The Word called a begotten God, John i. 18. Who is in heaven, John iii. 13. Is above all, John iii. 31. Stopping so arranged as to destroy express testimony, Rom. ix. 5. The Divine Sonship of Jesus as man: passages in which he is called the Son of God, or God is called his Father, altered, John iii. 17; vi. 65, 69; viii. 28, 38; ix. 35; x. 29, 32; xiv. 12, 28; xvi. 10; xvii. 1; xx. 17. Destroy; Christ came not to destroy men, Luke ix. 54—56. Divorce, Matt. xix. 9.

F.—Fasting, Matt. xvii. 21; Mark ix. 29; Acts x. 30; 1 Cor. vii. 5. Forgiveness, Mark xi. 26. Fore-knowledge of God. Acts xv. 18. Future state of those who perish, Matt. xxi. 44; Mark iii. 29; ix. 44, 46.

G.—Gift of God's chosen to Christ, John xvii. 11, 12, 24.

H.—House on rock, said to be well built instead, Luke vi. 48. Hypocrisy, Matt. xxiii. 14; Luke xi. 44.

J.—Justification. Being declared just, let us have peace, Rom. v. 1. Rom. xi. 6; Heb. x. 38.

L.—The Lord's prayer, in Matt. vi. 13; in Luke xi. 2, 4. The Lord's Supper, Luke xxii. 19, 20; 1 Cor. xi. 24—29.

M.—Man's state of ruin, Matt. xviii. 11. Mark, the last 12 verses treated as doubtful. Mary, the mother of Jesus, blest, Luke i. 28.

P.—Pierced with a spear, the body of Jesus said to have been while he was still living, Matt. xxvii. 49.

R.—Resurrection of Christ, evidence of it in Mark questioned, Mark xvi. 9—14. Omissions in Luke xxiv. 6, 9, 12. The resurrection of Christians, 1 Cor. xv. 51, 55. Riches, those who trust in them, Mark x. 24.

S.—The sun said to have been eclipsed when Christ was crucified, though the moon was full, and an eclipse impossible, Luke xxiii. 45. Separation from men of corrupt mind, 1 Tim. 6. 5.

APPROVED READINGS.—MATTHEW.

XIV. The Peshito-Syriac Text is in agreement with the following changes, which in the Revised English Version of 1881 were founded on deviations from the Received Greek Text.

MATTHEW i. 6. (And David) omit, the king. ii. 18. Omit, lamentation and. iii. 6. Add, the river (Jordan.) v. 27. Omit, to those of old time. vi. 12. (as we also) have forgiven, for, forgive. 18. Omit, openly. 34. Omit, the things (of itself.) vii. 2. Omit, again. 14. M. How, instead of, For (narrow.) 24. shall be compared, for, I will compare him. 29. their, for, the scribes. viii. 8. (say) by a word. 28. Gadarenes, for, Gergesenes. 32. into the swine, and all the herd. ix. 4. knowing, for, seeing (their thoughts.) 8. feared, for, marvelled. 13. Omit, to repentance. 35. Omit, among the people. x. 3. (Simon) the Zealous, for, the Canaanite. 10. staff, for, staves. xi. 2. by means of, for, two. 19. (by her) works, for, children. xii. 8. Omit, even (of the Sabbath.) 35. Omit, of the heart.

Ch. xiv. 6. (Herod's birthday) came, for, was kept. 12. corpse, for, body. 24. M. (was) many furlongs away from the land, instead of, in the midst of the sea. 25. (Jesus) came, for, went. 32. (had) gone up into, for, entered (the ship.)

Ch. xv. 4. Omit, commanded and. 6. the word, for, the command (of God.) 8. Omit, draw near to me with their mouth, and. 17. (Do ye) not, for, not yet (understand)? 22. (called out) omit, to him. 36. (to the) multitudes, for, multitude. 39. Magadan, Syriac, Magodu, for, Magdala.

Ch. xvi. 26. will be, for, is (a man profited?) xviii. 8. (cut) it, for, them (off.) xix. 3. (saying) omit, to him. 25. the, for, his disciples.

Ch. xxi. 7. he sat, for, they set him. 9. (went before) add, him. 28, (in) the, for, my (vineyard.)

Ch. xxii. 13. Omit, take him away, and. 23. (Sadducees), and said, for, who say. 32. He, for, God (is not God of the dead.) 35. Omit, and saying. 44. under, instead of, for the footstool of (thy feet.)

Ch. xxiii. 4. M. Omit, grievous to be borne. 7. Omit, Rabbi, once. 8. (One is your) Chief. Omit, the Anointed.

Ch. xxiv. 18. garment, for, garments. 27. Omit, also. 31.

M. a great trumpet, for, a great sound of a trumpet.   36. the, for, my (Father.)   37. Omit, also.   39. Omit, also.   49. shall eat and drink, for, (shall begin) to.

Ch. xxv. 13. Omit, in which the Son of man comes.   17. Omit, he also.   44. (answer) omit, him.

Ch. xxvi. 9. this, for, this ointment.   20. (with his twelve) add, disciples.   36. (said to) his (disciples.)   42. Omit, from me. 53. Put, now, after, give me.   60. Omit the second, they found it not.   (came two) omit, false witnesses.

Ch. xxvii. 2. Omit, Pontius.   10. I gave, as in M., for, they gave (them.)   22. Omit, to him.   35. Omit, that what was spoken by the prophet might be fulfilled,—They parted my garments among them, and upon my vesture they cast lots.

Ch. xxviii. 8. (they went) away from, for, out of.   9. Omit, And as they went to tell his disciples.

MARK i. 2. in the prophet Isaiah, for, in the prophets.   Omit, before thee.   5. all they of Jerusalem, and were immersed ; for, they of Jerusalem, and were all (immersed.)   11. in thee, for, in whom (I am well pleased.)   19. Omit, thence.   24. Omit, Let us alone.   27. among themselves, for, them.   42. Omit, when he had spoken.

Ch. ii. 2. Omit, immediately.   3. bringing to him, for, bringing.   17. Omit, to repentance.   20. in that day, for, in those days.   22. else the wine, instead of, the new wine.   26. under Abiathar, a chief priest ; Syriac, a chief of the priests.

Ch. iii. 5. Omit, whole as the other.   18. (Simon) the Zealous, for, the Canaanite.   34. Syriac, he looked on those who were sitting with him ; instead of, he looked round on those who sat round about him.

Ch. iv. 4. Omit, of heaven.   9. (he said) omit, to them.   18. (those who) have heard, for, who hear (the word.)   20. Omit, some, three times.

Ch. v. 9. he said to him, for, he answered and said.   11. on the mountain, for, on the mountains.   13. Omit, Jesus immediately.   Omit, they were.   14. (those who fed) them, for, the swine.   19. Omit, Jesus.   22. Omit, behold.   36. Omit, immediately.   38. they come, for, he comes.

Ch. vi. 12. made, for, were making (proclamation.)   15. (a prophet) as, for, or as (one of the prophets.)   26. (those reclining) omit, with him.   27. to bring (the head), instead of, (the head) to be brought.   33. (and knew) them, for, him.   Omit, and came together to him.   44. were, for, were about (five thousand.) 51. Omit, beyond measure.   55. (that region) omit, round about.

Ch. vii. 5. And, for, Then.   6. Omit, he answered, and.   8. Omit, ye do.   24. a house, for, the house.   25. (For), add, immediately.   28. Omit, for (even.)

Ch. viii. 1. Omit, Jesus.   7. (gave thanks) for them.   13.

Syriac, omits, again.   14. they, for, the disciples.   21. not yet, for, not.   25. (saw) all things, for, all persons.   28. (they) said, for, answered.   36. profit a man, for, shall it profit (him.)

Ch. ix. 12. Omit, answered and.   24. Omit, Lord.   33. they, for, he (came.)   38. (John) said, for, answered, saying.   Omit, who does not (follow us.)   Substitute (because he) did not, for, does not (follow us.)   41. naming that ye are, for, in my name, because ye are (of the Anointed.)   42. a millstone, add, of an ass.   45. Omit, into the unquenchable fire.

Ch. x. 1. to, for, by (beyond Jordan.)   35. (saying) to him.   52. him, for, Jesus.

Ch. xi. 10. Omit, in the name of the Lord.   14. Omit, Jesus.   19. M. They, for, he (went out.)   29. Omit, answered.   33. Jesus said, for, answered and said.

Ch. xii. 2. (of the) fruits, for, fruit.   17. Jesus said, for, And Jesus answered, and said.   23. Omit, when they shall rise.   24. Jesus said, for, And Jesus answered and said.   27. (but) omit, God (of the living.)   32. He, for, God (is one.)   43. who are casting, for, have cast (into the treasury.)

Ch. xiii. 2. Omit, answered and.   (left) add, here.   5. Omit, answered and.   8. the beginning, for, the beginnings.   9. shall stand, for, be brought (before rulers.)   15. (go down) omit, into the house.

Ch. xiv. 19. Omit, and another, Is it I?   20. Omit, answered and.   22. Omit, eat ye.   24. (which is shed) on behalf of, for, concerning (many.)   31. Omit, the more.   51. Omit, the young men.   52. (naked) omit, from them.   72. (And) add, immediately.

Ch. xv. 3. Omit, but he made no answer.   8. Omit, always.   41. (who) omit, also.   44. M. were already, for, had been long (dead.)

Ch. xvi. 8. Omit, quickly.   19. (the Lord), add, Jesus.

LUKE i. 26. (was sent) from, for, by (God.)   75. all our days, for, all the days of our life.   78. shall visit, for, has visited (us.)

Ch. ii. 2. This enrolment was the first; for, this, the first enrolment, took place (under the government.)   5. (Mary) his betrothed, omit, wife.   15. (that the shepherds) omit, the men.   22. of their, for, of her (purification.)   38. deliverance of, instead of, in (Jerusalem.)   42. Omit, to Jerusalem.

Ch. iv. 1, 2. Join, for forty days, with, led; instead of with, to be tempted.   8. Omit, Get thee behind me, Satan, for.

Ch. v. 15. (to be healed) omit, by him.   36. (no one) add, cuts off, . . . and (puts it on.)

Ch. vi. 1. Omit, the second-first.   5. Omit, also (of the sabbath.)   9. (on the) sabbath, for, sabbaths.   10. (said) to him, for, to the man.   Omit, whole.   17. add, a great (multitude of his disciples.)   38. with that, for, with the same (measure.)

H

Ch. vii. 11. Omit, many of (his disciples.)   28. Omit, For.
31. Omit, And the Lord said.   42. Omit, tell me.   44. (with
the hair) omit, of her head.

Ch. viii. 3. (who served) them, for, him.   9. Omit, saying.
20. Omit, [by some] who said.   29. he was commanding, for,
he commanded.   30. Omit, saying.   34. Omit, and went.
36. (those) omit, also (who saw.)   40. Omit, it came to pass.   47.
(Declared) omit, to him.   50. (answered) omit, saying.   51. (To
enter) add, with him.   52. Add, for (she is not dead.)

Ch. ix. 1. (his twelve) omit, disciples.   3. staff, for, staves.
50. (against) you, for, us ; (is for) you, for, us.   57. Omit, it came
to pass.

Ch. x. 1. Omit, also.   2. And, for, Therefore (he said.)   11.
(which cleaves to us) add, on our feet.   20. (rejoice) omit, rather.
21. in the Holy Spirit, for, in spirit.   35. Omit, when he departed.   39. (at the feet) of the Lord, for, of Jesus.

Ch. xi. 34. (is) thine eye, for, the eye.

Ch. xii. 1. M. Beware ye, first ; for, began to say first.   15. (guard
against) add, all (covetousness.)   22. your, for, the (body.)   23.
Add, For, (the life.)

Ch. xiii. 24. door, for, gate.   35. for I say, instead of, and
verily I say.   until, for, till the time come when (ye shall say.)

Ch. xiv. 5. Omit. answered and.   M. (whose) son, for, ass.   10.
(in the presence,) add, of all (those who.)   34. (but if) add, even
(the salt.)

Ch. xv. 17. (I perish) add, here.

Ch. xvi. 9. (that when) it, the mammon, for, ye (shall fail.)   14.
(The Pharisees) omit, also.   25. (he is now comforted) add, here.

Ch. xvii. 1. his, for, the (disciples.)   3. (if thy brother sin) omit,
against thee.   7. (will say, in Syriac, says immediately) add, to
him.   18. This verse a question.

Ch. xviii. 22. (when Jesus heard) omit, these things. Lee retains.

Ch. xix. 27. (and slay) add, them.   42. Syriac, Oh, if thou
hadst known those things which are for thy peace, at least in this
thy day !

Ch. xx. 1. (in one of) the, for, those (days.)   3. a, for, one
question.   24. Omit, answered and.   32. (last) omit, of all.
34. Omit. answered and.

Ch. xxi. 19. ye will possess, for, possess ye (your souls or lives.)
25. from terror at the roaring of the sea ; for, with perplexity, the
sea roaring.

Ch. xxii. 3. (Judas) called, for, surnamed (Iscariot.)   16. (eat) it,
for, of it.   36. Omit, therefore.   57. he denied [it], for, him.
70. M. ye say [the truth], because I am ; for, ye say that I am.

Ch. xxiii. 2. (turning aside) add, our (nation.)   and (saying.)
20. (Pilate spoke) add, to them.   35. (the rulers) omit, with them.
46. I commit, for, I will commit.   51. (who) omit, also himself
(was expecting.)

Ch. xxiv. 3. (the body) of Jesus, for, of the Lord Jesus. 5. (and bowed their) faces, for, face. 11. these, for, their words. 21. Omit, to-day. 29. (the day has) add, now, (declined.) 47. M. (repentance) for, instead of, and (the pardon of sins.) JOHN i. 19. (when the Jews sent) add, to him. 28. Bethany, for, Bethabara. 39. (come and) ye will see, for, see ye. ii. 22. (had said this) omit, to them. iii. 25. (with) a Jew, for, the Jews. iv. 17. (she said) add, to him. v. 30. (the will of) him, for, the Father (who sent me.) vi. 2. the, for, his (signs.) 11. (he distributed [these] to) those who were reclining; for, to the disciples, and the disciples to those who were reclining. 24. (they) omit, also (went into the boats.) 40. (For this is the will) of my Father; for, of him who sent me. 43. (Jesus) omit, therefore. 63. (the words which I) have spoken, for, speak. 68. (Peter) omit, therefore. 71. Simon Iscariot, for, Judas Iscariot.

Ch. vii. 33. (Jesus said) omit, to them. 34. (ye will not find) add, me. 36. add, me. 39. the Spirit, for, the Holy Spirit. M. (was not yet) add, given. 52. rises, for, has risen. 53. This verse is not in the Peshito.

Ch. viii. 1-11. These verses, and vii. 53, though not in the Peshito, may have been added by the Apostle, after the gospel was first written. 20. Omit, Jesus. 41, 48, 52. Omit, therefore, thrice.

Ch. ix. 8. a beggar, for, blind. 9. (others) add, No, but (he is like him.) 20. (answered) omit, them.

Ch. x. 26. because, instead of, for (ye are not.) 38. (and I) in the Father; Syriac, in my Father; for, in him.

Ch. xi. 12. (said) add, to him. 29. rose, for, rises (up.) came, for, comes. 31. supposing, for, saying. 41. Omit, where the dead was laid.

Ch. xii. i. Omit, who had died. (whom) add, Jesus (had raised up.) 4. (Iscariot) omit, [son] of Simon. 47. (and shall not) keep, for, believe (them.)

Ch. xiii. 26. Simon Iscariot, for, Judas Iscariot.

Ch. xiv. 2. Add, because (I go.) 14. (if ye shall ask) add, me. 16. (that he may) be, for, remain. 28. (because) I go, for, I said, I go. 30. (the ruler of) the, for, this (world.)

Ch. xv. 11. (that my joy may) be, for, remain (in you.)

Ch. xvi. 3. (they will do) omit, to you. 4. (that when) their, for, the (hour shall come.) 27. from the Father, for, from God.

Ch. xvii. 1. (thy Son) omit, also. 20. (who) trust, for, shall trust.

Ch. xviii. 11. the, for, thy (sword.) 14. (should) die, for, be destroyed. 18. (and Peter) add, also. 20. all, for, always (the Jews.) 29. (went out) add, to the outside. 31. (The Jews) omit, therefore. 37. M. Thou say'st [the truth], (because I am a king.)

xix. 11. (answered, in Syriac, said) add, to him.   35. (that ye) add, also.

xx. 16. (she said to him) add, in Hebrew.   19. were, for, were assembled.   29. Omit, Thomas.

xxi. 3. Omit, immediately.   25. Omit, Amen.

ACTS i. 14. (in prayer) omit, and supplication.

Ch. ii. 1. (were all) together, for, with one mind.   22. (as ye) omit, also.   30. Omit, would, as to the flesh, raise up the Anointed.   31. that he, instead of, his soul (was not to be left in Hades, Syriac, Shiul.)   40. (and exhorted) add, them.   43. (by the Apostles) add, in Jerusalem.

Ch. iii. 7. (raised) add, him.   11. (while) he, for, the lame man who had been healed.   20. (who has been) prepared, instead of, proclaimed (beforehand.)   21. Omit, all (his.)   22. Omit, to the fathers.   26. (his Son) omit, Jesus.

Ch. iv. 17. Omit, severely (threaten.)   27. (truly) add, in this city.   36. Joseph, for, Joses.

Ch. v. 5. (who heard of) it, instead of, these things.   16. (round about), omit, unto (Jerusalem).   18. Omit, their (hands.) 23. (standing) omit, without.   24. Omit, the [high] priest, and. 25. Omit, saying.   32. Omit, his (witness-bearers.)   Omit, also, (the Holy Spirit.)

Ch. vi. 8. full of [God's] favour, for, of trust.   13. Omit, blasphemous.

Ch. vii. 11. Egypt, for, the land of Egypt.   22. Add, his (words and deeds.)   32. Omit, God, before Isaac, and before Jacob.   43. of the god Rephan, for, of your god Remphan. 48. in places, for, in temples (made with hands.)

Ch. viii. 12. about the kingdom, for, about the things of the kingdom (of God.)   13. Add, great (miracles.)   37. Omit, And Philip said, If thou dost trust with thy whole heart, thou mayest.   And he answered and said, I believe that Jesus the Anointed, is the Son of God.

Ch. ix. 5, 6. Omit, it is hard for thee to kick against the pricks. And he, trembling and astonished, said, Lord, what dost thou wish me to do? and the Lord [said] to him.   6. But (stand up.)   8. (He saw) nothing, for, no one.   18. (he received sight) omit, forthwith.   19. he, for, Saul.   20. (was making proclamation about) Jesus, for, the Anointed.   21. From, and had come, to, (the chief) priests, not a question.   26. (And when) he, for, Saul. 31. (in the) assembly, for, assemblies.

Ch. x. 6. Omit, he will tell thee what thou must do.   7. (who spoke) to him, for, to Cornelius.   11. Omit, coming down to him. 12. Omit, and wild beasts.   21. Omit, who had been sent from Cornelius to him.   23. he arose and, for, Peter (went.)   48. (of the Lord) add, Jesus, the Anointed.

Ch. xi. 13. (send) omit, men.   20. (to the) Greeks, for, Greek-speaking [Jews.] 22. Omit, to go (as far as Antioch.) 25. he, for, Barnabas (went.)

Ch. xii. 13. he, for, Peter (knocked.) 20. he, for, Herod.

Ch. xiii. 1. Omit, certain (prophets.) 6. Add, the whole (island.) (a certain) add, man. 18. M. he nourished them, for, bore their conduct. 19. (he gave them their land) for an inheritance, instead of, by lot. 31. Add, now (his witness-bearers.) 42. (And as they went out) Syriac, from them, instead of, from the synagogue of the Jews. they, for, the Gentiles (besought.) 45. Omit, contradicting, and.

Ch. xiv. 8. Omit, being (a cripple.)

Ch. xv. 22. called, for, surnamed (Barsabas.) 34. Omit, But it seemed good to Silas to continue there. 36. the, for, our (brothers.) 37. wished, for, advised.

Ch. xvi. 7. the Spirit of Jesus, for, the Spirit. 16. to the house of prayer, for, to prayer. 17. (she) was following, for, followed. (who announce) to you, for, to us.

Ch. xvii. 5. (the Jews) omit, who were disobedient. 13. (stirring up) add, and disturbing. 14. as far as to the sea, for, as if to the sea. 26. [their] ordained, for, fore-ordained (times.) 27. (to seek) God, for, the Lord.

Ch. xviii. 5. he was restrained in speech, for, was oppressed in spirit. 7. Titus, for, Justus. 15. questions, for, a question. 19. they came, for, he came. 25. (concerning) Jesus, for, the Lord.

xix. 10. (of the Lord) omit, Jesus. 12. (spirits went out) omit, from them. 15. (the evil spirit said) add, to them. 35. Omit, goddess.

Ch. xx. 1. (the disciples) add, and comforted [them.] 7. (when) we, for, the disciples (were assembled.) 8. we, for, they (were assembled.) 19. Omit, many (tears.) 23. (bears witness) add, to me. 24. Omit, with joy. 29. (I know) omit, this. 32. Omit, [my] brothers.

Ch. xxi. 8. (We) omit, who were around Paul. 13. Add, Then (Paul.) 20. (glorified) God, for, the Lord. 22. Omit, the multitude must come together. 25. Omit, that they are to observe no such thing, but only. 26. Join, the next day, with, took the men ; not with, was purified.

Ch. xxii. 9. Omit, and were afraid. 16. (calling on) his name, for, the name of the Lord. 26. what art thou, for, take care what thou art (going to do.) 27. Art thou ? for, if thou art (a Roman.) 30. Omit, from his bonds.

Ch. xxiii. 6. (the son) of Pharisees, for, of a Pharisee. 9. some scribes, for, the scribes. 11. (Take courage) omit, Paul. 15. Omit, to-morrow. 34. (When) he, for, the Governor.

Ch. xxiv. 13. (nor can they prove) add, to thee. 20. what, for,

if any (wrong-doing.)   21. (judged) before, for, by (you.)   23.
Omit, or to come (to him.)   26. Omit, to set him free.
Ch. xxv. 2. (the chief) priests, for, priest.   6. not more than
eight or ten, for, more than ten (days.)   7. (stood round) add,
him.   18. (no accusation) add, of evil things, Syriac, no evil
accusation.   20. (as to inquiry about) these things, for, this.
Ch. xxvi. 4. Add, and (in Jerusalem.)   6. (made to) our, for,
the (fathers.)   12. (and commission) of, for, from (the chief
priests.)   14. saying to me, for, speaking to me and saying.
15. the Lord, for, he (said.)   17. Omit, now (I send thee.)   18.
that they may turn, for, to turn [them.]   25. Add, Paul (said.)
30. Omit, And when he had said these things.
Ch. xxvii. 2. (a ship) which was, for, we were (about to sail.)
12. (thence) omit, also.   34. (not a hair shall) perish, for, fall.
Ch. xxviii. 1. We, for, they (learned.)   16. we entered, for, came
to (Rome.)   Omit, the centurion delivered the prisoners to the
Chief of the army; but.   25. your, for, our (fathers.)   29.
Omit, And when he had said these things, the Jews went away,
and had much reasoning among themselves.
    ROMANS Ch. i. 16. Omit, of the Anointed.   24. Omit, also.
ii. 17. But if, for, Behold.   iii. 2. First, instead of, For first.
iv. 19. (not weakened in trust) he considered, for, he did not
consider (his body.)   Omit, now.   vi. 12. ([causing] you to
obey) the lusts of it, for, it, in the lusts of it.   vii. 6. We have
died to that, for, that has died (by which we were held.)
    Ch. viii. 1. Omit, but according to the Spirit.   11. (he who
raised up our Lord) Jesus the Anointed, for, the Anointed.   M.
because his Spirit, for, by means of his Spirit, who (dwells in you.)
20, and 21. upon hope that, for, upon hope; because (the creation.)
26. our weakness, for, our weaknesses.   28. God works all things
together; for, all things work together; Syriac, God helps in
everything (for good to those who.)   34. (Who) shall condemn,
for, condemns? Syriac, who is to condemn?
    Ch. ix. 28. Omit, in righteousness; for a purpose of cutting
short (will the Lord execute).   33. he, for, everyone (who trusts.)
    Ch. x. 1. (on behalf of) them, for, Israel.
    Ch. xi. 13. But, instead of, For.   21. neither will he spare;
Syriac, perhaps also he will not spare (thee); for, [beware] lest he
also spare not thee.
    Ch. xiii. 3. a terror to, for, the terror of (good works.)   9.
Omit, thou shalt not bear false witness.
    Ch. xiv. 4. the Lord, in Syriac, his Lord, instead of, God (is able.)
21. is made to stumble, for, he trips, or is made stumble, or becomes weak.   22. The trust which thou hast, for, hast thou trust?
    Ch. xv. 4. (were) written, instead of, fore-written (for our in-
struction.)   7. (has received) you, for, us.   15. from, for, by
(God.)

Ch. xvi. 6. (laboured much) for you; in Syriac, among you; instead of, us. 16. Add, all (the assemblies.) 20. Omit, Amen. 22. have written the letter by the Lord, for, salute you in the Lord.

1 CORINTHIANS i. 22. signs, for, a sign. 23. to the Gentiles; in Syriac, to the Syrians; for, to the Greeks.

Ch. ii. 1. the secret, for, the testimony (of God.) 4. Omit, of man's (wisdom.) 13. Omit, Holy (Spirit.)

Ch. iii. 14. shall remain, for, remains. iv. 2. Add, Here (moreover.) v. 3. Omit, as (absent.) 7. Omit, therefore (purge out.) 12. Omit, also. vi. 2. Add, Or, (know ye not.) 11. (of the Lord Jesus) add, the Anointed.

Ch. vii. 13. (let her not leave) her husband, for, him. 17. (as) the Lord, for, God (has imparted.) (as) God, for, the Lord (has called.) 29. M. that the time henceforth is shortened; for, the time is shortened, that henceforth. 38. (he who gives in marriage) add, his virgin daughter.

Ch. viii. 11. The verse not a question. (thy weak brother) is perishing, for, shall perish.

Ch. ix. 1. Put, free, and apostle, each in the other's place. 10. [should thresh] in hope of partaking; for, in hope, should be partaker of his hope.

Ch. x. 10. Omit, also (some). 17. M. Because, in Syriac, as, there is one loaf, we, who are many, are one body. 28. Omit, for the earth is the Lord's, and the fulness thereof.

Ch. xi. 22. M. Shall I praise you? In this I praise you not. 32. M. when we are judged by the Lord, for, when we are judged, (we are chastened) by the Lord.

Ch. xii. 12. (of the) omit, one (body.) 13. (been made to drink) one Spirit, for, into one Spirit.

Ch. xiv. 16. (if thou) dost, for, shalt (bless.) 18. I thank God, for, my God. 25. Omit, thus. 40. Add, But (let all things.)

Ch. xv. 6. (but some) omit, also. 31. Add, my brothers.

Ch. xvi. 3. M. I will send with letters ; in Syriac, a letter ; for, ye shall approve by letters. 7. For, in room of, But.

2. CORINTHIANS i. 8. concerning, for, on behalf of (our affliction.) 13. Omit, even (to the end.) 14. Add, our (Lord Jesus the Anointed.)

Ch. ii. 5. he has not grieved me [only], but, in some degree, all of you. 7. M. omit, rather.

Ch. iii. 14. M. and it is not revealed [to them] that it is done away in the Anointed; for, remains untaken away : which is done away in the Anointed. 17. Omit, there (liberty is.)

Ch. iv. 10. Omit, the Lord. v. 5. Omit, also. 12. Omit, For. 14. that one, for, that if one (died.) 18. Omit, Jesus. vi. 14. or, for, and (what in common has light with darkness ?)

Ch. vii. 13. (we have been comforted ;) add, and (in addition to) our, for, your (comfort, we have rejoiced the more exceedingly.) 16. Omit, therefore.

Ch. viii. 7. M. in our love for you, instead of, in your love for us.   19. and [to show] our, for, your (readiness.)   21. Add, For, (we provide.)   24. M. (and of our glorying) to them, instead of, (show ye) to them.

Ch. ix. 10. he will, or, may he (give [to you],...and increase your seed, and make great the fruits of your gifts.)

Ch. x. 7. (so also are we) omit, of the Anointed.

Ch. xi. 32. Omit, wishing (to take me.)

Ch. xii. 1. I ought to glory, but it is not of advantage [to me]; for, It is not of advantage to me to glory; (for I will come.)   5. on behalf of such a thing; Syriac, this thing; (I will glory.) (except in) omit, my (weaknesses.)   14. Add, this (third time.) 20. Strife, envying, for, strifes, envyings.

Ch. xiii. 4. M. (we are weak) with, for, in (him.)   (but we) Syriac, live, for, shall live.

GALATIANS i. 18. Cephas, for, Peter.   also in ii. 11, and 14. ii. 14. How is it? for, Why?   20. M. and no longer do I live; for, nevertheless I live, yet not I.   iii. 1. Omit, not to obey the truth.   Omit, among you.   12. he, for, the man (who does them.)   iv. 15. Where then is, for, what then was.   26. our mother, for, the mother of us all.   v. 19. Omit, adultery.   20. strife, for, strifes.   vi. 15. For neither is circumcision anything; instead of, For in the Anointed, Jesus, neither circumcision avails anything, (nor uncircumcision.)

EPHESIANS i. 4, 5. M. having beforehand, in his love, designed us ; for, (before him) in love; having beforehand designed us (for himself.)   6. which he has given us, for, with which he has favoured us.   18. the eyes of your heart; Syriac, hearts, for, of your understanding.   ii. 1. (dead in) add, your.   iii. 3. has been, for, he (made known to me.)   7. I have been made, for, was made (a servant.)   9. (what is) the stewardship, for, the fellowship (of the secret.)   (who has created all things) omit, by means of Jesus the Anointed.   iv. 32. M. (has forgiven) us, for, you.   v. 9. (the fruit of light, for, of the Spirit.   21. Syriac, in the love of the Anointed, for, in the fear of God.   29. (as) the Anointed, for, the Lord (does the assembly.)   vi. 19. boldly make known, for, boldly open my mouth.

PHILIPPIANS i. 14. (to speak the word) add, of God.   16. Syriac, some from good-will and love, for, from love (proclaim the Anointed, knowing.)   17. But those who proclaim the Anointed in strife, do it, not sincerely, but think to add affliction to my bonds.   28. of your salvation, for, to you of salvation.   ii. 5. have this mind, for, let this mind be (in you.)   12. Omit, as.   26. M. add, to see (you all.)   iii. 11. from among, for, of (the dead.)

COLOSSIANS i. 2. Omit, and from the Lord Jesus the Anointed.
3. to God the Father, for, to the God and Father. 6. (the world);
add, and increases, (and bears fruit.) 7. Omit, also. 14.
(redemption) omit, by means of his blood. 24. in those sufferings
which are, for, in my sufferings. ii. 1. on behalf of, for, concerning you. 13. (having forgiven) us, for, you. 15. M.
(having put off) the Syriac adds, his body; he made a show of
principalities and powers. 18. The Syriac seems to mean :—Let
no one desire, by humiliation of mind, to your condemnation, that
ye should subject yourselves to the worship of angels. iii. 15.
(Let the peace) of the Anointed, for, of God. 16. (singing) in
your hearts to God, for, in your heart to the Lord. 17. to God
the Father, for, to God and the Father. 22. (fearing) the Lord,
for, God.

1 THESSALONIANS i. 1. Omit, from God our Father, and the
Lord Jesus the Anointed. 4. my brothers, beloved by God ; for,
my beloved brothers, (your being chosen) by God. 7. an example,
for, examples. ii. 12. M. has called, for, is calling (you) 19.
Omit, the Anointed. iv. 8. to you, for, to us. 11. your hands,
for, your own hands. v. 3. Omit, For. 5. Add, For (all ye.)

2 THESSALONIANS ii. 2. (the day) of the Lord, for, of the Anointed.
4. (every) person, for, thing (called God.) 8. the Lord Jesus,
for, the Lord. 16. God our Father, for, our God and Father.
17. (and make) them, for you, [firm.]

1 TIMOTHY i. 1. (and of) omit, the Lord. 17. the only God,
for, the only wise God. ii. 7. (I speak the truth) omit, in the
Anointed. iii. 3. Omit, not greedy of base gain. 16. He was
revealed in flesh. The Syriac has not the name of God, but he,
cannot mean a human soul, for that would be no mystery ; nor an
angel, (Heb. i. 13); and therefore must mean God. iv. 12. Omit,
in spirit. 15. (manifest) to all, for, in all things. v. 4. (for
this is) omit, good and. vi. 12. Omit, also (thou hast been called.)
19. (may lay hold on) what is really life ; Syriac, true life; for,
eternal life.

2 TIMOTHY ii. 12. shall deny, for, deny. 13. Add, for, (he
cannot.) 19. (the name) of the Lord, for, of the Anointed. iv.
1. Omit, therefore.

TITUS i. 4. Omit, mercy.

PHILEMON 4. (I thank my God) always, for, always (making
mention.) 20. (my bowels) in the Anointed, for, in the Lord.

HEBREWS iii. 16. Two questions. For who were they who . . .
provoked him ? Were they not all who . . . by means of Moses?
iv. 7. as it has been before said ; Syriac, as it is above written ;
for, as it is said. v. 3. Syriac, on behalf of the people ; on

behalf of himself; on account of his sins; for, on account of the
people; on account of himself; on behalf of sins.　vi. 10. (and
the) love, for, labour of love.　vii. 4. (to whom) omit, even.
viii. 11. fellow-citizen, for, neighbour.　12. Omit, and their lawless deeds, (or iniquities.)　ix. 10. which are, for, and in (rules
of the flesh.)　11. M. (of the good things which) Greek, are
come; Syriac, he effected; for, were to come.　14. M. our, for,
your (conscience.)　28. (So) add, also (the anointed.)　x. 1.
they, for, it (can never.)　8. slain-offerings and gift-offerings,
for, slain-offering and gift-offering.　11. M. high-priest, for,
priest.　12. this [priest], for, he.　(sat down) for ever, for,
(offered) for ever.　15. Greek, after having said; Syriac, who has
said; for, after having before said.　30. Omit, says the Lord.
34. on those who were prisoners, for, on [me] in my bonds.
(knowing) that ye have, for, in yourselves that ye have.　xi. 13.
Omit, and were persuaded of [them.]　26. (the treasures) of, for,
in (Egypt.)　xii. 3. (who were adversaries to) themselves, for,
him.　18. (come near to) what, for, to the mountain which
(could be touched.)　20. Omit, or thrust through with a dart.
22. M. Greek, to tens of thousands of angels in general
meeting; Syriac, to the multitudes of tens of thousands of
angels; for, to tens of thousands of angels; to the general
meeting (and assembly of the first-born.)　26. I will shake, for,
I shake.　28. (with reverence and) fear, for, godly fear.　xiii.
6. I will not fear; what shall man do to me? for, and I will not
fear what man shall do to me.　9. (Be not) led away, for, led
about (by.)　15. And, for, Therefore (through him.)　21.
(working in) us, for, you.

　JAMES i. 26. Omit, among you.　ii. 5. of the, for, of this
(world.)　11. (If thou) dost not, for, shalt not (commit adultery,
but) dost, for, shalt (kill.)　18. Greek, without works; Syriac,
which is without works; for, without thy works.　24. Omit,
therefore.　iii. 9. (we bless) the Lord, for, God.　12. Greek,
nor [can] salt water yield sweet; Syriac, so also salt water cannot
be made sweet; for, so no spring can yield salt and sweet water.
iv. 12. Greek, [Only] one is the Lawgiver and Judge; Syriac, For
there is [but] one who appoints law and judgment; instead of,
[Only] one is the Lawgiver.　thy neighbour, for, another.　v.
11. Who have patiently endured, for, who patiently endure.

　1 PETER i. 22. Omit, by means of the Spirit.　24. (the glory)
of it, for, of man.　ii. 2. (ye may grow up) add, Greek, unto
salvation; Syriac, to life [-bliss].　25. (ye were) going astray,
for, (like sheep) which go astray.　iii. 8. (be) lowly, for, courteous,
or friendly.　9. for, instead of, knowing that (to [do] this.)　13.
(if ye be) zealous in, for, imitators of (what is good.)　15. the

Lord, the Anointed; for, the Lord God.   18. M. died, for, suffered.   21. (immersion saves) you, for, us.   iv. 1. (has ceased) M. Greek, from sins; Syriac, from all sins; for, from sin. 3. Omit, of life.   Greek, omits, for us (to have done); the Syriac has, that ye (have done.)   8. (love) covers, for, will cover.   9. (without) murmuring, for, murmurings.   14. Omit, on their part he is ill-spoken of, but on your part he is glorified.   16. in this name, for, on this account.   v. 5. (all of you) omit, be subject (one to another.)   (All of you) clothe yourselves, tightly girt, with humility one towards another.   14. in the Anointed, for, in the Anointed, Jesus.

1 JOHN i. 3. (we declare to you) add, also.   4. (that) our, for, your (joy.) The Syriac has, that our joy which is in you.   7. (the blood of Jesus) omit, the Anointed.   ii. 6. Omit, so.   7. My beloved, for, [My] brothers.   (which ye have heard) omit, from the beginning.   13. I have written, for, I write (to you, little children.)   24. The Greek omits, therefore; the Syriac has, And (ye.)   27. Greek, his (anointing); Syriac, the anointing which is from God; for, the same anointing.   continue ye, for, ye will continue.   29. (know ye that every one) add, also.   iii. 1. Greek, (that we should be called children of God) add, and [such] we are; Syriac, who has called us sons; [and] has also made us [sons.]   iii. 16. his (love), for, (the love) of God,   19. (our) heart, for, hearts.   v. 2. [when we] do, for, keep (his commands.) •7, 8. Omit, in heaven, the Father, the Word, and the Holy Spirit : and these three are one.   And there are three that bear witness on earth.   13. (These things I have written to you) omit, who trust in the name of the Son of God.   (that ye have eternal life), ye who trust; Syriac, have trusted; for, and that ye may trust (in the name of the Son of God.)   21. Omit, Amen.

XV. CONCLUSION.

These pages have been written with view to present known facts and testimonies with sufficient fulness to show the true worth of the Peshito-Syriac text of the New Covenant Writings.

It is submitted,—FIRST, that there is ground for belief that this text has been so correctly copied, that it has come down to us WITHOUT MATERIAL CHANGE FROM THE FIRST CENTURY. As Dr. Scrivener says, "The Syriac was cited by Melito as early as A.D. 170," and history leaves "no room to doubt what that version was." It was the Peshito. Part of it was left in India in the time of the Apostles, and the whole book of the N. C. was received there, and in Coordistan, as well as in Mesopotamia, not very long after the time of the Apostles. The copies in all those places must at that time have been alike, because the copies made from them do still, at this time, as Dr. Scrivener says, "exhibit a text in

every important respect the same." (See the previous p. 66.) "Literary history can hardly afford a more powerful case than has been
established for THE IDENTITY of the version of the Syriac now
called the Peshito WITH THAT USED by the Eastern Church, long
before the great schism had its beginning in the native land of the
blessed gospel;" that is, long before "the middle of the fifth
century," when the Syrian Christians were divided "into three,"
and eventually into yet more, hostile communions." Dr. Scrivener's
Introduction, 1883, pp. 312, 313.

An additional testimony, not mentioned in the preceding pages,
to the pure and unaltered state of the Peshito down to the middle
of the fifth century, has lately come to my knowledge. It is the
testimony of IBAS, bishop of Edessa. In a Syriac letter written to
a Persian before the year A.D. 449, he said,—"Those Scriptures
which have been granted [to us] by God, have not suffered
the least alteration." A copy of this letter is given by the Rev.
S. G. F. Perry, M.A., in his work, "The Second Synod of
Ephesus," 1881, p. 111. The Peshito, from its origin, was used at
Edessa; so that this testimony has a direct reference to it, as containing the Scriptures which God had granted them. Ibas was a
Nestorian, and suffered, for a time, deposition from his bishopric,
for denying that Mary was "the Mother of God." (Same, pp.
145-7.) His readiness to suffer rather than assent to an untruth,
gives weight to his testimony as to the purity of the Peshito down
to that time.

SECONDLY, It is submitted, that so far as THE REVISED ENGLISH
VERSION OF 1881, WAS BASED ON A NEWLY-FORMED GREEK TEXT,
the preceding comparison of that text with the Text of the Peshito,
(see these pp. 83-111,) proves it to be in a multitude of cases incorrect; that this incorrectness proves it to be unreliable; that the
Revisers, by following this faulty Greek text, have rejected passages
of much importance; that their changes have removed, and their
suggestions undermined, many divine testimonies; that some of
their suggestions tend to sanction errors; that for these reasons their
work, though it occupied so many persons, for so long a time, is unfit
for general use; and is not without danger of doing harm. This
comparison of their Greek text with that of the Peshito, sustains
the strong objections made to it by Dr. Scrivener, Dean Burgon,
and Canon Cook. (See these pp. 61-70.)

THIRDLY. THE FREEDOM OF THE PESHITO FROM THE MANY
FAULTY EXPRESSIONS AND MEANINGS OF THE GREEK TEXT OF THE
REVISERS, confirms all other proofs of its purity. Those Revised
Greek readings which agree with the Peshito, (see Section xiv. pp.
111-123) have, as a rule, little or no internal evidence against
them. But among the Revised Greek readings from which the
Peshito differs there are some which prove decisively that the
Greek copies are corrupt from which they are taken. The follow-

ing brief quotations from Dr. Scrivener's remarks on some of these will show the nature of this evidence.   Matt. xxvii. 28, clothed, for stripped him :—" a palpable impropriety "; p. 480 ; " an impossible reading ;" p. 543.   Matt. xxvii. 49.   The Saviour pierced before his death ;—" this gross corruption ;" p. 543.   Mark vi. 22.   Herod's daughter Herodias danced ; instead of, the daughter of Herodias :—a reading which "brings Mark into direct contradiction with Josephus, who expressly states that the wretched girl was named Salome," and was the daughter of Herod's brother Philip ; p. 544.   Mark xvi. 9-20 :—" all opposition to the authenticity of this paragraph resolves itself into the allegations of Eusebius," (an Arian), " and the testimony of Aleph and B."   " We can appeal to all extant manu-scripts excepting two ;" p. 590.   Luke ii. 14.   The Angelic Hymn sung at the nativity ;—" By the addition of a single letter to the end of the last line, the simple shepherds are sent away with a message, the diction of which no scholar has yet construed to his own mind."   " Solid reason and pure taste, revolt against " it ; p. 590.   The testimony for the common reading " cannot but over-power the transcriptural blunder of some early scribe ;" p. 592. Luke xxiii. 34.   " Father, forgive them :"—" It is almost incredible that acute and learned men should be able to set aside " the evi-dence for these words, " chiefly because D,"—a very corrupt Greek copy, " is considered especially weighty in its omissions, and B has to be held up, in practice if not in profession, as virtually almost impeccable."   " We cannot doubt that the system which entails such consequences is hopelessly self-condemned ;" p. 604.   John i. 18. " The only begotten God."   " Everyone must feel [the word] God to be untrue, even though for the sake of consistency he may be forced to uphold it."   This reading would introduce " a new, and, to us moderns, a strange term into Scripture ;" p. 605.   Acts iv. 25.   Some critical editors insert here " that which cannot possibly be right ;" the result of " setting up one or more of the oldest copies as objects of unreasonable idolatry ;" p. 549.   Acts. xii. 25, Barnabas and Saul, who were at Jerusalem (xi. 30), are said to have returned to Jerusalem.   " That the two Apostles returned from, not to, Jeru-salem is too plain for argument ;" p. 550.   Acts xxv. 13, having saluted Festus :   " The reading is manifestly false ;" p. 551. Acts xxviii. 13, took away, for, made a circuit : a " vile error of transcription ;" p. 551.   Romans v. 1, " let us have peace ;" " a reading which is manifestly unsuitable to the context ; p. 625.

The Revisers were led to give their countenance to the above impossible, or evidently false, readings, by the Greek Text of Drs. Westcott and Hort.   And Drs. Westcott and Hort, in the Intro-duction to their Greek Testament, do their utmost to commend their own Greek Text in opposition to the Peshito.   None of the above false readings occur in the Peshito.   This fact is one proof of its superiority to the Greek copies on which Drs. Westcott and Hort rely. The Peshito is true, where these are grossly false ; it is pure, where they are corrupt.

FOURTHLY, Have we not in the Peshito, that which all efforts have failed to produce by means of Greek copies, namely,—A TEXT WHICH, WITH SLIGHT EXCEPTIONS, IS PROVED TO BE A RELIABLE COPY OF THE INFALLIBLE WRITINGS GIVEN BY THE SPIRIT OF GOD. The inspiration of Scripture is being assailed with new energy, and from new quarters. The corruptions of the Greek text make it impossible to say that it is as pure and infallible as it was at first ; and it is admitted that the many most searching and unwearied endeavours which have been made to construct a Greek text which would have proof of being like the original Greek text, have failed. Dr. Schaff in America, and Dr. Scrivener here, have admitted this. (see the preceding pp. 53, 54.) Dr. Scrivener says that, " nothing short of a continuous, unceasing miracle," could have secured " the complete identity of all copies of Holy Scripture." (Introduction, p. 3.) But the marvellous likeness of the Syriac copies is proof that care and exactness in copying and in correcting copies, could prevent such incorrectness as there is in the Greek copies. It is evident that the Syrians, not only copied their Scriptures with care, but duly examined and corrected their copies. It is equally evident that many who made Greek copies did not do this. The result is, that while the Syriac copies prove their correctness by their wonderful agreement, the Greek copies vary perpetually, and often in almost every sentence ; baffling, by tens of thousands of variations, all attempts to find a pure text.

Is it not evident that God has, by his over-ruling care, provided for us in the Peshito an attested copy of what he has said, such as at the present time is felt to be A GREAT AND SPECIAL NEED ? Is there not reason to believe, with Wichelhaus, that the text from which the Syriac copies have been made "was exceedingly like the autographs of the Apostles ?" (On the Peshito, p. 264.) And does not Canon Cook justify this opinion, when he says, that " the Syriac Peshito " is one of the " authorities to which in some cases, a higher value is to be assigned, as *more ancient* and *better attested* than any [Greek] manuscripts ?" that it is " the version which probably comes *nearest to the autographs of the Evangelists ?*" and that " in the great majority of disputed readings that which has its decided support has a *prima facie* claim *to preference, if not to absolute acceptance ?*" (First Three Gospels, pp. 143-4.)

LASTLY, The early, the continuous, the uncontradicted Syrian testimony, that, as Jesudad said, THE PESHITO WAS " MADE BY THE CARE OF THADDÆUS AND OTHER APOSTLES," has an evident claim to calm and full consideration. The Syrian testimony that the Peshito was so made, lacks nothing which is held to entitle such testimony to belief. It is the same kind of testimony, and as credible, as that which is held to prove the Greek text to be of

Divine authority. Those who use the Peshito in India told Dr. Claudius Buchanan that whatever "*translations*" we might have in the west, their own Syriac Scriptures were "THE TRUE BOOK OF GOD," which they had possessed "in the mountains of Malabar for fourteen hundred years." (Pearson's Life of Buchanan, p. 70.) They contended that "the ORIGINAL language of the four Gospels was Syriac." (Buchanan's Researches, p. 95.) And even Dr. Westcott, when not under the influence of Dr. Hort, admits that "the Syriac Christians of Malabar," in claiming for the Peshito "the right to be considered as an EASTERN ORIGINAL of the New Testament," make a claim which "is not, to a certain extent, destitute of all plausibility." (On the Canon, p. 233.)

The fact that between the Greek words and the Syriac words, there is sometimes a want of that similarity of expression which a good translator is bound to use, implies that the Syriac was written under the care of persons, who, like the Apostles, had a right to vary their mode of expression at will, and tends to sanction the belief that both the Greek text, and the Syriac text, were made under Apostolic care.

It is also, in itself, most improbable that God should have guided his Apostles to make a perfect copy of his revealed will, (which is for the guidance of all), in the language of Gentiles only; and should have left his own nation without a perfect apostolic copy of it in their own tongue.

The Peshito-Syriac Text is therefore of great importance.

Index to the Introduction.

THE LETTER TO THE HEBREWS:

A TRANSLATION IN EVERY-DAY ENGLISH,

Of the Peshito-Syriac and the Received Greek Texts.

———✳———

The Peshito-Syriac Text.

HEBREWS I. 1–11.

THE LETTER TO THE HEBREWS.

I. 1. God, in all kinds of parts, and in all kinds of ways, spoke with our fathers by the prophets from of old; 2, and in these the last days, he has spoken with us by his Son, whom he has made inheritor of everything, and by whom he made the worlds; 3, who himself is the brightness of his glory, and the image of what he is, and who upholds everything by the might of his word; and who by means of himself effected the purging away of our sins, and sat down at the right hand of [God's] Greatness in the high [heavens]; 4, and he in everything is greater than angels, (a) in proportion as the name which he has inherited excels theirs.

5. For to whom from among the angels did God ever say,—Thou art my son, I to-day have begotten thee?—And again, —I will be to him for Father, and he shall be to me for Son?—6. Again too, when introducing the first-born into the world, he said,—Let all the angels of God worship him.

7. In reference to angels also, he said this,—Who made his angels spirit; and his servants, burning fire.

8. But in reference to the Son he said, —Thy throne, O God, is for ever and ever; a righteous sceptre [is] the sceptre of thy kingdom. 9. Thou hast loved justness, and hast hated wickedness; for this reason God, thy God, has anointed thee with the oil of joy, more than [he has] thy associates. 10. And again,— Thou from the beginning hast laid the foundations of the earth; and the heavens are the work of thy hands; 11, they shall pass away, but thou art firm; and they all as garments shall grow old;

The Greek Text.

HEBREWS I. 1–12.

THE LETTER OF PAUL TO THE HEBREWS.

I. 1. God, who of old, by the many parts [of his word], and in many ways, spoke to [our] fathers by the prophets, 2, has, in these last of the days, spoken to us by [his] Son, whom he has made inheritor of all things, by means of whom he also made the worlds; 3, who, being the forth-shining of [his] glory, and the stamped-image of what he himself is, and upholding all things by the word of his might; when he had by means of himself effected the purging away of our sins, sat down at the right hand of [God's] Greatness in the high [heavens]; 4, having become greater than the angels (a) in such high degree as he has inherited a name which excels theirs.

5. For to whom of the angels did he ever say,—Thou art my son, I to-day have begotten thee? And again,—I will be to him for Father, and he shall be to me for Son? 6. And again, when he introduces the first-born into the inhabited [earth], he says,—And let all the angels of God worship him.

7. And in reference to the angels he says,—Who makes his angels spirits, and his chief servants, a flame of fire.

8. But in reference to the Son,—Thy throne, O God, is for ever and ever; a sceptre of righteousness [is] the sceptre of thy kingdom. 9. Thou hast loved justness; and hated lawlessness. For this reason God, thy God, has anointed thee with the oil of great joy, more than [he has] those in fellowship with thee. 10. And,—Thou, O Lord, at the beginning, didst found the earth, and the heavens are works of thy hands; 11, they shall perish, but thou continuest; and they all, as a garment, shall grow old, 12, and

(a) Ver. 4. Both the Syriac word, and the Greek word, represented by the English word "angel," mean "messenger," that is, "a messenger [of God]." The word "angel" is the Greek word for "messenger" in an English form.

The Peshito-Syriac Text.	The Greek Text.
HEBREWS I. 12—14. II. 1—9.	HEBREWS I. 12—14. II. 1—9.

<table>
<tr><td>

12, and like as a cloak thou shalt fold them up, [and] they shall be changed. And thou, as thou art, wilt be, and thy years will not fail.

13. But to whom from among the angels has he ever said,—Sit thou at my right hand until I shall place thine enemies [for] a footstool beneath thy feet? 14, Are they not all spirits of service, who are sent forth on service, because of those who are about to inherit life [-bliss]? (a)

II. 1. For this reason we ought the more especially to be heedful of that which we have heard, lest we should fall. 2. For if the word which was spoken by means of angels was confirmed, and everyone who heard it and broke it, received the punishment which was just; 3, how shall we escape, if we shall neglect those things which are themselves our life [-bliss]; those which began to be spoken by our Lord, and were confirmed to us by those who heard [them] from him; 4, things to which God bore witness by signs and by wonders, and by various deeds of might, and by distributed [gifts] of the Spirit of Holiness, which were given according to his will?

5. For he has not put under angels the world which is to be, of which we are speaking. 6. But as the [sacred] writing bears witness, and says,—What is man that thou hast remembered him, and the son of man, that thou hast visited him? 7. Thou hast placed him a little lower than the angels; glory and honour hast thou put on his head, and thou hast made him rule over the work of thy hands. 8. And everything thou hast put under [him], beneath his feet. Now as to his having put everything under him, he has left nothing which is not put under [him]; but at present we do not yet see that everything is put under him. 9. But we see that on the head of him who was placed a little lower than angels, who is Jesus,there have been put, because of his having suffered death, both glory and honour; for he, by the

</td><td>

as a cloak thou shalt roll them up, and they shall be changed; but thou art the same, and thy years will not fail.

13. But to whom of the angels has he ever said,—Sit thou at my right hand until I place thine enemies [for] the footstool of thy feet? 14. Are they not all spirits of chief service, who are sent forth for service, because of those who are about to inherit salvation?

II. 1. For this reason we ought the more especially to give heed to the things which have been heard, lest by any means we fall away. 2. For if the word which was spoken by means of angels proved firm, and every breach [of it], and disobedience [to it], received just punishment, 3, how shall we escape, if we shall have neglected so great salvation, which was at first declared by means of the Lord, and was confirmed unto us by those who had heard [him]; 4, together with whom God bore witness by signs and wonders, and by various deeds of might, and by gifts of the Holy Spirit, distributed according to his will.

5. For he has not put under angels the inhabited [earth]which is to be, respecting which we are speaking. 6. But [there is] a place where one has borne witness, saying,—What is man that thou dost remember him, and the son of man that thou dost visit him? 7. Thou hast placed him a little lower than angels,thou hast crowned him with glory and honour,and hast placed him over the works of thy hands, 8, thou hast put under [him] all things, beneath his feet.—For in putting all things under him, he has left nothing which is not put under him; but at present we do not yet see all things put under him; 9, but we see him who was placed a little lower than angels, Jesus, because of his having suffered death crowned with glory and honour, in order

</td></tr>
</table>

(a) Ver. 14. The Syriac uses the word "life" where the Greek has "salvation;" the word "life" is used to denote a state of blessed existence, and is rendered in these pages "life-bliss."

The Peshito-Syriac Text.

HEBREWS II. 9—18. III. 1.

gracious favour of God, tasted death for every one. (a)

10. For it became him by means of whom [are] all things, and because of whom [are] all things, and [who] was introducing many sons into his glory, to fit perfectly the Head of their life [-bliss) by sufferings. 11. For he who made [them] holy, and those who were made holy, are all of them of one [family.] For this reason, he has not been ashamed to call them his brothers; 12, saying :—I will declare thy name to my brothers; and in the midst of the assembly, (b) I will praise thee. 13. And again:—I will trust on him.—And again,—Behold, I, and the sons whom God has given to me. 14. For because the sons shared flesh and blood, He also, in like manner, shared the same, that by his death he might make powerless him who holds the empire of death, who is Satan; 15, and might set free those, who, by fear of death, were all their lives placed under bondage. 16. For it was not from angels that he took [a body]; but [it was] from the seed,[the offspring] of Abraham that he took [one.] 17. For this reason it was right that He should in everything be made to be like his brothers; that he might be merciful, and a high priest faithful in the things of God, and might make atonement for the sins of the people. 18. For by this, that he suffered and was put to test, he is able to help those who are being tested.

III. 1. Therefore, my holy brothers, who have been called with a call which is from heaven ; look at this Chief-Messenger (c) and High Priest of our pro-

The Greek Text.

HEBREWS II. 9—18. III. 1.

that, by the gracious favour of God, he might taste of death for every one. (a)

10. For it became him because of whom [are] all things, and by means of whom [are] all things, when leading many sons into glory, to fit perfectly the Chieftain of their salvation by means of sufferings. 11. For both he who makes holy, and those who are made holy, [are] all of one [family]; for which reason he is not ashamed to call them brothers, 12, saying, —I will declare thy name to my brothers; in the midst of the assembly, (b) I will sing praise to thee.—13. And again,—I will trust on him.—And again,—Behold, I, and the children, whom God has given to me. 14. So then, since the children share flesh and blood, he also in like manner shared the same with [them]; that, by means of death, he might make powerless him who holds dominion over death, that is, the False-accuser ; 15, and might set these persons free ; who all, by fear of death, were held, through all their lives, in bondage. 16. For he does not indeed take on himself [the form] of angels; but he takes on himself [the form] of the seed,[the offspring] of Abraham. 17. Hence, he was bound to be made in all things like to his brothers, that he might become a merciful and faithful High Priest in things relating to God, in order to make atonement for the sins of the people. 18. For in that he has suffered, by having been put to test, he is able to help those who are being tested.

III. 1. So then, holy brothers, partakers of the heavenly calling, consider the Chief-Messenger (c) and High Priest of our profession, Jesus, the Anointed, 2,

---

(a) Ver. 9. Instead of the words rendered, "by the gracious favour of God," other Syriac manuscripts have two variations. The Greek does not seem to be correct, because the exaltation of Christ did not determine the object of his death. A reading older than the time of the Nestorians, was mentioned by Origen, who died about A.D. 254. It is, "For he, apart from Godhead." Some Nestorians adopted this reading. The Jacobites seem to have altered the position of "God," to suit their creed. They have in their copies,—"He, God, in his gracious favour, tasted death." The Peshito edited for the B. and F. Bible Society, partly by Dr. Buchanan, and partly by Dr. Lee, and which is founded on some ancient manuscripts, has the reading given above, which differs from that of the Jacobites only in the position of the word "God."

(b) Ver. 12. The word "church," used in the Common Version, does not give the meaning either of the Syriac or of the Greek word, both of which mean "assembly."

(c) Ver. 1. The Greek word is "apostolos," which, in English form, is "apostle." The meaning of the Greek word is, "one sent forth." It is translated "messenger" sometimes in the common E.V. See 2 Cor. viii. 23. Phil. ii. 25. The Syriac word has the same meaning. "Chief-messenger" seems to represent both the Syriac word, and the Greek word fitly, when used of the twelve, and of Jesus.

The Peshito Syriac Text.

fession, Jesus, the Anointed, 2, who [is] faithful to him who appointed him, even as Moses [was faithful] in respect of all his [God's] house.

3. For the glory of this [Messenger] is much greater than that of Moses, as to the degree in which the honour of the builder of a house is much greater than [that of] his building. 4. For every house is built by a man, but he, [Jesus,] who has built all things, is God.

5. And Moses, as a servant, was faithful in all [God's] house, to bear witness of those things which were to be spoken of by means of him. 6. But the Anointed, as Son, over his [God's] house ; and his house we [are], if unto the end we shall hold fast [our] confidence, and glorying in his hope. 7. Because the Spirit of Holiness has said,—To-day if ye will hearken to his voice, 8, harden not your hearts, so as to make him angry, as [did] the provokers; even as [they did] in the day of putting [me] to test, in the wildernsss ; 9, where your fathers put me to test, and to proof. They saw my works for forty years. 10. For this reason I was weary of that generation, and I said,— They are people whose heart errs, and they have not known my ways ;—11, so that I sware in my anger,—They shall not enter into my rest.

12. Take heed, therefore, my brothers, lest there should be in any one of you an evil heart which does not trust, and ye should depart from the living God. 13. But examine yourselves as to all days up to the day which is called to-day, lest any one of you should be hardened by the deception of sin. 14. For we have been made to share with the Anointed, if from the beginning unto the end, we shall continue in this fixed firmness. 15. As it is said,—To-day, if ye will hearken to his voice, harden not your hearts, so as to make him angry.— 16. For who were those who heard [him], and made him angry? Were they not all those who went out from Egypt by means of Moses? 17. And by whom was he wearied forty years, but by those who sinned, and whose bones fell in the wilderness? 18. And in reference to whom did he swear that they should not enter into his rest, but in reference to those who did not submit themselves ? 19. And we see that they were unable to enter, because they did not trust.

The Greek Text.

who [is] faithful to him who appointed him, even as Moses [was] also in respect of all his [God's] house.

3. For this [Messenger] has been honoured with more glory than Moses, in reference to the degree in which he who has built a house has more honour than the house. 4. For every house is built by some [man], but he [Jesus], who has built all things, [is] God.

5. And Moses indeed was faithful in all his [God's] house as a servant, that he might bear witness to the things which were to be spoken; 6, but the Anointed, as Son, over his [God's] house; whose house are we, if we retain [our] confidence and [our] glorying in [his] hope, firm to the end. 7. Because, as the Holy Spirit says,—To-day, if ye will hearken to his voice, 8, harden not your hearts, as in the provocation, in the day of putting to test, in the wilderness ; 9, where your fathers tested me, they put me to proof; and they saw my works forty years. 10. Therefore I was angry with that generation and said,—They always err in heart, and they have not known my ways; 11, so I sware in my anger,— They shall not enter into my rest.

12. Keep watch, brothers, lest there should be in any one of you a wicked heart of distrust, [shown] in departing from the living God. 13. But call yourselves to account for each day up to that which is called to-day, lest any one of you should be hardened by the deception of sin. 14. For we have become sharers with the Anointed, if we shall retain the beginning of [our] reliance firm unto the end ; 15, in [accord with] what is said,—To-day if ye will hearken to his voice, do not harden your hearts, as in the provocation. 16. For who were those who, having heard, provoked [him], but all, were they not, who went out from Egypt by means of Moses ? 17. And with whom was he angry forty years ? Was it not with those who sinned, whose limbs fell in the wilderness ? •18. And to whom did he sware that they should not enter into his rest, but to those who did not submit themselves? And we see that they were unable to enter, because of distrust.

The Peshito-Syriac Text.

HEBREWS IV. 1—15.

IV. 1. Let us therefore fear, lest, though the promise of an entrance into his rest is firm, there should be found any one among you who fails to enter. 2. For we also have been told of [it], as they were. But as to them, the word which they heard did not profit them; because it was not united with trust in those who heard it. 3. We then, those who trust, are to enter into rest; even as he said,—So I sware in my anger that they shall not enter into my rest?—For, behold, the works of God had been [going on] from the beginning of the world. As he said in respect of the sabbath-rest, —God rested on the seventh day from all his works.—5. And in this place, he said again,—They shall not enter into my rest. 6. Therefore, because there was a place [of rest] into which one or other will enter, and those who had before been told of it, did not enter, because they did not submit themselves; 7, again he fixed another day, after a long time, as it is above written, that David said,— To-day, if ye will hearken to his voice, harden not your hearts.—8. For if Jesus [Joshua] (a) the son of Nun had made them rest, he [God] would not have spoken afterwards of another day.

9. So then, it is firmly sure that the people of God are to keep a Sabbath-rest. 10. For he who has entered into his rest, he also has rested from his works, as God did from his.

11. Let us therefore strive earnestly to enter into that rest, lest we fall, like as they did who did not submit themselves. 12. For the word of God has life, and works out all things, and is of much sharper point than a sword with two edges; and enters even to the severance of life and of spirit, and of the joints, and of the marrow and bones; and judges the thoughts and purpose of the heart. 13. And there is no created thing which is hidden from his presence, but everything is naked and revealed before the eyes of him to whom we have to give account.

14. Because therefore we have a great High Priest, Jesus the Anointed, the Son of God, who has gone up to heaven, let us continue to profess him. 15. For we have not a high priest who is not able to have fellow-feeling with our weakness,

The Greek Text.

HEBREWS IV. 1—15.

IV. 1. Let us therefore fear lest, though a promise remains of entering into his rest, anyone of you should appear to have failed [to do so]. 2. For we also have been told the good tidings, as they were. But the word they heard did not profit them, not having been united with trust in those who heard [it]. 3. For we who have trusted are to enter into [his] rest, as he has said,—So I sware in my anger, —They shall not enter into my rest,— though [till he rested] the works had been coming into being from the foundation of the world. 4. For [there is] a place where he has spoken about the seventh day, thus,—And God rested on the seventh day from all his works.—5. And [he has said] in this [place] again,— They shall not enter into my rest. 6. Since therefore, it remains that some are to enter into it, and those who had before been told the good tidings, did not enter [it], because of insubmission; 7, again he fixes a certain day, saying by David, after so long a time,—To-day, as it has been said [already],—To-day, if ye will hearken to his voice, harden not your hearts. 9. For if Jesus, [Joshua] (a) had made them rest, he [God] would not have spoken afterwards about another day.

9. So then there remains for the people of God a keeping of Sabbath-rest. 10. For he who has entered into his rest, has also himself rested from his works, as God [did] from his own.

11. Let us therefore strive earnestly to enter into that rest, lest any one should fall by the same display of insubmission. 12. For the word of God has life and active force, and is sharper than any sword of two edges, and pierces even to the dividing of life and of spirit, and of the joints and marrow, and is a judge of the thoughts and purposes of the heart. 13. And there is no created thing which is hidden from his presence; but all things are naked and laid bare to the eyes of him, with whom is our account.

14. Having, therefore, a great High Priest, who has passed through the heavens, Jesus, the Son of God, let us hold fast our profession. 15. For we have not a high priest who is not able to have fellow-feeling with [us] in our

(a) Ver. 8. Jesus is the Greek form of a Hebrew word which is contracted from the Hebrew Jehoshua or Joshua. Jesus and Joshua have the same meaning.

The Peshito-Syriac Text.

but who, put to test in everything as we are, [was] without sin. 16. Let us, therefore, go near with confidence to the throne of his gracious favour, that we may receive mercies, and find gracious favour, for aid in time of affliction.

V. 1. For every high priest who is from among men, stands on behalf of men over those things which are of God, that he may offer gift-offerings, and offerings slain on behalf of sins. 2. And [he is] one who is able to humble himself, and to have fellow-feeling with those who are ignorant and erring; because that he also is clothed with weakness. 3. And because of that weakness, he is bound to offer [sacrifices], as on behalf of the people, so on behalf of himself, on account of his sins.

4. And no one takes to himself the honour, but he [takes it] who is called by God as [was] Aaron. 5. So also the Anointed did not take to himself the glory of being High Priest; but he [conferred it] who said to him,—Thou art my son, I to-day have begotten thee.—6. As also he said in another place,—Thou art a priest for ever, in the likeness of Melchizedec.

7. Also when he was clothed with flesh, he offered up prayer and intreaty with strong outcry, and with tears, to him who was able to bring him to life from death, and he was heard. 8. And though he was Son, [yet] from the fear and the sufferings which he endured, he learned obedience. 9. And thus he was made perfectly fit, and was the cause of life [-bliss], which is for ever, to all those who obey him. 10. And he was named by God,—A High Priest in the likeness of Melchizedec. 11. About him indeed, namely, this Melchizedec, we have much to say; and it is difficult to explain it, because ye are weak in your ability to hear. 12. For ye ought to be teachers, because of the time ye have been under teaching. But at present ye have again need to learn the things first written of the beginning of the words of God; and ye are in need of milk, and not of solid food. 13. Now every one whose food is milk, is unskilled in the word of justification, because he is a babe. 14. But solid food is that of the full[-grown]; who, because they search, have senses exercised to distinguish good and evil.

The Greek Text.

weaknesses, but one who has been put to test in all things, like as [we are], without sin. 16. Let us, therefore, go near with confidence to [his] throne of gracious favour, that we may take hold of mercy, and find gracious favour for seasonable help.

V. 1. For every high priest who is taken from among men, is appointed [to act] on behalf of men in things relating to God, that he may offer gifts and also offerings slain on behalf of sins; 2, being one who is able to deal gently with the ignorant and erring, since he himself also is clothed around with weakness; 3, and because of this weakness, he is bound to offer [sacrifices] on behalf of sins, as for the people, so also for himself.

4. And no one takes to himself the honour, but he [takes it] who is called by God, as was Aaron. 5. So also the Anointed did not take to himself the glory of becoming High Priest; but he [conferred it] who said to him,—Thou art my Son, I to-day have begotten thee. 6. As he says also in another [place],—Thou [art] a priest for ever of the same order as Melchizedec.

7. He, in the days of his flesh, when he had offered up prayers and intreaties, with strong outcry and tears, to him who was able to save him from out of death, and had been heard on account of his godly fear; 8, though he was Son, [yet] learned he obedience from the things which he suffered; 9, and having been made perfectly fit, he became the cause of eternal salvation to all those who obey him: 10, having been named by God, a High Priest of the same order as Melchizedec; 11, about whom we have much to say, and it is also difficult to explain, because ye have become weary in [your] ears. 12. For indeed, though ye ought to be teachers, because of the [length of] time, [yet] ye have again need that someone should teach you what are the simplest parts of the beginning of the words of God; and ye have become those who have need of milk, and not of solid food. 13. For every one who partakes of milk is unskilled in the word of justification, for he is a babe; 14, but solid food is that of the full-[grown], who, because of habit, have senses exercised to distinguish good and evil.

The Peshito-Syriac Text.

HEBREWS VI. 1–11.

VI. 1. For this reason, let us leave the beginning of the word of the Anointed, and let us go on to full[-growth]. Or are you again to be laying, for another foundation, the turning from dead works, and trust in God; 2, and the teaching of immersion, and of laying on of the hand; and the rising from the house of the dead, and the sentence of judgment which is for ever? 3. If the Lord permits, we will do this [which we propose].

4. But those cannot possibly be afresh renewed unto conversion, who have once gone down into immersion, (a) and have tasted of the gift which is from heaven, and have received the Spirit of Holiness, 5, and have tasted of the good word of God, and of the might of the world which is to be, 6, if they shall again sin, and shall crucify afresh the Son of God, and treat him with contempt. 7. For land which has drunk the rain which many times has come on it, and has produced herbage which is useful to those because of whom it is tilled, receives blessing from God. 8. But if it be [land] which produces thistles and thorns, it is rejected, and is not far from a curse, but its end is burning.

9. But we are persuaded with respect to you, my brothers, of those things which are excellent, and are related to life [-bliss], though we thus speak. 10. For God is not unjust, so as to forget your works, and your love, which ye have shown on account of his name, in that ye have done service to the holy ones, and are still doing service. 11. But

The Greek Text.

HEBREWS VI. 1–11.

VI. 1. Therefore let us forego mention of the beginning of [what relates to] the Anointed, and go on to fulness [of growth], not laying again the foundation of repentance from dead works, and of trust on God; 2, of the teaching of immersions, and of the laying on of hands; of the rising of the dead, and of the eternal sentence of judgment. 3 And this we will do, if God shall permit.

4. For it is impossible to renew again to repentance those who once have been enlightened, (a) and who have tasted of the heavenly gift, and become sharers of the Holy Spirit, 5, and have tasted of the good word of God, and of the mighty [miracles] of the age which is to be, 6, and have fallen away, crucifying afresh [as they do] for themselves the Son of God, and putting him to public shame. 7. For land which has drunk the rain which is often coming on it, and produces herbage fit for those because of whom it is also tilled, shares a blessing from God. 8. But if it produces thorns and thistles, [it is] rejected, and is near to a curse; to be burned is its end.

9. But we are persuaded with respect to you, beloved, of those things which are better, and which pertain to salvation, although we thus speak. 10. For God is not unjust, so as to forget your work, and the toil of that love which ye have shown towards his name, in having done service to the holy ones, and in doing it still. 11. But we desire that

---

(a) Ver. 4. The Syriac words, "have gone down into immersion," occupy the place of the Greek word which means, "have been enlightened." In Hebrews x. 32, the Syriac has, "The days in which ye received immersion;" instead of the Greek words, "the days in which ye, having been enlightened." In both passages, all the Syriac editions which I have, contain those same words; namely, Walton's Polyglot, 1653-7; Gutbir, 1663; Schaaf, 1717; British and Foreign Bible Society, 1816, founded partly on Indian manuscripts; the edition printed at Ooroomiah, in Persia, 1852, and believed to be founded on ancient Nestorian manuscripts of Coordistan; and the edition printed for the Maronites, from a Maronite manuscript, by the Roman Propaganda in 1703. Schaaf gives the various readings found in 13 editions, being the whole of those printed before his own; but there is no various reading in any of them of these passages. Of the Greek Text also, Tischendorf, in his 8th edition, gives no various reading, in either passage, as to these words. Immersion was, in the second century, called enlightening. Dr. Scrivener, writing in 1863 (on N.T. p. 511.) says that, "the worst corruptions of the New Testament originated within a hundred years after it was composed." Justin, the converted philosopher, and a martyr, said, A.D. 150, in his second defence of the Christians, addressed to the Emperor Antoninus, of baptism, "and this bath is called the enlightening, since those who learn these things are enlightened in the mind." The Greek word used by Justin, is the same as that of the Greek text in these two passages. –W, N.

we desire that each one of you should show this same earnestness to the extent of [having] the fulness of your hope even to the end ; 12, and that ye be not weary, but be imitators of those who, through trust and long patience of spirit, have inherited the promise.

13. For God, when he made promise to Abraham, because he had no one greater than he is to sware by, sware by himself, 14, and said,—Blessing, I will bless thee; and multiplying, I will multiply thee ;—15, and so he was long-patient in spirit, and received the promise. 16. For men swear by one greater than themselves; and with respect to every contention which there is among them, a sure end is [put] to it by an oath. 17. For this reason God wished to show the more fully to the inheritors of the promise that his promise is unchangeable, and bound it firmly by an oath ; 18, that, by two things which are unchangeable, in which it is impossible that God should lie, we, who have taken refuge in him, might have great comfort, and might hold fast the hope which is promised us: 19, which [hope] is to us like an anchor, which keeps our soul from being moved, and which enters within the veil; 20, which place Jesus entered beforehand on our behalf, and has become a Priest for ever in the likeness of Melchizedec.

VII. 1. Now this Melchizedec was King of Salem, a priest of God Most High. And he met Abraham when he returned from the slaughter of kings, and blessed him. 2. And Abraham separated for him tenths from everything there was with him. Now his name, if translated, is, King of Righteousness. And again, [he was] King of Salem, which is, King of Peace. 3. Neither his father, nor his mother was written in family records; nor the beginning of his days, nor the end of his life; but his priesthood, like [that of] the Son of God, remains for ever.

4. See ye then, how great this [priest was]! to whom Abraham, the head of the fathers, gave tenths and first-fruits.

5. For those who from among the sons of Levi receive the priesthood, have a command of the law to receive tenths from [their] people; they from their brothers, who also have come forth from

each of you should show this same earnestness to the extent of having the fulness of [your] hope unto the end; 12, so that ye may not be weary, but may be imitators of those who, through trust and long patience, are inheriting the promises.

13. For when God made promise to Abraham, since he could swear by no one greater, he sware by himself, 14, saying, —Surely, blessing, I will bless thee, and multiplying, I will multiply thee ;—15, And so he had long patience, and reached the promise. 16. For men indeed swear by one greater than [themselves], and [their] oath for confirmation, [puts] an end to every contention among them. 17. On which account God, wishing to show the more fully to the inheritors of the promise, the unchangeableness of his purpose, put between [them and him] an oath ; 18, that by means of two unchangeable things, in which it is impossible for God to lie, we, who have fled for refuge [to him], might have strong encouragement to keep fast hold of the hope which is set before us; 19, which [hope] we have as an anchor of the soul, fast and firm ; and which enters into the place within the veil; 20, which place, as forerunner, Jesus entered on behalf of us, having become a High Priest for ever, of the same order as Melchizedec.

VII. 1. For this Melchizedec, King of Salem, priest of God Most High, who met Abraham returning from the slaughter of the kings, and blessed him; 2, for whom Abraham separated a tenth part of all things also ; who [was], first, if [his name] is translated, King of Righteousness, and [who was] next also, King of Salem, which is, King of peace; 3, without father, without mother, without family-record, having neither beginning of days, nor end of life, but made in likeness to the Son of God, continues to be a priest perpetually.

4. Now consider ye how great this [priest was], to whom even Abraham, the chief father, gave a tenth out of the best of the spoils.

5. Even those who from among the sons of Levi receive the priesthood, have command, according to the law, to receive tenths from [their] people ; that is from their brothers, though these [are

The Peshito-Syriac Text.

HEBREWS VII. 5—22.

the loins of Abraham. 6. But this [priest], who is not written in their family-records, received tenths from Abraham [himself], and blessed him who had received the promise. 7. But without controversy, he who is less, is blessed by him who is greater than he.

8. And here men who die receive tenths; but there he [did so] of whom the [sacred] writing bears witness that he lives.

9. And as one might say, Levi also, who receives tenths, even he gave tenths by means of Abraham. 10. For he was still in the loins of his father when he met Melchizedec.

11. If therefore perfectness were by means of the priesthood of the Levites, through which the law was placed before the people, why was it needful that a different priest should arise, in the likeness of Melchizedec? In that case [God] would have said,—He shall be in the likeness of Aaron.

12. But as there was a change in the priesthood, so there was a change also in the law. 13. For he respecting whom these things were said, was born of another tribe, from which no one ever served at the altar. 14. For it is clear that our Lord arose from Judah, from a tribe respecting which Moses said nothing about priesthood. 15. And it is still better known, by this,—that [God] said, that a different priest, was to rise up in the likeness of Melchizedec; 16, one who is not [a priest] by the law of commands relating to the body, but by the might of a life which cannot be destroyed. 17. For [God] bears witness respecting him,—Thou art a priest for ever in the likeness of Melchizedec.—18. Now the change which was made as to the former command, [was] because of its weakness, and because there was no profit in it. 19. For the law perfected nothing; but a hope entered instead of it, which is better than it, and by which we draw near to God. 20. And [God] confirmed it to us by an oath. 21. For those priests were made without an oath; but this priest with an oath, as [God] said to him by means of David,—The Lord sware and will not lie,—Thou art a priest for ever in the likeness of Melchizedec.

22. In all this, better is that covenant of which Jesus has become Surety.

The Greek Text.

HEBREWS VII. 5—22.

but descendants] who have come forth from the loins of Abraham; 6, but the [priest] who has no family record among them, received a tenth from Abraham [himself], and blessed him who had received the promises. 7. Yet, without any contradiction, the less is blessed by the greater.

8. And here men who die receive tenths, but there he [received them], of whom witness is given that he lives.

9. And, so to speak, Levi also, who receives tenths, has given tenths by means of Abraham; 10, for he was still in the loins of his father when Melchizedec met him.

11. If, therefore, perfectness were by means of the Levitical priesthood, for the people were put under law [based] on it, what need still [existed,] that a different priest should arise, of the same order as Melchizedec, and that he should not be said [to be] of the same order as Aaron?

12. For the priesthood being changed, there has to be of necessity a change of law also; 13, for he, respecting whom these things are said, is one of another tribe, from which no one attends to the altar. 14. For it is clear that our Lord has arisen from out of Judah, as to which tribe Moses said nothing about priesthood. 15. And it is much more clear still that there arises a different priest, after the likeness of Melchizedec; 16, one who is made not after the law of a fleshly command, but after the might of a life which cannot be destroyed; 17, for [God] bears witness,—Thou art a priest for ever of the same order as Melchizedec. 18. For there is both the repealing of the preceding command, because of its weakness and unprofitableness, 19, (for the law perfected nothing), and also the introduction of a hope which is better, by means of which we draw near to God. 20. And [it is better], inasmuch as he was not [made] without an oath. 21. For they, indeed, are made priests without an oath, but he [was made] with an oath, by him who said to him,—The Lord sware, and will not repent,—Thou art a priest for ever of the same order as Melchizedec.

22. In such degree Jesus has become the Surety of a better covenant.

The Peshito-Syriac Text.

HEBREWS VII. 23–28. VIII. 1–7.

23. And those priests are many, because they die, and are not permitted to remain. 24. But because this [priest] stands for ever, his priesthood does not pass away. 25. And he is able to give life[-bliss] for ever to those who, by means of him, draw near to God; for he lives always, and offers up prayers on their behalf.

26. For a priest such as this, was also suitable for us,—one pure, and without malice; without blemish also; one separated from sins, and exalted higher than heaven. 27. And he has not the affliction of having every day to offer up slain offerings, as a chief priest has, first on behalf of his own sins, and then of [those of] the people; for [this last act] he did once only by offering up himself. 28. For the law appoints for priests men who are weak; but the word of the oath, which was made after the law, [appointed] the Son [of God], who is perfected for ever.

VIII. 1. But the chief of all these things is, that we have a High Priest who has sat down at the right hand of the throne of [God's] greatness in heaven; 2, and has become a servant of [his] holy house, and of that true tent-dwelling which God fixed, and not man. 3. For every high priest is appointed to offer up offerings [given] and offerings slain; for this reason it was right that this [priest] also should have something to offer up.

4. If, too, he were on the earth, he would not even be a priest, because there are priests who are offering up offerings such as those in the law; 5, priests who are doing service according to the likeness and the shadow of those things which [are] in heaven. As it was said to Moses, when he was making the tent-dwelling,—See, and make everything according to that likeness which was shown to thee in the mountain.

6. But Jesus, the Anointed, has now accepted a service which is as much better than that [service], as this covenant in which he is made Mediator, is also better than [that covenant]; and it has been given with promises which are better than those of that [covenant]. 7. For if the first [covenant] had been without fault, there would not have been any

The Greek Text.

HEBREWS VII. 23–28. VIII. 1–8.

23. And of those priests many have to be made, because by death they are forbidden to continue. 24. But this [priest], because he continues for ever, has a priesthood which does not pass away. 25. On this account, he is also able to save perfectly in all respects those who come to God through him; for he is always living to intercede on their behalf.

26. For he [is] such a High Priest as was suitable for us,—holy, without malice, undefiled, separated from sinners, and raised higher than the heavens; 27, one who has no necessity to offer up slain offerings daily, as the chief priests do, first on behalf of their own sins, then on behalf of those of the people; for he did this [last act] once for all, in having offered up himself. 28. For the law appoints men to be high priests, who have weakness; but the word of the oath, which was after the law, [appointed] the Son, who is perfected for ever.

VIII. 1. But that which is chief of the things now said [of him, is] that we have a High Priest of such kind that he has sat down at the right hand of the throne of [God's] greatness in the heavens, 2, a chief servant of the holy places, and of that true tent-dwelling which the Lord fixed, and not man. 3. For every high priest is appointed to offer up both gifts and slain offerings; hence it [was] necessary that this [priest] also should have something to offer up.

4. For if he were on earth, he would not even be a priest, because there are priests who offer up the gifts [which are] according to the law; 5, who do service in what is a representation and shadow of the heavenly things; according to which, Moses, when about to construct the tent-dwelling, was directed [to make it]; for [God] said,—See that thou make all things according to the pattern which was shown to thee in the mountain.

6. But he, [Jesus], has now accepted a service which is as much more excellent than [that of the law], as the covenant of which he is Mediator is also better than [it], and is planned upon better promises. 7. For if that first covenant had been faultless, no place would have been sought for a second. 8. For [God], finding fault with them, [the people]

place for this second. 8. For he [God] found fault with them [the people], and said,—Behold the days are coming, saith the Lord, in which I will complete with the family of the house of Israel, and with the family of the house of Judah, a new covenant; 9, not like that covenant which I gave to their fathers in the day in which I took them by their hand, and brought them out from the land of Egypt; for they did not continue in my covenant: also I despised them, saith the Lord. 10. But this is the covenant which I will give to the family of the house of Israel, after those days, saith the Lord ;—I will put, by gift, my law into their minds, and upon their hearts I will write it, and I will be their God, and they shall be my people. 11. And no one shall teach a son of his city, nor his brother, and say,—Know thou the Lord,—because they all shall know me, from the least of them [in age], to the oldest of them ; 12, and I will forgive them their iniquities, and their sins I will not remember any more. 13. By saying this,—A new [covenant],—he has made the first old in date; and that which is old in date, and old in age, is near to vanishing away.

IX. 1. Moreover in the first [covenant], there were commands of service, and a holy house in this world. 2. For in the tent-dwelling first made, there were the lampstand, and the table, and the bread of [God's] presence; and it was called,— The holy house. 3. But the inner tent-dwelling, which was within the second veil, was called,—The holy of holies.— 4. And there were in it the golden vessel of sweet odours, (a) and the ark of the covenant, which was covered all over with gold ; and there were in this, the golden jar in which was the manna, and the rod of Aaron which sprouted ; and the tables of the covenant ; 5, and above it, were the cherubim of glory, who overshadowed the place of atonement. But it is not the time to speak of each of those things which were so arranged. 6. And into the outer tent-dwelling the priests go at all times, and complete their service. 7. But into the tent-dwelling which was within it, the high priest goes once only in the year, alone, with that blood which he offers up on behalf of himself, and on behalf of the errors of the people. 8. Now, by

says,—Behold the days are coming, saith the Lord, in which I will complete with the house of Israel and with the house of Judah, a new covenant; 9, not according to the covenant which I made with their fathers, in the day when I took their hand to lead them out of the land of Egypt; for they did not continue in my covenant, and I cared not for them, saith the Lord. 10. For this [is] the covenant which I will make with the house of Israel after those days, saith the Lord ; I will put by gift, my laws into their mind, and upon their heart I will write them; and I will be their God, and they shall be my people ; 11, and they shall not teach each one his neighbour, and each one his brother, saying,—Know thou the Lord;—for all shall know me, from the least of them [in age], to the greatest of them; 12, for I will be merciful to their iniquities, and their sins and unlawful deeds I will remember no more. 13. By saying,—A new [covenant], he has made the first old in date; and that which is old in date and in age, is near to vanishing away

IX. 1. Moreover, the first [covenant] had also rules of service, and [its] holy place in this world. 2. For a tent-dwelling was prepared; [there was] the first, in which were the lamp-stand, and the table, and the setting forth of the loaves; which is called The holy [place]; 3, and after the second veil, [was] the tent-dwelling which is called,—The holy of holies; 4, having a golden censer, (a) and the ark of the covenant, covered all over with gold, in which was a golden jar holding the manna, and the rod of Aaron which sprouted, and the tables of the covenant ; 5, and above it [were] the cherubim of glory, overshadowing the place of atonement; respecting each of which things it is not [the time] now to speak. 6. And these things having been thus prepared, the priests go always into the first tent-dwelling, fulfilling [their] services; 7, but into the second, [enters] the high priest, alone, only once in the year, not without blood, which he offers up on behalf of himself, and of the sins of ignorance of the people: 8, [by which means] the Holy Spirit shows this, that

(a) Exodus XXX. 36.

The Peshito-Syriac Text.

this means, the Spirit of Holiness makes known, that the pathway of the holy ones (a) was not yet revealed, so long as the first tent-dwelling was standing. 9. And this [tent-dwelling] was a resemblance for that time in which offerings [given] and offerings slain, are offered up, which are not able to make perfect the conscience of him who offers them; 10, but have reference only to food eaten, and to drink, and to the immersion of different kinds of things; which [rules] were commands about the flesh, which were made binding until the time of reform.

11. But the Anointed, when he came, was High Priest of the good things which he effected; and he entered into that great and perfect tent-dwelling which has not been made by hands, and is no part of these created things; 12, and he did not enter by means of the blood of goats and young bulls, but he, by means of his own blood, entered once into the holy house, and obtained release which is for ever.

13. For if the blood of goats and young bulls, and if the ashes of a heifer which were sprinkled on those who were defiled, made them holy as to the purity of their flesh; 14, how much more, then, will the blood of the Anointed, who, through the Eternal Spirit, offered up himself, the spotless, to God, purify our conscience from dead works, so that we shall serve the living God!

15. For this reason he has become Mediator of a new covenant,—that by his death, he might be the means of release to those who have transgressed against the first covenant; so that those might receive the promised [gift], who have been called to the eternal inheritance. 16. For where there is a covenant, it implies the death of that [animal] which made it; 17, for only upon a dead [body] is it made firm; because as long as the [animal] which makes it, lives, there is no utility in it. 18. For this reason, the first [covenant] also was not made firm without blood. 19. For when every command had been enjoined by Moses, on all the people, according to the law, Moses took the blood of a

The Greek Text.

the pathway of the holy ones (a) had not yet been made manifest, while the first [tent-dwelling] was still standing; 9, which tent-dwelling was a resemblance for the period then following, during which both gifts and slain offerings are offered up, which are not able to make perfect, as to the conscience, him who serves [God]; 10, [having reference] only to the kinds of food eaten, and to drinks, and to various immersions, and to rules about the flesh; things which were made binding until the period of reform.

11. But when the Anointed had come, as High Priest of the good things which were to come, he, [passing] through that greater and more perfect tent-dwelling, which has not been made by hands; that is to say, is not of this [part] of the creation; 12, nor by means of the blood of goats and young bulls, but by means of his own blood, he entered once for all into the holy [place], having obtained eternal release by ransom.

13. For if the blood of bulls and of goats, and if the ashes of a heifer, sprinkled on the defiled, make [them] holy as to the purity of the flesh; 14, how much more shall the blood of the Anointed, who, through the Eternal Spirit, offered up himself, spotless, to God, purify your (b) conscience from dead works, that ye may serve the living God!

15. And the reason why he is Mediator of a new covenant is this, that by [his] death, suffered to give release by ransom from transgressions against the first covenant, those who have been called might receive the promised [gift] of the eternal inheritance. 16. For where there is a covenant, it is necessary that the death of that [animal] which makes the covenant, should be brought about. 17, For a covenant [is made] firm upon dead bodies; since it is of no force while the [animal] which makes it lives. 18. Hence, not even the first [covenant] has been dedicated without blood. 19. For when every commandment had been spoken according to the law, by Moses, to all the people, he took the blood of the young

(a) Ver. 8. Hebrews x. 19, 20.

(b) Ver. 14. Some Greek copies have "our" instead of "your," and agree with the Syriac in meaning.

The Peshito-Syriac Text.

heifer, and water, with scarlet wool and hyssop, and sprinkled [the blood] on the books, and on all the people; 20, and said to them,—This is the blood of that covenant which has been commanded by God. 21. Also on the tent-dwelling, and on all the vessels of service, he sprinkled part of the blood. 22. Because, by the law, every thing is purified by blood; and without the shedding of blood there is no forgiveness.

23. For it was necessary that those things which are a likeness of heavenly things, should be purified by those [slain offerings]; but these heavenly things, with slain offerings, which are better than those. 24. For it was not into the holy house which was made by hands, that the Anointed entered; which [house] is a likeness of the true one; but he entered into heaven, that he might appear before the face of God on our behalf.

25. Also it was not [necessary] that he should offer up himself many times, like as the high priest does [his offerings], and enters, every year, into the holy house, with blood which is not his own. 26. Otherwise he ought to have suffered many times from the beginning of the world. But now, at the end of the world, he has offered up himself once, by being himself slain, that he might put away sin utterly. 27. And like as there is appointed for men to die once, and after their death, judgment; 28, so also the Anointed was offered up once, and in himself he slew the sins of many; and then the second time he is to appear, without the sins, for the life [-bliss] of those who expect him.

X. 1. For in the law there was a shadow of the good things which were to come; it was not the presence of those things. For this reason, the same slain offerings which have been offered up every year, have never been able to perfect those who offered them. 2. For if they [the offerings] had made [them] perfect, [those who offered] would then doubtless have rested from their offerings; because the conscience of those who had once been purified, would not thenceforth have smitten them on account of s ns. 3. But in those slain offerings, they call their sins to remembrance every year. 4. For it is not possible for the blood of bulls and of goats to purge

The Greek Text.

bulls and goats, with water and scarlet wool and hyssop, and sprinkled both the book itself, and all the people, 20, saying, —This is the blood of the covenant, which God has commanded [to be made] with you.—21. And he sprinkled with blood, in like manner, both the tent-dwelling, and all the vessels of [God's] service. 22. And according to the law, all things are purified in part by blood, and without shedding of blood there is no forgiveness.

23. It was necessary, therefore, that the representations of the things in the heavens should be purified by these things, but that the heavenly things themselves [should be purified] by slain offerings better than these. 24. For the Anointed has not entered into the holy [place] made by hands, which corresponds with the true, but into heaven itself, to appear now before the face of God, on our behalf.

25. Nor [was it necessary] that he should offer up himself often, like as the high priest enters into the holy [place], yearly, with blood other than his own; 26, since [if it had been necessary], he ought to have suffered often from the foundation of the world; but he has appeared now once, at the end of the ages, for the utter putting away of sin, by being a slain offering himself. 27. And even as there is appointed for men to die once, and after this, judgment; 28, so the Anointed, having been once offered up, that he might take on himself the sins of many, will appear a second time, without sin, to [give] salvation to those who wait for him.

X. 1. For the law, having but a shadow of the good things which were to come, not the very presence of those things, is never able, by the same slain offerings which they offer up year by year, continually, to perfect those who draw near to [God]. 2. For [otherwise] would they not have ceased to be offered? because those who serve [God], having been once purified, would no longer have had any consciousness of sins. 3. But in those [slain offerings there is] a calling of sins to remembrance year by year. 4. For it is impossible for the blood of bulls and of goats to take away sins. 5. Therefore he, [the Anointed], when entering into the world says,—Slain offering and

The Peshito-Syriac Text.

away sins. 5. For this reason, when he [the Anointed], entered into the world, he said,—Slain offerings and gift-offerings, thou hast not desired; but with a body thou hast clothed me; 6, and offerings burnt whole on behalf of sins, thou hast not asked for. 7. Then I said, —Behold, I myself come, for in the beginning of the books it is written of me, that I may do thy will, O God.

8. At first he said,—Slain offerings, and gift-offerings, and offerings burnt whole on behalf of sins. thou hast not desired : —which were offered up by the law; 9, and after this he said,—Behold, I come, that I may do thy will, O God.—By this, he abolished the first, that he might set firm the second. 10. For, by this will of his, we have been made holy, by the offering up of the body of Jesus the Anointed, once only.

11. For every chief priest who has been standing and serving every day, has been offering up the same slain offerings, which have never been able to purge away sins. 12. But this [Priest] offered up one slain offering on behalf of sins, and sat down at the right hand of God for ever ; 13, and waits, thenceforth, until his enemies be placed for a footstool beneath his feet. 14. For by one offering, he has perfected for ever those who have been made holy by him.

15. The Spirit of holiness also bears witness to us [of this], for he has said,—16, This is the covenant which I will give to them after those days, saith the Lord, —I will put by gift my law into their minds, and on their hearts I will write it ; 17, and their iniquity and their sins I will not remember.—18. But where there is forgiveness of sins, no offering on behalf sins is demanded.

19. We have therefore, my brothers, confidence in entering the holy house by the blood of Jesus, and by that pathway of life [-bliss), 20, which he has now newly made for us through the veil, which is his flesh. 21. And we have a high priest over the house of God. 22. Let us draw near, therefore, with a true heart, and with confidence of trust: our hearts sprinkled and purified from an evil conscience, and our body washed in pure water. 23. And let us persevere in

The Greek Text.

gift-offering thou hast not desired, but a body thou hast prepared for me; 6, in offerings burnt whole and for sin thou hast had no pleasure ; 7, then I said,—Behold, I come, [as] in the beginning of the book it is written of me, to do, O God, thy will.

8. At first he says,—Slain offering, and gift-offering, and offerings burnt whole and for sin, thou hast not desired, nor hast had pleasure in them ;—which are offered up according to the law ; 9, then he says,—Behold, I come, to do, O God, thy will.—He abolishes the first, that he may establish the second. 10. By the which will, we have been made holy, by means of the offering up of the body of Jesus, the Anointed, once for all.

11. And every priest stands doing service daily, and offering up many times the same slain offerings, which are never able to take away sins; 12, but he, after having offered up one slain offering on behalf of sins, sat down for ever at the right hand of God ; 13, thenceforth waiting till his enemies be placed for a footstool of his feet. 14. For by one offering he has perfected for ever those who are made holy.

15. And the Holy Spirit also bears witness [of this] to us ; for after he had said beforehand,—16, This is the covenant which I will make with them after those days, saith the Lord ;—I will put by gift my laws upon their heart, and upon their minds I will write them ;—[he said], —17, And their sins and their lawless deeds, I will remember no more.—18. But where there is forgiveness of these, no longer [is there] any offering for sin.

19. Having, therefore, [my] brothers, confidence for entering into the holy [place], by the blood of Jesus, 20, by the new and living way which he has dedicated for us, through the veil, that is, his flesh; 21, and [having] a Great Priest over the house of God, 22, let us draw near with a true heart, in the fulness of trust, having been sprinkled, as to our hearts, [and purified] from an evil conscience; and having been bathed, as to the body, in pure water. 23. Let us

The Peshito-Syriac Text.

the profession of our hope, and not turn aside; for he is trustworthy who has promised us. 24. And let us look one on another, prompting to love and to good works. 25. And let us not desert our assembly, as the custom of some is; but exhort ye one another; so much the more as ye see that that day comes near.

26. For if any one should sin of his own will, after he has received knowledge of the truth, thenceforth there is no slain offering to be offered up on behalf of sins. 27. But there will be judgment of might, and the fierceness of the fire which is to devour enemies. 28. For if he who has broken the law of Moses, dies without mercy upon the mouth of two and of three witnesses; 29, how much more fully, think ye, shall he receive capital punishment, who treads on the Son of God, and deems the blood of his covenant [to be] as that of every man; [that] by which he was to be made holy; and has treated with contempt the Spirit of merciful favour. 30. We know him who has said,—To me belongs avengement, and I will repay.—And again,—The Lord will judge his people. —31. Great is the fearfulness of falling into the hands of the living God.

32. Therefore remember the former days,—those in which ye received immersion, and bore patiently a great conflict of sufferings, under reproach and infliction; 33, and in which ye were gazing-stocks; and also took part with those who bore these things. 34. And ye grieved for those who were imprisoned; and ye bore with joy the seizure of your goods, because ye know that ye have a possession in heaven which is better, and passes not away. 35. Therefore destroy not the confidence which ye have, and for which there will be a great reward. 36. For patient endurance is needful for you, that ye may do the will of God, and receive what is promised. 37. Because little is the time, and very little, to when,—He will come who is to come, and will not delay.—38. But,—He who is righteous will have

The Greek Text.

maintain our profession of hope undeparted from; for trustworthy is he who has promised. 24. And let us take notice one of another, to promote love and good works; 25, not leaving off the assembling of ourselves together, as the custom of some [is]; but exhorting [one another], and so much the more as ye see the day come near.

26. For if we sin willingly after we have received the knowledge of the truth, no slain offering for sins any longer remains; 27, but a fearful expectation of judgment, and the fierceness of that fire which will devour the adversaries. 28. He who has broken the law of Moses, dies without compassion, on [the word of] two or three witnesses; 29, how much worse punishment, think ye, shall he be deemed to deserve, who has trodden under foot the Son of God, and has regarded the blood of the covenant by which he was to be made holy, as mere common [blood], and has treated with proud scorn, the Spirit of merciful favour? 30. For we know him who has said,—To me [belongs] avengement; I will repay, saith the Lord;—and again,—The Lord will judge his people.—31. It is a fearful thing to fall into the hands of the living God.

32. But remember the former days, in which, having been enlightened, (a) ye bore patiently a great conflict of sufferings; 33, both by being made gazing-stocks by reproaches and inflictions; and by having become sharers in common with those who were so treated. 34. For ye had fellow-feeling with [me] in my bonds, (b) and ye took joyfully the seizure of your goods, knowing that ye have in yourselves (c) a better possession in heaven, and one which continues. 35. Cast not away, therefore, your confidence, which has great recompense of reward. 36. For ye have need of patient endurance; in order that, having done the will of God, ye may receive what is promised. 37. For [after] still a very little time,—He who is to come, will come, and will not delay.—38. But,—The righteous person will live by means of trust;—and

---

(a) Ver. 32. Compare VI. 4.

(b) Ver. 34. Some Greek copies, for "with me in my bonds," have "with the prisoners," like the Syriac.

(c) Ver. 34. Some Greek copies have only "that ye have," without "in yourselves."

The Peshito-Syriac Text.

life [-bliss] through trust in me.—And,—
If he becomes weary, my soul has no
pleasure in him.—39. But we are not of
the weariness which leads to destruction, but of trust, which causes us to
possess our soul.

XI. 1. Moreover, trust is persuasion
about things hoped for, as if they were
things done ; and it is a revealing of
those things which are not seen. 2. And
on account of it witness was borne to
the ancients.

3. For by trusting, we understand that
the worlds were formed by the word
of God, and that those things which are
seen, came to be from those things which
are not seen.

4. By trusting, Abel offered up to God
a slain offering, which was much better
than [the offering] of Cain ; and because
of it, witness was borne respecting him
that he was righteous ; and God bore
witness respecting his offering ; and because of it also, though he is dead, he
speaks.

5. By trusting, Enoch was taken away,
and did not taste of death ; and he was
not found, because God had taken him
away. For even before he took him
away, witness was borne respecting him
that he pleased God. 6. But without
trusting, no one is able to please God.
For he who draws near to God must
trust in that he is, and will be the
rewarder of those who seek him.

7. By trusting, Noah, when he was
spoken to about things which were not
seen, feared, and made for himself
an ark, to preserve the lives of his
household ; by which [ark] he condemned
the world, and became an inheritor of
the righteousness which is by trust.

8. By trusting, Abraham, when he was
called, obeyed [the command] that he
should go forth to the place which he
was, in the future, to receive for an inheritance ; and went forth when he
knew not whither he was going. 9. By
trusting, he lived without any fixed
dwelling in that land which had been
promised to him, as if [he were] in a
foreign [land] ; and dwelt in tents with
Isaac and Jacob, the inheritors of the
same promise. 10. For he was expecting

The Greek Text.

if he draw back, my soul has no pleasure
in him. 39. But we are not of the draw-
ing back [which leads] to destruction,
but of trust, [which leads] to the possession of the soul.

XI. 1. Now trust is assurance of things
hoped for ; conviction of things not seen.
2. For by it the ancients had witness
borne to them.

3. By trusting, we understand that the
worlds have been formed by the word of
God, so that the things seen have not
come into being from out of things which
are apparent.

4. By trusting, Abel offered up to God
a slain offering, which was better than
[the offering] of Cain ; through which
witness was borne that he was righteous;
God bearing witness respecting his gifts;
and by means of that [offering], he,
though dead, still speaks.

5. By trusting, Enoch was taken
away, so as not to see death ; and he
was not found, because God had taken
him away ; for before he was taken away,
witness had been borne that he was
well-pleasing to God. 6. But without
trust, it is impossible to please [him]
well ; for he who comes to God must
trust in that he is, and that he will be
the giver of reward to those who seek
him earnestly.

7. By trusting, Noah, having been told
[by God] about things not yet seen,
moved by godly fear, prepared an ark,
for the salvation of his household ; by
means of which [ark], he condemned the
world, and became an inheritor of that
righteousness which is according to
trust.

8. By trusting, Abraham, when called
to go forth into the place which he was
afterwards to receive for an inheritance,
obeyed, and went forth, not knowing
whither he was going. 9. By trusting,
he dwelt without fixed abode in the land
of promise, as in a foreign [country],
dwelling in tents, with Isaac and Jacob,
inheritors with him of the same promise ; 10, for he was expecting the city
which has its foundations ; whose Designer and Builder [is] God.

The Peshito-Syriac Text.

the city which has a foundation, whose Designer and Maker is God.

11. By trusting, Sarah, who was barren, received strength to receive seed, and gave birth when not at the fit time of her years; because she firmly believed that he was trustworthy who had promised her.

12. For this reason, by one who was incapable from age, were begotten as many as the stars which are in heaven, and as the sands which are on the sea-shore, which are numberless.

13. These all died trusting, and received not what was promised them; but from afar they saw it, and rejoiced in it, and professed that they were strangers and without fixed dwelling on earth. 14. But those who say these things, show that they are seeking their own city. 15. And if they had been seeking that city from which they had gone out, they had time to return, [and] go to it again. 16. But at present it is known that they were desiring a [city] which is better than it; the one which is in heaven. For this reason, God was not ashamed to be called their God; for he prepared for them a city.

17. By trusting, Abraham, when put to test, offered up Isaac, and lifted to the altar his only son;—him whom he had received by promise. 18. For it had been said to him,—In Isaac a seed shall be called thine. 19. And he thought within himself,—The hands of God are able even to raise him from among the dead;—and for this reason, he was given [back] to him in the likeness [of a resurrection].

20. By trusting in that which was to be in the future, Isaac blessed Jacob and Esau.

21. By trusting, Jacob, when dying, blessed each one of the sons of Joseph, and worshipped, [leaning] on the head of his staff.

22. By trusting, Joseph, when dying, made mention of the leading forth of the sons of Israel; and gave commandment about his bones.

23. By trusting, the parents of Moses hid him, after he was born, for three months; because they saw that he was a beautiful child; and feared not on account of the command of the king.

The Greek Text.

11. By trusting, Sarah also herself received power for the deposit of seed, and brought forth when past the fit time of life, because she esteemed him trustworthy who had promised.

12. Therefore, even by one, and by him when partly dead, there were begotten as many as the stars of heaven in multitude, and like the sands which are on the sea-shore, which cannot be numbered.

13. These all died, trusting without having received the things promised, but having seen them from afar, and having been persuaded of [them], and having embraced [them], and professed that they were strangers, and without fixed dwelling, on earth. 14. For those who say such things, make it manifest that they are seeking a country of their own. 15. For if, indeed, they had been calling to mind that [country] from which they went out, they would have had opportunity to return. 16. But at present [we know] that they were desiring a better one, that is, a heavenly one. Therefore God is not ashamed of them, [nor] of being called their God; for he has prepared for them a city.

17. By trusting, Abraham, when put to test, offered up Isaac; he who had received the promises offered up even his only son, 18, respecting whom it had been said,—In Isaac a seed shall be called thine;—19, for he had taken into account that God was able even to raise him up from among the dead; from among whom he also received him, by a resemblance [of resurrection].

20. By trusting, with respect to things to come, Isaac blessed Jacob and Esau.

21. By trusting, Jacob, when dying, blessed each of the sons of Joseph, and worshipped, [leaning] upon the top of his staff.

22. By trusting, Joseph, when dying, made mention of the going forth of the sons of Israel, and gave commandment about his bones.

23. By trusting, after Moses was born, he was hidden three months by his parents, because they saw that the child was beautiful; and they feared not the command of the king.

The Peshito-Syriac Text.

HEBREWS XI. 24—38.

24. By trusting, Moses, when he became a man, refused to be called the son of the daughter of Pharaoh; 25, and chose for himself to be in affliction with the people of God, instead of, for a little time, delighting in sin. 26. And he deemed reproach [on account] of the Anointed, to be wealth far exceeding the treasure of Egypt; for he was looking at the recompense of reward. 27. By trusting, he left Egypt, and feared not on account of the wrath of the king; and he hoped as one who saw God, who cannot be seen.

28. By trusting, they kept the passover, and the sprinkling of the blood, that he who was destroying the firstborn might not come near them.

29. By trusting, they passed through the sea of Suph, as if on dry land; though the Egyptians were swallowed up in it, when they had dared to enter it.

30. By trusting, the walls of Jericho fell, when they had been gone round seven days.

31. By trusting, Rahab the harlot perished not with those who obeyed not; because she had received the spies with peace.

32. What more shall I say? For I have little time to tell about Gideon, and Barak, and Samson, and Jephthah, and David, and Samuel, and the rest of the prophets: 33, who, by trusting, conquered kingdoms, and worked righteousness; who received things promised, and shut the mouths of lions; 34, who quenched the might of fire, and were delivered from the edge of the sword; who were made strong from weaknesses, and were mighty in battle, and overthrew the camps of enemies. 35. Who gave to women their sons, by the rising [to life] of the dead. And others died by tortures, and did not hope to be delivered, that they might have a better rising [to life]. 36. Others moreover went through mockings and scourgings; others were delivered up to bonds and prisons; 37, others were stoned; others were sawn asunder; others died by the edge of the sword; others went about clothed in the skins of sheep and of goats; and [they were] needy, and afflicted, and harassed; 38, men of whom the world was not worthy; and they lived like wanderers, in desert, and in moun-

The Greek Text.

HEBREWS XI. 24—38.

24. By trusting, Moses, when he became a man, refused to be called the son of the daughter of Pharaoh; 25, choosing to be ill-treated together with the people of God, rather than to have for a season the enjoyment of sin. 26. For he deemed reproach [on account] of the Anointed, greater wealth than the treasures in Egypt; for he looked onward to the recompense of reward. 27. By trusting, he left Egypt, without fearing the wrath of the king, for he steadfastly went on as seeing him who cannot be seen.

28. By trusting, he kept the passover, and the outpouring of the blood, that he who destroyed the first-born might not touch them.

29. By trusting they passed through the Red Sea, as by dry land; which the Egyptians, attempted [to pass], and were swallowed up.

30. By trusting, the walls of Jericho fell, after they had been gone round for seven days.

31. By trusting, Rahab the harlot perished not with those who obeyed not, she having received the spies with peace.

32. And why should I say more? For time will fail me to tell fully about Gideon, and Barak, and Samson, and Jephthah, and David, and Samuel, and the prophets; 33, who, by means of trusting, subdued kingdoms, worked righteousness, obtained things promised, stopped the mouths of lions, 34, quenched the power of fire, escaped the edge of the sword, were made strong from weakness, became mighty in war, turned back the armies of foreign foes. 35. Women received their dead, by their rising again [to life]; and others were tortured, and did not accept deliverance, that they might have a rising again [to life], which was better. 36. And others underwent mockings and scourgings, and also bonds and imprisonment; 37, they were stoned, they were sawn asunder, they were tempted, they died by murder of the sword; they went about in sheeps' skins, and goats' skins; they were in need, were afflicted, were ill-treated; 38, of whom the world was not worthy; they wandered in deserts, and in mountains, and in caves, and in the clefts of the earth.

The Peshito-Syriac Text.

tains, and in caverns, and in clefts of the earth.

39. And of all these to whom witness was borne on account of their trust, none received what was promised; 40, because God had provided, with view to our benefit, that they should not be made perfect without us.

XII. 1. For this reason, let us also, who have all those witness-bearers surrounding us like clouds, put away from us all weights, also sin which is always made ready for us, and let us run with patient endurance this race which is set before us. 2. And let us look on Jesus, who is the Beginner and the Perfecter of our trust; who, for the sake of the joy which was to be his, endured patiently the cross, and yielded himself to shame, and sat down at the right hand of the throne of God.

3. See ye, therefore, how much he patiently endured from those sinners who were adversaries to themselves, (a); that ye may not be weary, nor your soul become faint. 4. Not yet have ye come to blood in the contest against sin. 5. And ye have forgotten the teaching which speaks to you as to sons,—My son, slight not the chastening of the Lord, nor let thy soul faint when thou art reproved by him. 6. For whom the Lord loves he chastens, and uses the rod to those sons in whom he delights.—7. Therefore endure chastening patiently. Because God is dealing with you as with sons. For what son is there whom his father does not chasten? 8. But if ye are without that chastening with which everyone is chastened, ye are strangers, and not sons. 9. And if our fathers of flesh chastened us, and we revered them, how much more, on that account, ought we to submit ourselves to the Father of spirits, and have life [-bliss]. 10. For they chastened us, for a little time, according to their pleasure; but God [chastens us] for our benefit, that we may share his holiness. 11. But all chastening, while it lasts, is counted a thing, not of joy, but of sadness; yet, in the end, it bears fruits of peace and righteousness to those who have been exercised by it.

12. For this reason, strengthen your relaxed hands, and your trembling knees;

The Greek Text.

39. And of all these to whom, through trusting, witness was borne, none received what was promised; 40, God having provided for us what is better, that they, without us, should not be made perfect.

XII. 1. Therefore let us also, who have so great a cloud of witness-bearers surrounding us, put away every weight, and sin which readily besets [us], and run with patient endurance the race set before us; 2, looking away to Jesus, the Originator and Perfecter of trust; who, on account of the joy set before him, patiently endured the cross, despising the shame, and sat down at the right hand of the throne of God.

3. For consider him who patiently endured such hostile speech by sinners against him (a), that ye may not be weary, fainting in your souls. 4. Not yet have ye resisted unto blood, contending against sin. 5. And ye have forgotten the admonition which talks with you as with sons,—My son, slight not the chastening of the Lord, nor faint when reproved by him; 6, for whom the Lord loves he chastens; and applies the rod to every son whom he tenderly embraces.—7. If ye endure chastening patiently, God is dealing with you as with sons. For what son is there whom a father does not chasten? 8. But if ye are without chastening, of which all [sons] have partaken, then ye are bastards, and not sons. 9. Besides, we had the fathers of our flesh to chasten us, and we gave them reverence; shall we not much rather submit ourselves to the Father of spirits, and live? 10. For they, for a few days, chastened us according to what pleased them; but he [does it] for our benefit, that we may share his holiness. 11. But all chastening, while present, seems not to be a thing of joy, but of grief; but afterwards, it yields the peaceful fruit of righteousness, to those who have been exercised thereby.

12. Therefore make use anew of the drooping hands, and of the unstrung

---

(a) Ver. 3. Some Greek copies have, "against themselves."

13, and make right paths for your feet; that a lame limb may not slip, but be cured.

14. Pursue peace with every one, and holiness, for without this no one sees our Lord. 15. And take ye heed lest anyone be found among you who is destitute of the merciful favour of God; and lest any root of bitterness should put forth its shoot, and harm you; and by it many be defiled. 16. And lest any one be found among you who is a fornicator and loose-liver, like Esau, who for one meal of food sold his right as first-born. 17. For ye know that also afterwards he desired to inherit the blessing, and was rejected; for he did not find room for repentance, though he sought the [blessing] with tears.

18. For ye have not come near to burning fire, and to what could be touched, nor to darkness, and to blackness, and to tempest; 19, nor to the sound of the trumpet, and to the voice of words; as to which voice, those who heard it intreated that no words might be spoken to them again; 20, for they were not able to endure patiently that which was commanded, that even if an animal went near the mountain, it should be stoned; (a) 21, and so fearful was the sight, that Moses said,—I fear and tremble.

22. But ye have come near to that mount Zion, and to that city of the living God, to that Jerusalem, which [are] in heaven; and to the multitudes of tens of thousands of angels; 23, and to the assembly of the first-born who are written in heaven; and to God, the Judge of all; and to the spirits of the righteous who have been perfected; 24, and to Jesus, the Mediator of the new covenant; and to the sprinkling of his blood, which speaks better things than that of Abel.

25. Take ye heed, therefore, lest ye refuse [to hear] him who speaks with you. For if those escaped not, who refused [to hear] him who spoke with them on earth, how much less shall we, if we refuse [to hear] him who has spoken with us from heaven. 26. Whose voice shook the earth; but, at present, he has promised and said,—Again I will, for once,

knees; 13, and make right paths for your feet, that the lame [limb] may not be turned aside, but may be cured.

14. Pursue peace with all, and holiness, without which no one will see the Lord. 15. Take heed, by oversight, lest anyone should be destitute of the merciful favour of God; lest any root of bitterness should spring up, and give trouble, and by means of it many be defiled ; 16, lest there should be any fornicator, or profane person, like Esau, who, in exchange for one [meal] of food sold his right as first-born. 17. For ye know that also afterwards, when he wished to inherit the blessing, he was rejected; for he found no place of repentance, though he sought the [blessing] earnestly with tears.

18. For ye have not come near to a mountain which could be touched, and which burned with fire; and to blackness, and darkness, and tempest; 19, and to the sound of a trumpet, and to the voice of words, by which voice, those who heard it, intreated that no word more might be addressed to them; 20, for they could not endure what was commanded ;—Even if a beast touch the mountain, it shall be stoned, or thrust through with a dart. (a) 21. And so fearful was the manifestation that Moses said,—I fear exceedingly and tremble.

22. But ye have come near to mount Zion, and to the city of the living God,—the heavenly Jerusalem; and to tens of thousands of angels; 23, to the universal meeting and assembly of the first-born who have been written in the roll of heaven; and to God the Judge of all; and to the spirits of the righteous made perfect; 24, and to Jesus the Mediator of the new covenant, and to [his] blood of sprinkling, which speaks better things than that of Abel.

25. See that ye refuse not him who speaks. For if those escaped not who refused him when speaking on earth, much more shall not we, if we turn away from him [speaking] from heaven. 26. Whose voice then shook the earth; but now he has promised, saying,—Still once, I shake not only the earth, but also the heaven.—27. And this,—Still

(a) Ver. 20. The words, "or thrust through with a dart," are not in the Syriac text, nor in some Greek copies.

shake not only earth, but also heaven.–
27. This then which he has said,–For
once,–shows the changing of those
things which are to be shaken, because
these have been made that those which
are not to be shaken may continue.

28. And, therefore, because we have
received a kingdom which is not to be
shaken, may we have merciful favour,
by which we may serve and please God
with reverence and fear ; 29, for our God
is a devouring fire.

XIII. 1. Let love of brothers continue
among you. 2. And forget not kindness
to strangers; for by means of it, some
have been honoured to receive, without
knowing it, angels. 3. Remember those
who are in bonds, as if ye were bound
with them. Keep in memory those who
are afflicted, as being yourselves clothed
with flesh.

4. Marriage is honourable in all, and
their bed is pure; but fornicators and
adulterers God will judge.

5. Let not your mind love money; but
let what ye have satisfy you; for the
Lord himself has said,–I will not forsake
thee, nor draw back my hands from thee.
–6. And it is ours to say with confidence,
–My Lord is my Helper; I will not fear;
what can man do to me?

7. Remember your leaders–those who
spoke to you the word of God ; consider
the completion of their courses, and
imitate their exercise of trust.

8. Jesus, the Anointed, is the same
yesterday, and to-day, and for ever.

9. Be not led away by teachings foreign
[from ours], and of varied kinds ; for it is
good for us to strengthen our hearts by
merciful favour, not by kinds of food ;
because those who have walked in these,
have not been helped [thereby].

10. Moreover, we have the altar from
which it was not lawful for those to
eat who did service in the tent-dwelling.
11. For the flesh of those animals, the
blood of which the high priest took into
the holy house on behalf of sins, was
burned outside the camp. 12. For this
reason, Jesus, that he might make his
people holy by his blood, suffered outside
the city. 13. And therefore, let us also go
out to him outside the camp, bearing
his reproach. 14. For we have not

once,–points out the changing of the
things to be shaken, as of things which
have been made in order that those
which are not to be shaken may continue.

28. Therefore may we, who are receiv-
ing a kingdom which is not to be shaken,
have merciful favour, by means of which
we may serve God in a way well-pleasing
to him, with reverence and godly fear;
29, for our God is a consuming fire.

XIII. 1. Let brotherly love continue.
2. Forget not kindness to strangers ; for
by means of it, some, unconsciously,
have entertained angels. 3. Remember
those in bonds, as bound with [them] ;
those who are ill-treated, as being yourselves also in the body.

4. Marriage is honourable in all, and
[its] bed [is] undefiled ; but fornicators
and adulterers God will judge.

5. Live without love of money; be
content with what ye have; for he himself has said,–Surely I will not forsake
thee, nor, as surely, will I leave thee ;–
6, so that we boldly say,–The Lord is my
helper; and I will not fear. What shall
man do to me?

7. Remember your leaders, those who
spoke to you the word of God. Consider
the close of their course, and imitate
their exercise of trust.

8. Jesus the Anointed is the same
yesterday, and to-day, and for ever.

9. Be not led about by teachings
various and foreign [from ours]; for it is
good that the heart be made firm by
merciful favour, not by kinds of food, by
which those have not been profited who
have walked in them.

10. We have the altar from which those
who do service [as] in the tent-dwelling
have no authority to eat. 11. For the
bodies of those animals, the blood of
which, [shed] on account of sin, is taken
by the high priest into the holy [place],
are burned outside the camp. 12. Therefore Jesus also, that he might make [his]
people holy by means of his own blood,
suffered outside the gate. 13. Therefore
let us come out to him, outside the camp,
bearing his reproach. 14. For we have

The Peshito-Syriac Text.

HEBREWS XIII. 14—25.

a continuing city here, but are expecting that which is to be.

15. And through him let us offer up slain-offerings of praise, at all times, to God; which [praise] is the fruit of lips which give thanks to his name.

16. And forget not kindness and the giving of gifts to the poor; for by these slain offerings man pleases God.

17. Be persuaded by your leaders, and submit to them; for they keep watch on behalf of your souls, as those who have to give an account of you; that they may do this with joy, and not with sighs; because that would not be of advantage to you.

18. Pray for us, for we are confident that we have a good conscience; for in everything we desire to conduct ourselves well. 19. I more especially beg you to do this, that I may quickly return to you.

20. Now may the God of peace, who brought up from the house of the dead the Great Shepherd of the flock, by the blood of the eternal covenant, who is Jesus, the Anointed, our Lord; 21,—may he perfect you in every good work, that ye may do his will; and may he work in us that which is good in his sight, by means of Jesus the Anointed; to whom [be] glory for ever and ever. Amen.

22. Now I beg of you, my brothers, that ye exercise forbearance under the word of exhortation, because it is in few words I have written to you.

23. Know ye also that our brother Timothy has been set free; and if he should come soon, I will see you with him.

24. Give my wish of peace to all your leaders, and to all the holy ones.

All those who are of Italy wish you peace.

25. Merciful favour be with you all. Amen. (b)

The Greek Text.

HEBREWS XIII. 14—25.

not here a continuing city, but we seek that which is to be.

15. Through him therefore, let us offer up the slain offering of praise, at all times, to God; that is, the fruit of lips which give thanks to his name.

16. And forget not to do good and give gifts, for with such slain offerings God is well pleased.

17. Be persuaded by your leaders, and submit; for they keep watch on behalf of your souls, as those who will give account; that they may do this with joy, and not with sighing; for that [would be] unprofitable for you.

18. Pray ye for us; for we are confident that we have a good conscience, and desire to conduct ourselves well in all things. 19. And I more especially beg you to do this, that I may be restored to you the sooner.

20. And may the God of peace, who brought up from among the dead the Great Shepherd of the sheep, by the blood of the eternal covenant, our Lord Jesus, 21, may he make you perfect in every good work, so as to do his will; working in you (a) what is well-pleasing in his sight, by means of Jesus the Anointed; to whom be glory for ever and ever. Amen.

22. Now I beg of you, [my] brothers, to bear with the word of exhortation, for in few words I have written to you.

23. Know ye that our brother Timothy has been set free; with whom, if he should come soon, I will see you.

24. Give greetings to all your leaders, and all the holy ones.

Those who are of Italy greet you.

25. Merciful favour be with you all. Amen.

(a) Ver. 21. Some Greek copies have, "us" instead of "you."

(b) Ver. 25. The Syriac copies state, at the end of this letter, that it was written from Italy. Jacobite copies say,—Finished is the letter to the Hebrews, which was written from Roman Italy, and was sent by the hands of Timothy.—The Maronite edition of 1703 says,—that it was "written from Italy," and adds, "and to God be glory for ever." The Ooroomiah edition of 1852, supposed to represent Nestorian copies of Coordistan, has,- Finished is the letter to the Hebrews, which was written from Italy.

THE LETTER OF JAMES

TO THE CHRISTIANS OF THE TWELVE TRIBES SCATTERED AMONG THE GENTILES.

The Peshito-Syriac Text.	The Greek Text.
THE LETTER OF JAMES, A CHIEF MESSENGER.	**THE LETTER OF JAMES.** (a)
JAMES I. 1–11.	JAMES I. 1–11.

I. 1. James, a servant of God, and of our Lord Jesus the Anointed:—
To the twelve tribes which are sown among the Gentiles;—Peace.

2. Let it be all joy to you, my brothers, when ye enter into many and various trials. 3. For ye know that the testing of [your] trust, makes you to possess patient endurance. 4. But let there be in patient endurance itself, a complete work, that ye may be perfect and complete, and may be lacking in nothing.

5. But if any one of you lacks wisdom, let him ask [it] of God, who gives to all largely, and does not reproach ; and it will be given him. 6. But let him ask in the exercise of trust, without doubting. He who doubts is like the waves of the sea, which the wind disturbs. 7. And let not that man think that he will receive anything from the Lord, 8, who doubts in his mind, and is disturbed in all his ways.

9. And let the brother of lowly [lot] glory in his high position ; 10, and the rich in his becoming lowly ; because, like the flower of herbage, so he is to pass away. 11. For the sun rises in its heat, and dries up the herbage, and its flower

I. 1. James a bond-servant of God, and of the Lord Jesus the Anointed;—
To the twelve tribes which are in the dispersion ; Joy.

2. Deem it all joy, my brothers, when ye fall into various trials; 3, for ye know that the testing of your trust, patient endurance. 4. But let [your] patient endurance do a complete work, that ye may be complete and whole, lacking in nothing.

5. But if any one of you lacks wisdom, let him ask [it] of God, who gives to all liberally, and does not reproach ; and it will be given him. 6. But let him ask in the exercise of trust, without any doubting ; for he who doubts is like a wave of the sea, driven by the wind, and tossed about. 7. For let not that man think that he will receive anything from the Lord. 8. A man of two minds [is] unstable in all his ways.

9. And let the brother of lowly [lot] glory in his high position; 10, but let the rich one [glory] in making himself lowly; because, like the flower of herbage he will pass away. 11. For the sun rises, with [its] burning heat, and dries up the

---

(a) Title. The seven letters,—that of James, the 1st and 2nd of Peter, the 1st, 2nd and 3rd of John, and that of Jude, have been called, in the titles of them, in many copies, "Catholic," that is, General. Chrysostom (A.D. 386–403) speaks of "three catholic letters," meaning probably James, 1st Peter, and 1st John. Cyril of Jerusalem (A.D. 348–386) speaks of "the seven catholic letters of James, Peter, John and Jude." So do Epiphanius (A.D. 403); Athanasius (A.D. 326–373); and Amphilochius (about A.D. 380). Why were they so called? They were not addressed to all Christians. Leontius (about A.D. 590) says that "the seven catholic letters, were called catholic because they were not written to one nation as those of Paul were, but generally to all." But those of James and Peter state that they were written solely to the Hebrews dispersed among the Gentiles. Ebed Jesu, (A.D. 1298–1318) spoke of "the three letters which are called catholic, those of James, Peter and John," as "signed by the apostles in every language." (Dr. Badger's Nestorians, Vol. II. p. 362.) As at Pentecost, the Hebrews from all parts heard the apostles speak in all the languages of the nations in which they dwelt; so, according to Ebed Jesu, these letters were signed by the apostles in them all, and were therefore, at the least, written in both Syriac and Greek. See Westcott on the canon, Appendix D.

The Peshito-Syriac Text.

JAMES I. 11—25.

falls off, and the beauty of its appearance perishes; so also is the rich man to wither away in the midst of his proceedings.

12. Blessed is the man who endures trials patiently, for when he shall have been proved [faithful], he is to receive the crown of life [-bliss], which God has promised to those who love him.

13. Let no one say, when he is tempted, —I am tempted by God;—for God is not tempted by evil things, and he tempts no one. 14. But each one is tempted by his own eager desire; and he desires, and is drawn on; 15, and this eager desire becomes pregnant, and gives birth to sin; and sin, when it has been perfected, gives birth to death. 16. Do not err, my beloved brothers. 17. From above comes down every good and complete gift, from the Father of lights; with whom there is nothing of change, nor the shadow of change. 18. He himself willed and begat us (a) by the word of truth, that we might be a first-fruit of those whom he creates.

19. And be ye, every one of you, my beloved brothers, quick to hear, and slow to speak; slow also to anger; 20, for the anger of man works not the righteousness of God. 21. For this reason put far away from you all pollution, and the abounding of evil, and receive with lowliness the word which has been planted in our nature, which is able to impart life [-bliss] to your souls.

22. But be ye doers of the word, and not hearers only; and do not deceive yourselves. 23. For if a person be a hearer of the word, and not a doer of it, he is like to him who views his face in a mirror; 24, for he sees himself, and goes away, and forgets what he was. 25. But every one who looks into the complete law of freedom, and continues in it, is not a hearer of what is heard and forgotten, but a doer of deeds; and he will be blessed in what he does.

The Greek Text.

JAMES I. 11—25.

herbage, and the flower of it falls off, and the beauty of its appearance perishes. So also will the rich man wither away in the midst of his proceedings.

12. Blessed is the man who endures trial patiently; for when he has been approved, he will receive the crown of life, which the Lord has promised to those who love him.

13. Let no one when tempted say,—I am tempted by God;—for God cannot be tempted by evil things, and he himself tempts no one. 14. But each one is tempted by being drawn out and enticed by his own eager desire; 15, then the eager desire becomes pregnant, and brings forth sin; and sin, when completed, brings forth death. 16. Do not err, my beloved brothers; 17, from above is all giving of good, and every complete gift; it comes down from the Father of lights, with whom there can be no change, nor the shadow of turning. 18. He willed and begat us, (a) by the word of truth, that we might be a first-fruit of those whom he has created.

19. So then, my beloved brothers, let every man be quick to hear, slow to speak, slow to anger; 20, for the anger of man does not work out the righteousness of God. 21. Therefore put away all filthiness, and the abounding of wickedness, and receive with meekness the implanted word, which is able to save your souls.

22. But be ye doers of the word, and not hearers [of it] only, deluding yourselves. 23. For if any one is a hearer, and not a doer of the word, he is like a man who views his natural face in a mirror; 24, for he views himself, and goes away, and immediately forgets what sort of person he was. 25. But he who looks into the complete law, that of liberty, and continues [in it], he, not being a hearer who forgets, but a doer of [what is to be] done, will be blessed in what he does.

(a) Ver. 18. The Common English Version has, "he begat us." The Revised Version substitutes for those words, "he brought us forth;" that is, as a mother brings forth children. The word "he" implies that God, the Father, is represented in this passage as being what is impossible in nature, both father and mother to his children. The word "he" makes the words "bring forth" utterly inconsistent. No man is a mother; and it is difficult to conceive how intelligent men brought themselves to believe that words so contradictory in themselves, and so much at variance with other parts of scripture, express the true meaning of God's word in this place.

The Peshito-Syriac Text.

JAMES I. 26, 27. II. 1–16.

26. And if a person thinks that he is serving God, and restrains not his tongue, but deceives his heart, his service is in vain. 27. For pure and holy service, before God, the Father, is this; —to visit orphans and widows in their afflictions, and for a person to keep himself unstained by the world.

II. 1. My brothers, do not retain trust in the glory of our Lord Jesus, the Anointed, [together] with wrong regard for persons. 2. For if there shall enter into your congregation a person with rings of gold, or in beautiful clothes; and there shall enter a poor person in dirty clothes; 3, and ye pay regard to him who wears the beautiful clothes, and say to him,—Sit thou here in a beautiful [seat];—and say to the poor person,—Stand thou there,—or,—Seat thyself here, before the stool of our feet; —4, will ye not have double-dealing within you, and be expounders whose thoughts are evil? 5. Hear ye, my beloved brothers; has not God chosen the poor of the world, but rich in trust, to be inheritors of that kingdom which God has promised to those who love him? 6. But ye have despised the poor man. Do not the rich exalt themselves over you, and drag you to the house of judgment? 7. Do they not revile the Good Name after which ye are called? 8. If in this ye fulfil the law of God, as it is written, —Thou shalt love thy neighbour as thyself,—ye do well. 9. But if ye have wrong regard for persons, ye commit sin, and are accused by the law as law-breakers. 10. For he who keeps the whole law, save that he sins in one thing, is condemned by the whole law. 11. For he who said, —Thou shalt not commit adultery,—is he who said,—Thou shalt not commit murder.—If then thou dost not commit adultery, but dost commit murder, thou art a breaker of the law.

12. So speak ye, and so do, as those who are to be judged by the law of freedom. 13. For judgment is to be without mercy on him who shows not mercy. Ye are to be exalted by mercy above condemning judgment.

14. Of what use is it, my brothers, for a person to say,—I have trust,—if he has not the works [of it]? Can his trust make life [-bliss] his? 15. If such as a brother or sister be naked, and in need of food for the day; 16, and one of you says to them,—Depart in peace, warm

The Greek Text.

JAMES I. 26, 27. II. 1–16.

26. If anyone among you seems to be religious, yet bridles not his tongue, but deceives his heart, his religion is in vain. 27. Pure and undefiled religion, before [our] God and Father, is this;—to visit orphans and widows in their affliction, and to keep one's self unstained by the world.

II. 1. My brothers, do not hold [your] trust in the glory of our Lord Jesus, the Anointed, [combined] with wrong regard for persons. 2. For if there should enter into your synagogue, a man with gold rings, in splendid clothing, and there should enter a poor person in dirty clothing; 3, and ye regard him who wears the splendid clothing, and say to him,—Sit thou here in a good place;— and say to the poor person,—Stand thou there,—or,—Sit here under my footstool; —4, would you not be, within yourselves, partizans, and judges with evil thoughts? 5. Hear ye, my beloved brothers! has not God chosen the poor of this world [to be] rich in trust, and inheritors of the kingdom which he has promised to those who love him! 6. But ye have dishonoured the poor man. Do not the rich oppress you? and themselves drag you to the judgment-seats? 7. Do they not revile that Good Name after which ye are called? 8. If indeed ye fulfil the royal law, according to the [holy] writing,—Thou shalt love thy neighbour as thyself,—ye do well. 9. But if ye have wrong regard for persons, ye commit sin, and are accused by the law as law-breakers. 10. For whoever shall keep the whole law, except that he fails in one [command], has become [by the voice] of all, guilty. 11. For he who said,—Thou shalt not commit adultery, —said also,—Thou shalt not commit murder.—And if thou dost not commit adultery, but dost commit murder, thou hast become a law-breaker.

12. So speak ye, and so do, as those who are to be judged by the law of liberty. 13. For judgment [will be] without mercy on him who has not shown mercy. And mercy is to glory in setting aside condemning judgment.

14. Of what use [is it], my brothers, for any one to say that he has trust, if he has not works [of trust]? Can such trust save him? 15. And if a brother or sister be such as are naked, and in want of daily food; 16, and one of you says to them,—Depart in peace, be ye warmed,

JAMES II. 16—26. III. 1—7.

yourselves, and eat till ye are satisfied; —and yet ye do not give them that of which the body has need, of what use is it? 17. So also trust which has no works, is dead, while alone. 18. For [if] some one says [to him],—Thou for thyself hast trust, and I for myself have works:—19. Show me thy trust which has no works, and I will show thee my trust by means of my works. 19. Thou dost trust for true that God is but one; thou dost well. The devils also trust it, and tremble. 20. Art thou willing to know, O feeble man, that trust which has no works, is dead? 21. Was not our Father Abraham declared righteous by means of works [of trust], because he lifted up Isaac his son upon the altar? 22. Seest thou that his trust gave aid to his works, and that by means of works his trust was made perfect? 23. And that the [holy] writing was fulfilled which says,—Abraham trusted in God, and it was reckoned to him with view to righteousness; and he was called the friend of God? —24. Seest thou that by means of works [of trust] a man is declared righteous, and not by means of trust without [them]? 25. So also was not Rahab the harlot declared righteous by means of works, because she received the spies, and sent them forth by another road? 26. As the body without the spirit is dead, so trust, without works, is dead also.

III. 1. Let there not be many teachers among you, my brothers; but know ye, that [if] we are condemned, [our] condemnation is greater. 2. For in many things we all err. Whoever errs not in word is a perfect man, who is able to keep his whole body in subjection also. 3. For, behold, we put bits into the mouths of horses, so that they may be subject to us; and we turn about their whole body. 4. Huge ships also, when strong winds drive them, are turned about by a small rudder, to the place which the will of the steerer predetermines. 5. So the tongue also is a small member, and yet it exalts itself. A small flame also sets on fire many woods; 6, and the tongue is a fire, and the world of of sin is like a wood; and the tongue being itself in the midst of our members, blackens our whole body; and it sets on fire the whole train of our generations, which run on like wheels; and it is also itself set on fire by fire [from hell]. 7. For all the natures of beasts and of

JAMES II. 16—26. III. 1—7.

and well fed;—and yet ye do not give them the things of which the body has need,—of what use [is it]? 17. So also trust, if it has not works, is dead, by itself. 18. But will someone say [to him],—Thou hast trust, and I have works?—Show me thy trust without thy works, and I will show thee my trust by means of my works. 19. Thou dost trust for true that God is but one. Thou dost well. The devils also trust it, and tremble. 20. But art thou willing to know, O thoughtless man, that trust without works [of trust] is dead? 21. Was not Abraham our Father declared righteous by means of works, when he offered up Isaac his son upon the altar? 22. Seest thou that his trust worked in union with his works, and that by means of works trust was made complete? 23, and that the [holy] writing was fulfilled which says,—Abraham trusted in God, and it was reckoned to him with view to righteousness; and he was called the friend of God?—24. Do you see, therefore, that by means of works a man is declared righteous, and not by means of trust only? 25. And in like manner was not Rahab the harlot also declared righteous by means of works, when she received the messengers and sent them forth by another road? 26. For as the body without the spirit is dead, so trust without [its] works is dead also.

III. 1. Be not many teachers, my brothers; for ye know that we, [if condemned], shall receive greater condemnation. 2. For we are all faulty in many things. If anyone be not faulty in word, he is a complete man, able to bridle the whole body also. 3. Behold, we put bits into the mouths of horses, that they may obey us, and we turn about their whole body. 4. Behold, ships also, though they are so large, and are driven by rough winds, are turned about by a very small rudder, to the place which the will of the steersman may choose. 5. So also the tongue is a little member, and yet it is very boastful. Behold how large a wood a little fire sets ablaze! 6. And the tongue is a fire; it is the world of unrighteousness; the tongue is so placed in the midst of our members, that it soils the whole body; it sets on fire also, the run of successive generations; and it is set on fire by hell. 7. For every nature of beasts and of birds, of creeping things, and of things in the sea, is to be tamed,

JAMES III. 7–18. IV. 1–7.

JAMES III. 7–18. IV. 1–7.

birds, of things moving in the sea and on dry land, have been made subject to the nature of man; 8, but the tongue no man is able to tame; this is an evil which cannot be stopped; it is full of deadly poison. 9. For with it we bless the Lord and Father, and with it we curse men who are made in the likeness of God. 10. And from the same mouth come forth curses and blessings. These things, my brothers, ought not to be so done. 11. Is it possible for sweet water and bitter to come forth from one spring? 12. Or can a fig-tree, my brothers, bear olives? or a vine, figs? So salt water also cannot be made sweet.

13. Who is there among you who is wise and learned? Let him set forth his works, with lowly wisdom, by means of good courses of conduct. 14. But if there is bitter jealousy among you, or a spirit of strife in your hearts, boast not against the truth, nor lie. 15. Because this wisdom comes not down from above, but is earthly, from thoughts of self, and from devils. 16. For where there is jealousy, and a spirit of strife, there also is disturbance, and everything which is evil. 17. But the wisdom which is from above is pure, and full of peace; it is lowly and obedient; it is full of mercy and of good fruits; there is in it no love of division, nor wrong regard for persons. 18. The fruits also of righteousness are sown in quietness by those who make peace.

IV. 1. From what [cause] is it that there are wars and contentions among you? Are they not from eager desires which wage war by means of your members? 2. Ye eagerly desire, and yet have not; ye kill also, and envy, and yet nothing comes into your hands; ye contend and carry on wars, and yet get nothing; because ye do not ask. 3. Ye ask, and receive not, because ye ask in an evil way; that ye may nourish your eager desires. 4. Ye adulterers, know ye not that [to be in] friendship with this world, is to act as an enemy of God? He therefore who resolves to be a friend of this world, is an enemy of God. 5. Or think ye that the [holy] writing has said without reason, that the spirit which dwells in us covets eagerly through envy? 6. But our Lord has given us greater merciful help. For this reason it says,—God brings low the lifted up, and gives merciful help to the lowly.—7. Therefore submit yourselves to God.

and has been tamed, by the nature of man. 8. But no man is able to tame the tongue; it is an irrepressible evil; it is full of deadly poison. 9. With it we bless him who is God and Father, and with it we curse men who are made in the likeness of God. 10. Out of the same mouth come forth blessing and cursing. These things, my brothers, ought not to be so. 11. Does the spring send forth from the same opening sweet water and bitter? 12. Can a fig-tree, my brothers, bear olives? or a vine, figs? So, no spring [can] give salt water and sweet.

13. Who among you is wise and learned? Let him set forth his works with meekness of wisdom, by means of [his] good course of conduct. 14. But if ye have bitter jealousy, and a spirit of strife in your heart, glory not against the truth, nor lie against it. 15. This is not the wisdom which comes down from above, but is earthly, selfish, devilish. 16. For where jealousy and a spirit of strife are, there is disquiet, and every bad deed. 17. But the wisdom which is from above, first, is pure, next, peaceable, gentle, obedient, full of mercy and of good fruits, without love of disagreement, and without hypocrisy. 18. And the fruit of righteousness is sown in peace by those who make peace.

IV. 1. Whence [come] wars and contentions among you? [Come they] not hence? Out of your pleasures which make war by your members? 2. Ye eagerly desire, and yet have not; ye kill and jealously covet, and ye are unable to obtain; ye contend and make war, but have not, because ye do not ask; 3, ye ask, and receive not, because ye ask in an evil way; that ye may spend [what ye get] on your pleasures. 4. Ye adulterers and adulteresses, know ye not that [to be in] friendship with this world, is to act as an enemy of God? Whoever resolves to be a friend of the world, makes himself an enemy of God. 5. Or think ye that without reason the [holy] writing says, that the spirit which dwells in us covets and leads to envy? 6. But he gives greater merciful help. Therefore it says,—God resists the proud, but gives merciful help to the humble. 7. Submit yourselves therefore to God. Oppose the False-accuser, and he will flee from

The Peshito-Syriac Text.

JAMES IV. 7–17. V. 1–6.

Resist Satan also, and he will flee from you. 8. Draw near also to God, and he will draw near to you. Cleanse your hands, ye sinners; be holy in your hearts, ye of divided mind. 9. Humble yourselves and mourn; let your laughter also be turned into mourning, and your joy into grief. 10. Humble yourselves before the Lord, and he will exalt you.

11. Speak not one against another, my brothers; for he who is speaking against his brother,or is condemning his brother, is speaking against the law, and condemning the law; and if thou condemnest the law, thou art not a doer of the law, but its judge. 12. For there is but One who makes law, (a) and passes sentence of judgment; One who is able to give life [-bliss], and to destroy. But thou, who art thou, who art condemning thy neighbour?

13. What too shall we say about those who say,—To-day or to-morrow we will go into a city,—whichever it may be,—and do business there one year, and trade and get gain;—14, and yet they know not what will be on the morrow. For what is our life but a vapour, which is seen for a little time, and then vanishes, and is at an end. 15. Instead of their saying,—If the Lord shall please, and we shall live, we will do this or that. —16. They glory in their boasting; all glorying such as this is of evil [kind]. 17. And he who knows what is good, and does it not, has on him sin.

V. 1. O ye rich ones! wail and weep on account of the miseries which are to come upon you. 2. For your wealth is to rot and stink; and your suits of clothing are to be eaten by the moth; 3, your gold and your silver will rust, and their rust will bear witness against you, and will eat your flesh. Ye have made a fire-pile for yourselves, for the last days. 4. Behold, the pay of the labourers who have reaped your lands, which ye have wrongfully kept back, cries out; and the outcry of the reapers has entered into the ears of the Lord of Armies. 5. For ye have lived in luxury upon the earth; and in excesses; and have nourished your bodies as in a day when [fatlings] are killed. 6. Ye condemned and killed the Righteous One; and will he not rise up against you?

The Greek Text.

JAMES IV. 8–17. V. 1–6.

you. 8. Draw near to God, and he will draw near to you. Cleanse your hands, ye sinners, and purify your hearts, ye double-minded. 9. Be in distress, and mourn, and weep; let your laughter be turned into mourning, and your joy into downcast grief. 10. Humble yourselves before the Lord, and he will exalt you.

11. Speak not one against another,[my] brothers. He who is speaking against his brother, and is condemning his brother, is speaking against the law, and is condemning the law; but if thou condemnest the law, thou art not a doer of the law, but a judge. 12. There is but one Lawgiver, (a) who is able to save, and to destroy. Thou, who art thou, who condemnest thy neighbour?

13. Come now, ye who say,—To-day or to-morrow we will go into that city, and do business there one year, and trade, and get gain;—14, ye who do not know what will be on the morrow. For what is your life? It is a vapour, which appears for a little time, and then vanishes away. 15. Instead of your saying, —If the Lord shall please, we shall both live and do this or that. 16. But now ye glory in your boastings; all such glorying is evil. 17. He therefore who knows how to do good, and does it not, has on him sin.

V. 1. Come now, ye rich men, weep and howl over your coming miseries. 2. Your wealth is to become rotten; your [changes] of clothing also are to be moth-eaten; 3, your gold and your silver are to rust, and their rust will be for a testimony against you, and will eat your flesh; ye have heaped up treasures [to be] as a fire in the last days. 4. Behold, the pay of the labourers who have reaped your fields, which is by you, through fraud, withheld, cries out; and the cries of those who reaped have entered into the ears of the Lord of Armies. 5. Ye have lived in luxury on the earth, ye have indulged yourselves in excesses; ye have nourished your hearts as in a day of killing [for a feast]. 6. Ye condemned, ye murdered the Righteous One. Is he not fighting against you?

(a) Ver. 12. Some Greek copies have "one Lawgiver and Judge."

The Peshito-Syriac Text.

7. But ye, my brothers, be patient until the coming of the Lord ; like the farmer, who is expecting the precious fruits of his land, and waits patiently for them, until he shall receive the earlier and the later rain. 8. So also be ye patient, and fix firmly your hearts; for the coming of our Lord has come near. (a)

9. Do not groan complainingly one against another, my brothers; that ye may not be condemned; for behold, judgment is standing before the door.

10. Take as an example for yourselves, my brothers, the prophets who spoke in the name of the Lord, that ye may bear your afflictions with long-suffering patience. 11. For, behold, we ascribe blessedness to those who patiently endured. Ye have heard of the patient endurance of Job, and ye have seen the ending which the Lord worked out for him ; because the Lord is merciful and kind.

12. But before everything, my brothers, be not swearers; not by heaven, nor by earth, nor by any other oath. But let your speech be,—yes, yes, and no, no; that ye may not be under sentence of condemnation.

13. If any one of you shall be in affliction, let him pray ; and if he shall be joyful, let him sing ; 14, and if he be unwell, let him call for the elders of the assembly, and let them pray over him, and anoint him with oil in the name of our Lord ; 15, and the prayer of trust shall make him well who is unwell ; and our Lord shall raise him up ; and if sins shall have been committed by him, they shall be forgiven him.

16. Confess also your faults one to another; and pray one for another that ye may be restored to health ; for great is the power of the prayer which a righteous man prays. 17. Even Elijah was a man who suffered as we do; and he prayed that rain might not fall on the earth ; and it fell not for three years and six months. 18. And again he prayed, and the heavens gave rain, and the earth gave its fruits.

The Greek Text.

7. Be patient, therefore, [my] brothers, until the coming of the Lord. Behold, the farmer expects the precious produce of the earth, and waits patiently for it until he receives the early and later rain. 8. Be ye also patient; fix firmly your hearts ; for the coming of the Lord has come near. (a)

9. Groan not one against another, [my] brothers, that ye may not be condemned. Behold, the Judge stands before the doors.

10. Take ye, my brothers, for an example of the endurance of evil, and of long-suffering patience, the prophets who spoke in the name of the Lord. 11. Behold, we call those blessed who patiently endure. (b) Ye have heard of the patient endurance of Job ; and have seen the ending [given] by the Lord ; that the Lord is very compassionate and full of pity.

12. But before all things, my brothers, swear not ; neither by the heaven, nor by the earth ; nor by any other oath ; but let your yes be yes, and your no, no; that ye may not fall under condemnation.

13. Does any one among you suffer evil? let him pray. Is any one cheerful? let him sing to the harp. 14. Is any one among you unwell? let him call to him the elders of the assembly, and let them pray over him, and anoint him with oil in the name of the Lord ; 15, and the prayer of trust shall save him who is sick, and the Lord shall raise him up ; and if he shall have committed sins, he shall be forgiven.

16. Confess one to another your faults ; and pray, one on behalf of another, that ye may be restored to health. The earnest petition of a righteous man avails much. 17. Elijah was a man who suffered as we do; and he prayed earnestly that it might not rain ; and it rained not on the earth, for three years and six months. 18. And he prayed again, and the heaven gave rain, and the earth brought forth its fruit.

(a) Ver. 8. In Matt. x. 23, Jesus said to the twelve,—ye shall not have gone through the cities of Israel, till the Son of man be come.—He came in power, though not in person, in the destruction of the Jewish nation and worship.

(b) Ver. 11. Some Greek copies have "endured" instead of "endure."

The Peshito-Syriac Text.

JAMES V. 19, 20.

19. My brothers, if any one of you shall err from the way of truth, and one shall turn him from his error: 20, let him know that he who turns the sinner from the error of his way, raises his soul to life [-bliss] from death, and covers [through forgiveness] the multitude of his sins. (a)

The Greek Text.

JAMES V. 19, 20.

19. [My] brothers, if any one among you shall err from the truth, and one shall turn him to [it]; 20, let him know that he who turns the sinner from the error of his way, will save a soul from death, and will cover [through forgiveness] a multitude of sins. (b)

(a) Some Syriac copies have this note at the end of this letter :—" Finished is the letter of James, a Chief Messenger."

(b) Many Greek copies of this letter have no note at the end. One of them has this :—" The end of the letter of the holy apostle James, the brother of God."—Mary was called, and is still called by some,—" The mother of God."—By " the brother of God," was doubtless meant James the brother of Jesus, who is called by Paul, in Gal. i. 19, " James, the brother of our Lord." Compare Mark vi. 3.

THE FIRST LETTER OF PETER

TO HEBREW CHRISTIANS WHO WERE DWELLING IN FOREIGN COUNTRIES.

The Peshito-Syriac Text.

NEXT: A LETTER OF PETER, CHIEF MESSENGER; SIMON CEPHAS. (a)

I PETER I. 1—8.

I. 1. Peter, a Chief Messenger of Jesus the Anointed;—

To the Chosen, who have no fixed dwelling-place; who are sown in Pontus, and in Galatia, and in Cappadocia, and in Asia, and in Bithynia; 2, who were chosen by the fore-knowledge of God, the Father, to be obedient, by being made holy by the Spirit, and to be sprinkled with the blood of Jesus the Anointed :—

May merciful favour and peace be given to you abundantly.

8. Blessed be God, the Father of our Lord Jesus the Anointed, who in his great mercy begat us anew, through the rising [from death] of our Lord Jesus the Anointed, to [give us] hope of life [-bliss], 4, and an inheritance which cannot be destroyed, nor be defiled, nor fade away; which is prepared for you in heaven; 5, [for you], who yourselves are kept by the power of God, and by means of trust, for that life [-bliss] which is prepared, that it may be revealed in the last times; 6, in which [last times] ye will be joyful for ever, though at this time, ye are saddened a little by the various trials which are passing over you; 7, in order that the testing of your trust, which [testing] is of more worth than [that of] refined gold, which has been tested by fire, may be seen to be for fame, and for honour, and for glory, at the revealing of Jesus the Anointed; 8, whom ye have not seen, yet whom ye love; and through trust in whom ye rejoice greatly, with a glorified joy, which cannot be

The Greek Text.

THE FIRST GENERAL LETTER OF PETER. (a)

I PETER I. 1—8.

I. 1. Peter, a Chief Messenger of Jesus the Anointed ;—

To the Chosen, who have no fixed dwelling-place; who are of those who are dispersed in Pontus, Galatia, Cappadocia, Asia, and Bithynia ;—2, [chosen] according to the foreknowledge of God the Father, to obedience, by being made holy by the Spirit, and to the being sprinkled with the blood of Jesus the Anointed ;—

May merciful favour and peace be given to you abundantly.

8. Blessed [be] God, the Father of our Lord Jesus the Anointed, who, according to his great mercy, begat us anew, to a living hope through the resurrection of Jesus the Anointed from among the dead, 4, [and] to an inheritance which cannot be destroyed, nor defiled, nor can fade away; one which is reserved in the heavens, 5, for you, who are kept by the power of God, through trust; that ye may have the salvation [which is] in readiness to be revealed in the last time; 6, at which [last time] ye are to rejoice greatly, though now, since it is needful, ye are a little grieved by various trials; 7, [sent] that the testing of your trust, which [testing] is of much more worth than that of perishing gold, though it be tested by fire, may be found to be for praise, and honour, and glory, at the revealing of Jesus the Anointed; 8, whom, without having seen, ye love; in whom, though now ye see him not, yet, trusting, ye rejoice greatly with joy which cannot be spoken, and is made glorious;

(a) The Titles given to this letter, both in Syriac, and in Greek copies, vary. The above occur only in some of the copies. The word Catholic, that is General, occurs in many of the Greek titles. The statement of Ebed Jesu (see note on James) that the letters called "general" were signed by the apostles in various languages, confirms belief that this letter, which was written to Hebrews, was written or signed by the apostle in the Syriac language of the Hebrews, as well as in Greek.

The Peshito-Syriac Text.

I PETER I. 8—22.

spoken; 9, because ye will receive, as recompense of your trust, the life [-bliss] of your souls.

10. Respecting which life [-bliss], the prophets made diligent search, when they prophesied about that gift of merciful favour which was in the future to be given to you; 11, and they searched into what the time was of which the Spirit of the Anointed who dwelt in them was giving notice, and bearing witness, as that in which the sufferings of the Anointed, and the glory which was to follow them, were to be in the future. 12. And all that they searched into was revealed to them; because it was not about themselves that they inquired; but about us, respecting whom they were prophesying those things which have now been revealed to you by means of those which we have announced to you, by the Spirit of Holiness who has been sent from heaven. Into which very things angels also greatly desire to look.

13. For this reason gird up the loins of your minds, be perfectly watchful, and hope for the joy which is to come to you at the revealing of our Lord Jesus the Anointed, 14, as obedient sons; and share not again those former strong desires which ye had when not in a state of knowledge; 15, but be ye holy in all your courses of conduct, as he is holy who called you. 16. Because it is written, —Be ye holy, as also I am holy.—17. And if ye call him Father, before whom there is no wrong regard for persons, and who judges everyone as his works are, conduct yourselves with fear during this time of your having no fixed dwelling-place; 18, for ye know that it was not with silver which wears away with age, nor with gold, that ye were set free from your worthless works. which ye received from your fathers; 19. but with the precious blood of that Lamb, who is the Anointed, in whom there is no spot nor blemish; 20, who beforehand was set apart for this very [purpose], from before the foundations of the world, and has been revealed in the last of the times, because of you, 21, who, through him, have trusted in God, who raised him up from the house of the dead, and gave him glory, that your trust, and your hope, might be in God; 22, that your souls might be made holy by obedience to the truth; and might be filled with love which has no wrong regard for

The Greek Text.

I PETER I. 9—23.

9, because ye have to receive, as the end of your trust, the salvation of [your] souls.

10. Respecting which salvation, the prophets made diligent inquiry and search, who prophesied about the gift of merciful favour to you; 11, searching as to what the time [was], or what the kind of time, which the Spirit of the Anointed who was in them, was making known, when bearing witness beforehand to the sufferings awaiting the Anointed, and the glories to come after them. 12. To whom it was revealed that they were setting forth, not for themselves, but for us, the things which have now been announced to you by means of those who have told you the good message, by the Holy Spirit, who has been sent from heaven. Into which things angels greatly desire to look.

13. Therefore gird up the loins of your mind, be perfectly watchful, and hope for the gift of merciful favour which is to be brought to you, at the revealing of Jesus the Anointed, 14, as obedient children; and be not conformed to the strong desires of that former time when ye were in your ignorance; 15, but like as he who called you is holy, be ye yourselves also holy in all [your] conduct; 16, because it is written,—Be ye holy, because I am holy.—17. And if ye call him Father, who judges without wrong regard for persons, according to the work of each, pass the time of your having no fixed dwelling-place, in fear; 18, knowing that it was not by perishable things,— by silver or by gold, that ye were set free by ransom from your useless course of life, delivered to you by your fathers, 19, but by the precious blood of the Anointed, as of a lamb without spot and without blemish; 20, who, indeed, was fore-ordained before the foundation of the world, but was made manifest in the latest times, because of you, 21, who, through him, are trusting in God, who raised him up from among the dead, and gave him glory, that your trust and hope might be in God. 22. As ye have purified your souls by obedience to the truth, by means of the Spirit, that ye may have brotherly love, which is without hypocrisy; love ye one another with a pure heart, fervently; 23, because ye have been

The Peshito-Syriac Text.

I PETER I. 22—25. II. 1—10.

persons; that ye might love one another with a pure and perfect heart; 23, as those who have been begotten anew, not by seed, [the life of] which perishes with age, but by that which does not so perish;—by the living word of God which is firm for ever. 24. Because,—All flesh [is as] grass, and all its beauty as a flower of the field; the grass dries up, and the flower fades away; 25, but the word of God is firm for ever;—and this is the word which ye have heard spoken.

II. 1. Therefore put away from you all malice, and all deception; also wrong regard for persons, and envying, and false-accusing; 2, and be as little infants, and desire earnestly the word, as that pure and spiritual milk by which ye will grow up into life [-bliss]; 3, if ye have tasted, and have seen, that the Lord is good; 4, to whom ye draw near; [and] who is the living stone whom the sons of men rejected, but who is chosen and honoured by God. 5. And ye also as living stones have been built up, and are spiritual temples; also holy priests, to offer up spiritual (b) slain-offerings which are acceptable before God through Jesus the Anointed.

6. For it is said in the [holy] writing,—Behold, I place in Zion a stone, chosen and honoured, at the head of the corner; and he who trusts in it shall not be ashamed.—7. To you therefore who are trusting,this honour has been given; but to those who obey not, 8, it is a stone of stumbling, and a stone kicked against; and they stumble against it, in that they obey not the word; those who were appointed to [do] this. 9. But ye are a tribe chosen to be priests of [God's] kingdom; [ye are] a holy people; a multitude delivered, that ye may declare the praises of him who called you out of darkness into his surpassing light; 10, ye, who before were not accounted [God's] people, but now are the people of God; ye, to whom also mercy had not come; but on whom mercy has now been outpoured.

The Greek Text.

I PETER I. 23—25. II. 1—10.

begotten anew, not by perishable, but by imperishable seed, by means of the living word of God, which continues for ever. 24. Because,—All flesh is as grass, and all the glory of man as the flower of grass. The grass is dried up, and its flower falls off; 25, but the word of the Lord continues for ever.—And this is the word, the good message of which has been told you.

II. 1. Therefore put away all malice, and all deception; also hypocrisies. and envyings, and all slanders; 2, and as babes just born,desire earnestly the pure milk of the word, that by it ye may grow, (a) 3, if ye have tasted that the Lord is kind, 4, to whom ye draw near; [even to that] living stone who has been rejected by men, but who with God is chosen and in honour. 5. And be yourselves as living stones, are built up; [ye who are] a spiritual house, a holy priesthood, to offer up spiritual slain-offerings, which are acceptable to God through Jesus the Anointed.

6. Therefore this occurs also in the [holy] writing,—Behold, I place in Zion a stone for the head of the corner, which is chosen and in honour, and he who trusts on it shall not be put to shame. 7. For you, therefore, who are trusting, is this honour; but to those who obey not, —That stone which the builders rejected, has become the head of the corner;—8, and,—A stone of stumbling, and a rock kicked against;—[to those] who stumble by disobeying the word; to [do] which they also were appointed. 9. But ye are a chosen race, a royal priesthood, a holy nation, a people to be [God's] possession, that ye may tell forth the noble deeds of him who called you out of darkness into his marvellous light; 10, ye who once were not [God's] people, but are now the people of God; ye who had not received mercy, but now have received mercy.

(a) Ver. 2. Some Greek copies add, "into salvation," agreeing with "life [-bliss]" in the Syriac.

(b) Ver. 5. The word "spiritual" is not in all the Syriac copies. It is inserted in the edition printed for the Maronites at Rome; in that of Ooroomiah, supposed to represent Coordistan; and in that by Dr. Lee, 1816, supposed to represent copies from India. These copies agree with the Greek Text.

The Peshito-Syriac Text.

11. My beloved, I beg of you, as persons away from home, and as having no fixed dwelling-place [here], to separate yourselves from all those strong desires of the body which wage wars against the soul; 12, and [to take care] that your courses of conduct before all the sons of men be good [courses]; that those who speak against you evil words may see your good works, and may glorify God, in the day which puts [you] to test.

13. And submit yourselves, because of God, to all the sons of men; to kings because of their authority; 14, and to judges, because they are sent from him for the punishment of wrong-doers, and for the praise of those who do good deeds. 15. Because it is the will of God that thus, by your good works, ye should shut the mouth of those foolish persons who know not God; 16, as sons who are free, yet not as those whose freedom is made by them a covering to hide their malice; but as the servants of God. 17. Honour everyone; love your brothers; fear also God; and honour kings.

18. And those servants who are among you:—Submit yourselves to your masters, with fear; not only to the good and mild, but also to the harsh and severe. 19. For before God there is merciful favour for those who, because [they have] a good conscience, endure patiently sorrows which come on them unjustly. 20. But what praise is due to those who endure patiently inflictions because of their wrong-doings? But when ye do what is good, and they afflict you, and ye bear it patiently, ye have then great praise with God. 21. For to [do] this ye were called; because also the Anointed died on our behalf, and left us this example, that ye might walk in his footsteps; 22, in his who committed no sin, nor was deceit found in his mouth; 23, of him who was reviled, yet reviled not; and suffered, yet threatened not; but committed the judgment of himself to the Judge who is righteous. 24. And he bore our sins, all of them; and carried them up in his body to the cross; that we might be dead to sin, and have life [-bliss] by his righteousness; for by his wounds ye have been healed. 25. For ye were going astray like sheep, but have been turned now to the Shepherd and Guardian of your souls.

III. 1. So also ye wives, submit yourselves to your husbands; that ye, by

The Greek Text.

11. Beloved, I beseech you, as persons away from home. and having no fixed dwelling-place [here], to abstain from fleshly strong desires which make war against the soul; 12, and to maintain a good course of conduct among the Gentiles, so that so far as they speak against you as evildoers, they may, on account of your good works which they behold, glorify God in the day when he visits [you.]

13. Submit yourselves, therefore, because of the Lord, to every [authority] created by men; whether to the king, as supreme; 14, or to rulers, as sent, through him, for the punishment, indeed, of evildoers, but for the praise of those who do what is good; 15, for it is the will of God, that thus, by doing what is good, ye should silence the ignorance of foolish men; 16, as free, yet not as having freedom [to make it] a cloak to cover malice; but as bond-servants of God. 17. Honour all; love the brotherhood; fear God; honour the king.

18. Ye household servants, submit yourselves to your masters with all fear; not only to the good and mild, but also to the perverse. 19. For if any one, because of conscience toward God, bears griefs patiently, when suffering unjustly, this [has his] merciful favour. 20. For what glory [have ye], if, when ye sin and are struck with the hand, ye bear it patiently? But if ye bear [this] patiently, when ye do what is good, and yet suffer, this has merciful favour with God. 21. For to [do] this ye were called; because also the Anointed suffered on our behalf, leaving us an example, with intent that ye should follow in his footsteps; 22, [in his] who committed no sin, nor was deceit found in his mouth; 23, who, when reviled, reviled not in return; when he suffered, threatened not; but committed [himself] to him who judges righteously; 24, who himself carried up our sins in his own body on to the cross, in order that we might be dead to the sins, and might live by the righteousness [of him,] by the wounding of whom ye have been healed. 25. For ye were as sheep which go astray; but ye have now been turned to the Shepherd and Overseer of your souls.

III. 1. Likewise, ye wives, submit yourselves to your own husbands: that good lines of conduct, which give no offence, may possess those who obey not the word; 2, when they see that ye conduct yourselves with fear and chasteness. 3. And do not adorn yourselves with outward adornments, such as interweavings of your hair, or ornaments of gold, or finer clothes. 4. But adorn yourselves in the hidden person of the heart, with a lowly spirit, which is imperishable: an adornment of surpassing excellence in the sight of God. 5. For so also of old those holy women who hoped in God adorned themselves, and were submissive to their husbands; 6, as Sarah submitted herself to Abraham, and called him,—My lord. Her daughters are ye, by good works, while by no terror made to waver.

7. And ye husbands, likewise, dwell with your wives according to knowledge; and hold them in honour as delicate vessels; because also they are inheritors with you of the gift of eternal life [-bliss]; that ye may not be hindered in your prayers.

8. Finally, [I intreat] you to be all in agreement; and to feel suffering with those who suffer; and to love one another; and to be merciful and lowly. (a) 9. And that to no one ye return evil for evil; nor reviling for reviling; but do the contrary of these, bless ye. For to [do] this ye were called, that ye might inherit blessing. 10. Let him therefore who,—Desires life [-bliss], and loves to see good days, keep his tongue from evil, and his lips from uttering deceit; 11, let him depart from evil, and do good; let him also seek peace, and pursue it. 12. Because the eyes of the Lord are upon the righteous, and his ears [are ready] hear them; and the face of the Lord is against those who are evil. (b)—13. And who is he who will do you evil, if ye be zealous (c) [in doing] things good? 14. Yet if it should happen that ye suffer on account of righteousness, blessed are ye; and fear not those who try to put you in fear, nor be disturbed; 15, but holily honour in your hearts the Lord, the Anointed; and be ready, in reply to everyone who asks you to speak about the hope in which ye

even if some obey not the word, they may, without a word [spoken], be gained by means of the [good] conduct of [their] wives ; 2, by observing your chaste conduct [joined] with fear. 3. Let your adorning be, not that which is outward ; that of braiding the hair, and wearing articles of gold, or putting on [better] clothes. 4. But let the hidden person of the heart [be adorned] with the imperishable [ornament] of a meek and quiet spirit, which is, in the sight of God, of great worth. 5. For thus of old the holy women also who hoped in God, adorned themselves; and were submissive to their own husbands; 6, as Sarah obeyed Abraham, calling him lord; and of her, ye have become children, by doing what is good, and not being deterred by any terror.

7. Likewise, ye husbands, dwell with [your wives] according to knowledge; and give honour to the wife as to the weaker vessel; and [dwell] as joint inheritors of the favour-gift of life, for the end that your prayers be not hindered.

8. Finally, be ye all of the same mind, have fellow-feeling, have brotherly love, be compassionate, be friendly. (a) 9. Return not evil for evil, nor reviling for reviling, but, on the contrary, bless ye; for ye know that to [do] this ye were called, that ye might inherit blessing. 10. For,—Let him whose wish it is to love life, and to see good days, restrain his tongue from evil, and his lips from uttering deceit; 11, let him depart from evil, and do good, let him seek peace, and pursue it. 12. Because the eyes of the Lord [are] upon the righteous, and his ears [listen] to their request; but the face of the Lord is against those who do evil. (b) 13. And who is he who will harm you, if ye be imitators of (c) that which is good? 14. But even if ye should suffer because of righteousness, blessed [are ye]. And be not terrified by their [attempt] to terrify; nor be disturbed. 15. But holily honour in your hearts the Lord God. (d) And be ye always prepared, [in reply] to every one who asks you for an account of the hope which is in you, to give your defence with meekness and fear: 16, keeping a good conscience, so that in whatever

---

(a) Ver. 8. Some Greek copies have "humble," instead of "friendly."

(b) Ver. 12. Ps. xxxiv. 12–16.

(c) Ver. 13. Some Greek copies have "zealous for," instead of "imitators of."

(d) Ver. 15. Some Greek copies have "the Anointed," instead of "God."

The Peshito-Syriac Text.

I PETER III. 15—22. IV. 1—5.

trust, to give your defence, with lowliness and fear: 16, keeping meanwhile a good conscience, so that those who speak against you as against bad men, may be ashamed, as those who have misrepresented the good courses which ye follow, by [the will of] the Anointed. 17. For it is gain to you that ye should suffer evil things while doing good deeds,—if indeed such be the will of God, instead of when doing evil deeds. 18. Because that also the Anointed died for once on behalf of our sins, the righteous one on behalf of sinners. that he might bring you near to God. He died indeed in body, yet lived in spirit. 19. And he made proclamation to those souls which were kept in hold in the abodes of the departed; 20, those which of old were disobedient in the days of Noah, when the forbearance of God commanded the making of an ark, for hope of their repentance; into which only eight persons entered, and were kept alive by the waters. 21. In likeness to which example, ye also have life[-bliss] through immersion; (not when ye wash the body from filth, but when ye make profession in [the name of] God with a pure conscience), and through the rising [to life] of Jesus the Anointed; 22, who has been exalted to heaven, and is at the right hand of God; and angels, authorities, and powers are made subject to him.

IV. 1. If therefore the Anointed suffered [death] in the flesh on your behalf, arm yourselves to [effect] the same purpose; for everyone who dies as to his body, has ceased from all sins; 2, so that thenceforth, so long as he is in the body, he lives, not [to do] the [natural] desires of the sons of men, but to [do] the will of God. 3. For the time which has passed away, is sufficient for you to have done in it the will of the profane, by unchaste licentiousness, and by drunkenness, and by gratified lust, and by song-singing, and by the worship of devils. 4. And lo! they now are astonished, and speak evil of you, because you do not gratify lust together with them, as in that former [course of] unchaste licentiousness; 5, they who will have to give account to God, who is in the future to judge the dead and the living.

The Greek Text.

I PETER III. 16—22. IV. 1—5.

[it be] that they speak against you as evildoers, those who talk spitefully of your good conduct in [the service of] the Anointed, may be ashamed. 17. For it is better that ye should suffer while doing good, if this be the will of God, than while doing evil. 18. Because the Anointed also suffered for once [death] for sins, he the righteous on behalf of the unrighteous, that he might bring us to God; put to death indeed in flesh, but made to live in [his] spirit; 19, in which he also went and made proclamation to the spirits in prison; 20, which formerly were disobedient, when the forbearance of God was waiting in the days of Noah, while the ark was being prepared; [by entering] into which few, that is eight, persons were saved by means of water; 21, corresponding to which [event], immersion also now saves us, (not the putting away of the filth of the flesh, but the act of a good conscience making request to God), through the resurrection of Jesus the Anointed; 22, who has gone into heaven, and is at the right hand of God; angels, and authorities, and powers, having been made subject to him.

IV. 1. Therefore, since the Anointed has suffered in flesh on our behalf, do ye also arm yourselves [to effect] the same purpose; because he who has suffered [death] in respect of the flesh, has ceased from sin; 2, with view to live what remains of his [time] in flesh, no longer in [doing the natural] desires of men, but in [doing] the will of God. 3. For the time of life (a) which has passed, is sufficient for us (a) to have done the will of the Gentiles, by going on in unchaste actions, in [gratified] natural desires, in drunkenness, in festivities of dance and song, in drinking-bouts, and in lawless idolatries; 4, as to which [course], they think it strange that you do not run with them in the same career of unchaste licentiousness, and speak evil of you; 5, they, who will have to give account to him who is in readiness to judge the living, and the dead.

(a) Ver. 3. Some Greek copies have not "of life." Some have not "for us." These last copies agree with verse 4, which has "you," not "we." In both cases these copies agree with the Syriac.

6. For because of this [judgment], announcement was made also to the dead, that they might be judged as men [will be who are] in the flesh, and might live unto God in spirit.

7. Moreover, the end of all has come near; for this reason be sober-minded, and give yourselves watchfully to prayer.

8. And before everything, let there be ardent love among you one toward another; for love covers [by forgiveness] a multitude of sins.

9. And be ye kind to strangers, without murmuring.

10. And let everyone of you serve his neighbours with the gift which he has received from God, as good stewards of the different favour-gifts of God. 11. Let everyone who shall speak, speak as the word of God [does]; and let everyone who serves, [do so] as from the power which God gives him; that in all things which ye do, God may be glorified by means of Jesus the Anointed; whose are glory and honour for ever and ever. Amen.

12. My beloved, be not astonished by the trials which come to you, as if something foreign [from what ought to be], were happening to you; because they come to test you. 13. But rejoice that ye share the sufferings of the Anointed, that so also when his glory shall be revealed, ye may rejoice and be glad exceedingly. 14. And if ye are reproached on account of the name of the Anointed, blessed are ye; because the glorious Spirit of God rests on you. 15. Only let no one of you suffer as a murderer, or as a thief, or as a doer of evil deeds. 16. But if one suffers as a Christian, let him not be ashamed; but let him glorify God on account of [bearing] this very name. 17. Because it is a time in which judgment will begin from the house of God; but if it begins from us, what is to be the end of those who

6. For with view to this [judgment] a good message was sent to the dead also, that they might be judged according to men [who are] in the flesh, but live according to God in spirit.

7. But the end of all things has come near ; (a) be ye, therefore, sober-minded, and watchful as to prayers.

8. And before all things have fervent love one towards another, for love will cover [by forgiveness] a multitude of sins.

9. Receive each other kindly as visitors, without murmurings.

10. According to the favour-gift which each has received, use it for serving one another, as good stewards of the various favour-gifts of God. 11. If anyone speaks, [let him speak] as the words of God [speak]; if any one serves, [let him do so] as by the strength which God supplies; that in all things God may be glorified by means of Jesus the Anointed; whose is the glory, and whose the dominion, for ever and ever. Amen.

12. Beloved, do not look on the putting of you into the fire to test you, which is happening among you, as strange; as if a strange thing were happening to you; 13. but in that ye share the sufferings of the Anointed, rejoice; that also, when his glory shall be revealed, ye may rejoice with exceedingly great joy. 14. If ye are reproached on account of the name of the Anointed, blessed [are ye]; because the Spirit of glory and of God rests upon you. By them he is blasphemed; but by you he is glorified. (b) 15. For let not anyone of you suffer as a murderer, or a thief, or an evil-doer, or an overseer of another's [charge]. (b) 16. But if [one suffers] as a Christian, let him not be ashamed ; but let him glorify God on this account. 17. For the time [is one in which] inflicted judgment is to begin at the house of God; and if [suffered]

(a) Ver. 7. Compare Matt. xxiv. 14. "Then shall the end come;" and verse 16, "Then let those who are in Judea flee to the mountains." The end referred to by Peter may be that end of the Hebrew dispensation and worship.

(b. b.) Neither the words, "By them he is blasphemed, but by you he is glorified," verse 14: nor the words, "as an overseer of another's [charge];" verse 15: are in any of my copies of the Peshito Syriac text; namely Walton's, 1653–7; Gutbir's, 1663; the Maronito, 1703; Schaaf's, 1717, and his readings of all previous editions; Lee's, 1816; and the Nestorian of Ooroomiah, 1852. Most of the Greek copies have those words, but this testimony of the Peshito-Syriac is entirely against them.

The Peshito-Syriac Text.

I PETER IV. 17—19. V. 1—12.

obey not the message of God ? 18. And if the righteous man enters life [-bliss] with difficulty, where will the ungodly person and the sinner be found ? 19. For this reason, let those who suffer by the will of God, intrust, by good deeds, their souls to him as to [their] trustworthy Creator.

V. 1. I also beseech the elders who are among you,—I, an elder, your associate, and one who bears witness to the sufferings of the Anointed, and who is to share his glory, which is in the future to be revealed ;—2. Tend as shepherds the flock of God which is committed to you, and take care of it spiritually, not by being urged, but willingly ; not for polluted gains, but with your whole heart ; 3, not as lords of the flock, but as those who are to set them a good example ; 4, that when the Chief Shepherd shall be revealed, ye may receive from him a crown of glory which fades not away.

5. And ye younger, submit yourselves to your elders ; and be tightly wrapped round with humility of mind, one towards another ; because God is opposed to those who exalt themselves, and gives favour-gifts to the humble. 6. Therefore humble yourselves [while] under the mighty hand of God, that it may exalt you at the fit time. 7. And cast all your anxious care on God, for he himself cares for you. 8. Be watchful, and mindful ; because your enemy, Satan, like a lion, roars, and walks about, and seeks for someone to devour. 9. Therefore resist him, and be firm in trust ; and know that these same sufferings are happening also to your brothers who are in the world.

10. Now to the God of favour-gifts, who has called us to his eternal glory by means of Jesus the Anointed. [and] who has granted us that, by bearing patiently these little afflictions, we should be strengthened, and made firm, and be made to stand in him for ever,—11, to him be glory, and dominion, and honour, for ever and ever. Amen.

12. These, as I think them, few things, I have written to you by means of

The Greek Text.

I PETER IV. 17—19. V. 1—12.

first by us, what will be the end of those who obey not the good message of God ? 18. And if the righteous man is saved with difficulty, where will the ungodly one and the sinner appear ? 19. So that let even those who suffer, according to the will of God, intrust, by well-doing, their souls to [him] as to [their] trustworthy Creator.

V. 1. The elders who are among you, I beseech,—I, who am a fellow-elder, and a witness-bearer to the sufferings of the Anointed, and who am to share the glory which in the future is to be revealed ;—2. Tend as shepherds the flock of God [which is] among you, taking the oversight, not constrained by necessity, but willingly ; nor for vile gain, but with readiness of mind ; 3, nor as being lords of [God's] possessions, but being examples to the flock ; 4, and when the Chief Shepherd shall be made manifest, ye will receive the crown of glory which fades not away.

5. Likewise, ye younger, submit yourselves to the elders ; and all of you submit yourselves one to another ; (a) and wrap yourselves round with humility ; for God opposes the proud, but gives favour-gifts to the humble. 6. Humble yourselves, therefore, under the mighty hand of God, that he may exalt you at the fit time ; 7, and cast all your anxious care on him, for he cares for you. 8. Be cautious, be watchful ; for your adversary, the false-accuser, as a roaring lion, walks about, seeking someone to devour ; 9, whom resist, firm in trust, knowing that the same sufferings are taking place among those of your brotherhood who are in the world.

10. And to the God of all gracious favour, who has called us to his eternal glory by Jesus the Anointed, [and] who himself [is] to perfect you, to fix [you] firmly, to strengthen you, and to give [you] a sure foundation, by means of your having suffered a little,—11, to him be glory and dominion for ever and ever. Amen.

12. I have written to you in few [words], as I think, by means of Salvanus, the

---

(a) Ver. 5. In this verse some Greek copies have no repetition of " submit yourselves ; and that part of the verse reads nearly as the Syriac does, thus,—" and all of you, wrap yourselves round with humility one towards another."

The Peshito-Syriac Text.

I PETER V. 12—14.

Silvanus, a trustworthy brother; and I persuade [you to believe], and I bear witness, that this is God's true gift of favour,—this in which ye stand.

13. The chosen assembly which is in Babylon, and Mark, my son, wish you peace. 14. Give wish of peace one to another, with a holy kiss. Peace be with all of you who are in the Anointed. Amen.

The Greek Text.

I PETER V. 12—14.

trustworthy brother, exhorting [you], and bearing witness that this is the true gracious favour of God in which ye stand.

13. The [assembly] in Babylon, chosen together with [you], salutes you; also Mark, my son. 14. Salute ye one another with a kiss of love. Peace to you all who are in Jesus the Anointed. Amen.

THE FIRST LETTER OF JOHN,

ONE OF THE TWELVE CHIEF MESSENGERS.

The Peshito-Syriac Text.

NEXT: THE LETTER OF JOHN, THE CHIEF MESSENGER.

I JOHN I. 1–10. II. 1–2.

I. 1. We declare to you him who was from the beginning; him whom we heard, and saw with our eyes; [him whom] we saw, and touched with our hands; him who is the Word of Life. 2. And the Life was revealed; and we saw, and do bear witness, and proclaim to you, the Life which is for ever; that [Life] which was with the Father, and was revealed to us. 3. And that which we saw and heard, we make known to you also, that ye may be in association with us; and our own association is with the Father, and with his Son, Jesus the Anointed. 4. And these things we write to you, that our joy which is in you may be made full.

5. And this is the message which we heard from him, and declare to you,— that God is light, and that in him is no darkness at all; 6, and that if we say that we are associated with him, and yet walk in darkness, we are liars, and go not in the path of truth; 7, but that if we walk in the light, as he is in the light, [he and] we are associated one with another, and that the blood of Jesus his Son purifies us from all our sins. 8. And that if we say that we have no sin, we deceive ourselves, and the truth is not in us; 9, but that if we confess our sins, he is trustworthy and righteous in that he will forgive us our sins, and will purify us from all our wickedness. 10. And that if we say that we have not sinned, we make him a liar, and his word is not with us.

II. 1. My sons, I write these things to you, that ye may not sin; and yet, if any one sins, we have One who pleads with the Father,—Jesus, the Anointed, the Righteous One. 2. For he himself is the atonement for our sins, and not on

The Greek Text.

THE GENERAL FIRST LETTER OF JOHN.

I JOHN I. 1–10. II. 1–2.

I. 1. That which was from the beginning, that which we have heard, that which we have seen with our eyes; that which we beheld, and our hands touched, as the Word of Life, [we declare to you]; 2, and the Life was made manifest; and we have seen, and do bear witness, and declare to you the Eternal Life which was with the Father, and was manifested to us; 3, that which we have seen, and have heard, we declare to you, that ye also may have association with us; and our association is with the Father, and with his Son Jesus the Anointed. 4. And these things we write to you that your (a) joy may be made full.

5. And this is the message which we have heard from him, and declare to you, —that God is light, and that in him there is no darkness at all; 6, that if we say that we are associated with him, and yet walk in darkness, we lie, and do not act according to truth; 7, but that if we walk in the light as he is in the light, [he and] we are associated one with another, and that the blood of Jesus, the Anointed, (a) his Son, purifies us from all sin; 8, that if we say that we have no sin, we deceive ourselves, and the truth is not in us; 9, that if we confess our sins, he is trustworthy and righteous, so that he will forgive us [our] sins, and will purify us from all unrighteousness: 10, that if we say that we have not sinned, we make him a liar, and his word is not in us.

II. 1. My little children, I am writing these things to you, that ye may not sin; and yet if anyone shall sin, we have One who pleads with the Father, Jesus, the Anointed, the Righteous. 2. And he himself is the atonement for our

---

(a. a.) In verses 4 and 7, some Greek copies have—"our" for "your;" and have not "the Anointed."

The Peshito-Syriac Text.

I JOHN II. 2–14.

behalf of ours only, but also on behalf of [those of] the whole world. (a)

3. And by this we are made conscious that we know him ;—if we keep his commands. 4. For he who says,—I know him,—and yet does not keep his commands, is a liar, and the truth is not in him. 5. But in him who keeps his word, the love of God is in very truth made complete; for by this we know that we are in him. 6. He who says,—I am in him,—ought himself to walk in the same ways in which he [Jesus] walked.

7. My beloved, I am not writing to you a new command, but an old command, which ye received from the beginning; and the old command is that word which ye heard.

8. Again, I am writing to you a new command; which [fact] is true in respect of him, and in respect of you; because darkness has passed away, and the True Light has begun to be seen. 9. He therefore, who says that he is in the Light, and yet hates his brother, is in the darkness until now. 10. He who loves his brother continues in the Light, and there is no stone of stumbling in respect of him. 11. But he who hates his brother is in darkness, and walks in darkness, and knows not whither he goes, because darkness has blinded his eyes.

12. I write to you, sons, because your sins have been forgiven you, because of his name. 13. I write to you, fathers, because ye have known him who was from the beginning. I write to you, young men, because ye have conquered the evil one. I have written to you, boys, because ye have known the Father; 14, I have written to you, fathers, because ye have known him who was from

The Greek Text.

I JOHN II. 2–14.

sins, and not for ours only, but also for [those of] the whole world. (a)

3. And by this we know that we know him,—if we keep his commands. 4. He who says,—I know him,—and does not keep his commands, is a liar, and the truth is not in him; 5, but whoever shall keep his word, in him the love of God is truly completed. By this we know that we are in him. 6. He who says that he continues in him, ought himself also to walk so as he [Jesus] walked.

7. [My] brothers, (b) I am not writing to you a new command, but an old command, which ye had from the beginning; the old command is the word which ye heard from the beginning. (c)

8. Again; I am writing to you a new command; which [fact] is true in respect of him, and in respect of you; because the darkness passes away, and the True Light now appears. 9. He who says that he is in the Light, and yet hates his brother, is in the darkness until now. 10. He who loves his brother continues in the Light, and in respect of him there is no stumbling-block. 11. But he who hates his brother, is in the darkness, and walks in darkness, and knows not whither he goes, because the darkness has blinded his eyes.

12. I write to you, little children, because your sins have been forgiven you because of his name. 13. I write to you, fathers, because ye have known him [who was] from the beginning. I write to you, young men, because ye have conquered the evil one. I write (c) to you, little children, because ye have known the Father. 14. I have written to you, fathers, be-

---

(a) II. 2. This letter, like the letters of Peter and James, seems to have been written to Hebrew Christians. "Our sins;" seem to be those of Hebrews, who "walked in light," and who were "purified from all sins;" i. 7. "[Those of] the whole world," must, of necessity, mean the sins of those in the whole world, who "walk in the light, and are purified from sins," as in the case of Hebrews. Atonement is the "purging away of sins;" Heb. i. 3. Atonement extends to none but to those who, by its efficacy, are brought to "trust in the blood of Jesus;" Rom. iii. 25. Whenever sins were atoned for, under the law, they were forgiven. Lev. v. 10, 13, 16, 18. etc. If sins remain unpardoned, at last, it is proof they were not atoned for, were not "purged away." James, Peter, and John laboured chiefly among the Hebrews. Gal. ii. 9.

(b) II. 7. Some Greek copies have, like the Syriac, "beloved," instead of "brothers."

(c. c) Verses 7, 13. Some Greek copies have not, "from the beginning;" ver. 7; and some have, "I have written," instead of "I write," ver. 13; and are like the Syriac.

the beginning. I have written to you, young men, because ye are strong, and the word of God dwells in you, and ye have conquered the evil one. 15. Love not the world, nor anything which is in it: for in him who loves the world the love of the Father is not. 16. For everything which there is in the world, consists of what the body desires, and what the eyes desire, and what the world glories in; things which are not of the Father, but are of the world. 17. And the world is passing away; both it and what it desires; but he who does the will of God continues for ever.

18. My sons, it is the last period; and as ye have heard,—A false pretender to be the Anointed is to come;—and now there are many false pretenders to be the Anointed, and from this we know that it is the last period. 19. They went out from us, but they were not of us; for if they had been of us, they would have continued with us. But they went out from us, that it might be known that they were not of us.

20. And ye have an anointing from the Holy One, and ye discern what every man is. 21. I have not written to you because ye know not the truth, but because ye know it, and that no lie is a part of the truth. 22. Who is a liar, unless he be one, who denies that Jesus is the Anointed? And this is a false pretender to be the Anointed. He who denies the Father, denies also the Son. 23. And he who denies the Son, does not trust in the Father also. He who makes profession of the Son, makes profession of the Father also. 24. And what ye have heard from the beginning, let that continue with you. For if that which ye have heard from the beginning shall continue with you, ye yourselves also will continue in the Father and in the Son. 25. And this is the promise which he has promised us,—life [-bliss] which is for ever.

26. These things I have written to you because of those who try to lead you astray. 27. And yet also, if the anointing which ye have received from him shall continue with you, ye will not need that anyone should teach you; but, as the anointing which is from God teaches you about everything, and is true, and

cause ye have known him [who was] from the beginning. I have written to you, young men, because ye are strong, and the word of God continues in you, and ye have conquered the evil one. 15. Love not the world, nor the things [which are] in the world. If any one loves the world, the love of the Father is not in him. 16. For everything which there is in the world, that which the flesh desires, and that which the eyes desire, and the vain glory of life,—is not of the Father, but is of the world. 17. And the world is passing away; and what it desires; but he who does the will of God continues for ever.

18. Little children, it is the last period; and even as ye have heard,—The foe of the Anointed is to come;—and now many foes of the Anointed exist; from which we know that it is the last period. 19. They went out from us, but they were not of us; for if they had been of us, they would have continued with us; but [they went out] that it might be made manifest that they all are no part of us.

20. And ye have an anointing from the Holy One, and ye know all things. 21. I have not written to you because ye know not the truth, but because ye know it, and that no lie is part of the truth. 22. Who is the liar, unless it be he who denies that Jesus is the Anointed? This is the foe of the Anointed,—he who denies the Father and the Son. 23. No one who denies the Son, has the Father; he who makes profession of the Son, has the Father also. 24. Ye, therefore, let that which ye have heard from the beginning, continue in you. If that which ye have heard from the beginning shall continue in you, ye yourselves also will continue in the Son, and in the Father. 25. And this is the promise which he has promised us,—the life which is eternal.

26. These things I have written to you respecting those who try to lead you astray. 27. And as to yourselves, the anointing which ye have received from him, continues in you, and ye need not that anyone should teach you; but as the same anointing teaches you respecting all things, and is true, and is no lie,

The Peshito-Syriac Text.

has no lie in it, continue ye in that which is according to what it has taught you.

28. And now, my sons, continue ye in him, that when he shall be revealed, we may not be ashamed on account of him, but may have confidence when he comes. 29. If ye know that he is righteous, know also that everyone who works righteousness is from him.

III. 1. And see ye how great is the love of the Father toward us, who has called us sons, and has also made us sons. For this reason the world knows not us, because it also knew not him. 2. My beloved, we are now sons of God, and it has not been revealed, up to the present time, what in the future we shall be; but we know that when he shall be revealed, we are to be in his likeness, and are to see him as he is. 3. And everyone who has this hope with respect to him, makes himself pure as he is pure. 4. But he who commits sin, works wickedness; for all sin is wickedness. 5. And ye know that he was revealed to take away our sins; and that in him there is no sin. 6. And everyone who continues in him, does not sin; and everyone who sins, has not seen him, nor known him. 7. My sons, let no one lead you astray. He who works righteousness, is righteous, like as also the Anointed himself is righteous. 8. And he who commits sin, is of Satan; because Satan himself has been a sinner from the beginning; and the Son of God appeared for this reason,—that he might undo the works of Satan. 9. Everyone who has been begotten by God, does not commit sin; because his seed is in him, and he is unable to sin, because he has been begotten by God. 10. By this the sons of God are distinguished from the sons of Satan;—everyone who works not righteousness, and who loves not his brother, is not of God. 11. Because this is the command which ye have heard from the beginning,—that ye love one another; 12, [that ye be] not like Cain, who was of the evil one, and killed his brother. And for what reason did he kill him, but because his works were evil, and those of his brother righteous?

13. And be not astonished, my brothers, if the world is hating you. 14. We know that we have passed from death to life

The Greek Text.

continue ye in that which is according to what it has taught you.

28. And now, [my] little children, continue ye in him, that when he shall be made manifest, we may have confidence, and may not be ashamed on account of him, when he comes. 29. If ye know that he is righteous, know ye that everyone who works righteousness has been begotten by him.

III. 1. See ye what kind of love [-gift] the Father has given us, that we should be called children of God. For this reason the world knows not us, because it know not him. 2. Beloved, we are now children of God, and what we shall be has not yet been made manifest; but we know that if he shall be made manifest, we shall be like him, because we shall see him as he is. 3. And everyone who has this hope, [founded] on him, makes himself pure, even as he is pure. 4. Everyone who commits sin, breaks the law also; and sin is the breach of the law. 5. And ye know that he was made manifest, that he might take away our sins, and that in him there is no sin. 6. Everyone who continues in him does not sin; everyone who sins, has not seen him, nor known him. 7. Little children, let no one lead you astray; he who does righteousness, is righteous, even as he [Jesus] is righteous. 8. He who commits sin is of the False-accuser; because the False-accuser has been sinning from the beginning. For this end the Son of God was made manifest,—that he might undo the works of the False-accuser. 9. Everyone who has been begotten by God, does not commit sin, because his seed continues in him; and he is unable to sin, because he has been begotten by God. 10. By this the children of God are manifest, and the children of the False-accuser;—everyone who works not righteousness, is not of God; nor is he who loves not his brother. 11. Because this is the message which ye have heard from the beginning,—that we should love one another; 12, [that we should] not be like Cain, who was of the evil one, and slew his brother. And why did he slay him? Because his own works were evil, and those of his brother were righteous.

13. Be not astonished, my brothers, if the world is hating you. 14. We know that we have passed out of death into

The Peshito-Syriac Text.
I JOHN III. 14—24. IV. 1—4.

by this,—that we love the brothers. He who loves not his brother, continues in death. 15. For everyone who hates his brother, is a murderer ; and ye know that life which is for ever, cannot be continuing in anyone who is a murderer.

16. By this we know the love which he [Jesus] has toward us,—that he gave his life on our behalf ; and it is also right for us to give our lives on behalf of our brothers. 17. And he who has worldly property, and sees that his brother is in need, and shuts up his compassion from him ; how can the love of God be in him ? 18. My sons, let us not love one another in words and in tongue, but in works and in truth. 19. And by this we get knowledge that we are of the truth, and persuade our heart [of it], before he comes. 20. And if it be [true] that our heart is condemning us, how much more [must] God [be doing so], who is greater than our heart, and knows everything. 21. My beloved, if our heart does not condemn us, we have confidence before God ; 22, and everything which we ask, we receive from him, because we keep his commands, and are doing things which are good in his sight. 23. And this is his command,—that we trust in the name of his Son, Jesus the Anointed, and love one another as he commanded us. 24. And he who keeps his commands is kept in him ; and he [Jesus] dwells in him. And by this we understand that he dwells in us, by his Spirit whom he has given us.

IV. 1. My beloved, trust not in all [who say they speak by] the Spirit, but decide by testing them whether they are from God; because many false prophets have gone out into the world. 2. By this the Spirit of God is known; everyone who says [that he speaks by] the Spirit, and professes that Jesus the Anointed has come in the flesh, is from God. 3. And everyone who[says that he speaks by] the Spirit, but does not profess that Jesus has come in the flesh, is not from God. But he is from that false anointed one, of whom ye have heard that he was to come, and who now already is in the world. 4. But ye are of God, [my] sons, and have conquered them ; because, greater is he who

The Greek Text.
I JOHN III. 14—24. IV. 1—4.

life, because we love the brothers ; he who loves not [his] brother, continues in death. 15. Everyone who hates his brother is a murderer, and ye know that no murderer has eternal life continuing in him.

16. By this we know the love of God, (a) —that he [Jesus] laid down his life on our behalf ; and we ought to lay down [our] lives on behalf of [our] brothers. 17. But he who has worldly property, and sees that his brother has need, and shuts up his compassion from him ; how can the love of God be continuing in him ? 18. My little children, let us not love in word, nor in tongue ; but in work, and in truth. 19. And by this we know that we are of the truth, and shall persuade our hearts [of it] before him. 20. Because, if our heart condemns us, [God does so]; because God is greater than our heart, and knows all things. 21. Beloved, if our heart does not condemn us, we have confidence toward God. 22. And whatever we ask, we receive from him, because we keep his commands, and do those things which are pleasing in his sight. 23. And this is his command,— that we trust in the name of his Son, Jesus the Anointed, and love one another, as he gave us command [to do]. 24. And he who keeps his commands, continues in him, and he [Jesus] in him. And by this we know that he continues in us, by the Spirit whom he has given us.

IV. 1. Beloved, trust not in everyone [who says he speaks by] the Spirit, but test those who [say they speak by] the Spirit, as to whether they are from God; because many false prophets have gone out into the world. 2. By this know ye the Spirit of God ;—everyone who [says that he speaks by] the Spirit, and professes that Jesus the Anointed has come in the flesh, is from God. 3. And every-one who [says that he speaks by] the Spirit, but does not profess that Jesus the Anointed has come in the flesh, is not from God. And this is that foe of the Anointed, of whom ye have heard that he was to come, and who now already is in the world. 4. Ye are of

---

(a) Ver. 16. Some Greek copies are without "of God." The meaning then is, "we know [his] love,"—that of Jesus; as in the Syriac.

is in you than he who is in the world. 5. And these are of the world. For this reason they speak what is of the world, and the world hears them. 6. But we are of God; and he who knows God hears us; and he who is not of God does not hear us. By this we understand who it is [who speaks by] the Spirit of truth, and who by the spirit of deception.

7. My beloved, let us love one another; because love is of God, and everyone who loves has been begotten by God, and knows God; 8, because God is love; and everyone who does not love, does not know God. 9. By this has been made known the love which God has for us;—that God has sent his only Son into the world, that we might have life [-bliss] by means of him. 10. The love consisted in this,—it was not in that we loved God, but in that God himself loved us, and sent his Son to be an atonement on behalf of our sins. 11. My beloved, if God has so loved us, we also ought to love one another. 12. No one has ever seen God; but if we love one another, God is continuing in us, and his love is made complete in us. 13. And by this we know that we are continuing in him, and that he is continuing in us,—that he has given us of his Spirit. 14. And we have seen, and we bear witness, that the Father sent his Son [to be] a Saviour for the world. 15. Whoever professes that Jesus is the Son of God, God is continuing in him, and he is continuing in God. 16. And we have trusted in, and have known, the love which God has toward us; for God is love; and everyone who is continuing in love, is continuing in God. 17. And by this his love for us is made complete, so that we shall have confidence in the day of judgment; —[namely] because such as he is, such also are we in this world.

18. There is no fear in love, but perfect love casts out fear; because we fear [when] in danger; so that he who fears is not made complete in love.

19. For this reason let us love God, because he first loved us.

20. But if anyone shall say,—I love God,—and yet hates his brother, he is a liar; for he who loves not his brother who is seen, how is he able to love God who is not seen? 21. And this command we have received from him,

God, little children, and have conquered them; because greater is he who is in you than he who is in the world. 5. They are of the world; for this reason they speak what is of the world, and the world hears them. 6. We are of God; he who knows God hears us; he who is not of God, does not hear us; by this we know him [who speaks by] the Spirit of truth, and him [who speaks by] the spirit of deception.

7. Beloved, let us love one another; for love is of God, and everyone who loves has been begotten by God, and knows God; 8, he who loves not, knows not God, for God is love. 9. By this has been made manifest the love of God in respect of us,—that God has sent his only Son into the world that we might live by means of him. 10. In this is the love,—not in that we loved God, but in that he loved us, and sent his Son [to be] an atonement for our sins. 11. Beloved, if God has so loved us, we also ought to love one another. 12. No one has ever seen God; if we love one another, God is continuing in us, and his love is made complete in us. 13. By this we know that we are continuing in him, and he in us,—because he has given us of his Spirit. 14. And we have seen, and we bear witness, that the Father has sent his Son [to be] the Saviour of the world. 15. Whosoever shall profess that Jesus is the Son of God, God is continuing in him, and he in God. 16. And we know, and have trusted in, the love which God has in respect of us. God is love; and he who is continuing in love, is continuing in God, and God in him. 17. By this his love for us is made complete, with view to our having confidence at the day of judgment,—[namely] because such as he is, [such] are we also in this world.

18. There is no fear in love; but perfect love casts out fear; because fear has [in view] punishment; and he who fears is not made complete in love.

19. Let us love him, because he first loved us.

20. If anyone shall say,—I love God,—and yet shall hate his brother, he is a liar; for he who loves not his brother whom he has seen, how is he able to love God whom he has not seen? 21. And this command we have received from

The Peshito-Syriac Text.

that everyone who loves God, love his brother also.

V. 1. Everyone who is trusting in that Jesus is the Anointed, has been begotten by God; and everyone who loves him who begat, loves also him who has been begotten by him. 2. And by this we know that we love the sons of God, when we are loving God, and are doing his commands. 3. For this is the love of God that we keep his commands; and his commands are not burdensome. 4. Because everyone who has been begotten by God, conquers the world. And this is the victory which has conquered the world, our trust. 5. For who is he who conquers the world, but he who is trusting in that Jesus is the Son of God?

6. This is he who came by means of water and of blood,—Jesus the Anointed; he came not by water only, but by water and by blood; and the Spirit bears witness, because the Spirit is [the Spirit of] truth. 7. Because there are three who bear witness [in heaven,—the Father, the Word, and the Holy Spirit, and these three are one. 8. And there are three that bear witness on earth](a), —the Spirit, and the water, and the blood; and these three are [united] in one. 9. If we receive the witness borne by men, how much more [should we receive] the witness borne by God, who is [so] great? and this is the witness which God has borne respecting his Son.

10. Everyone who trusts in the Son of God, has this witnessing within himself.

Everyone who does not trust in God, has made him a liar, by not trusting in the witness borne by God respecting his Son. 11. And this is the witness borne,—that God has given to us life [-bliss] which is for ever, and that this life [-bliss] is in his Son. 12. Everyone who has the Son, has also life [-bliss]; and everyone who has not the Son of God, has not life [-bliss].

13. I have written these things to you that ye may know that ye have life [-bliss] which is for ever,—ye who have trusted in the name of the Son of God.

The Greek Text.

him, that he who loves God, love his brother also.

V. I. Everyone who is trusting in that Jesus is the Anointed, has been begotten by God; and everyone who loves him who has begotten, loves also him who has been begotten by him. 2. By this we know that we love the children of God, —when we love God, and keep his commands. 3. For this is the love of God, that we keep his commands, and his commands are not burdensome. 4. For everyone who has been begotten by God conquers the world; and this is the victory which has conquered the world, —our trust. 5. Who is he who conquers the world, but he who is trusting in that Jesus is the Son of God?

6. This is he who came by means of water and of blood, Jesus the Anointed; not by water only, but by water and by blood. And it is the Spirit that bears witness, because the Spirit is the [Spirit of] truth. 7. Because there are three who bear witness [in heaven; the Father, the Word, and the Holy Spirit: and these three are one. 8. And there are three that bear witness on earth], (a) the Spirit, and the water, and the blood, and the three are [united] in the one [testimony]. 9. If we receive the witness borne by men, the witness borne by God is greater; because this is the witness which God has borne respecting his Son.

10. He who trusts in the Son of God has the witnessing in himself.

He who does not trust in God, has made him a liar; because he has not trusted in the witness borne by God respecting his Son. 11. And this is the witness borne,—that God has given to us eternal life, and that this life is in his Son. 12. He who has the Son, has the life; he who has not the Son of God, has not the life.

13. I have written these things to you who trust in the name of the Son of God, that ye may know that ye have eternal life, and that ye may trust (b) in the name

---

(a) Verses 7 and 8. Many good copies, both Syriac and Greek, do not contain the words from "in heaven" to "on earth." They are not in the editions representing Syriac copies of the Maronites, (1703), of the Nestorians of Coordistan, (1852), or of India, (1816).

(b) Verse 13. Some good Greek copies of this verse are like the Syriac, and read thus,—"These things I have written to you, that ye may know that ye have eternal life, ye who are trusting in the name of the Son of God."

The Peshito-Syriac Text.

I JOHN V. 14—21.

14. And this is the confidence which we have in him,—that as to everything which we ask of him, [which is] in accord with his will, he hears us. 15. And if we are persuaded that he hears us with respect to what we ask of him, we are confident that we have received already [the gift of] those things which we have asked of him.

16. If anyone shall see that his brother is sinning a sin which does not condemn [him] to death, let him ask, and life[-bliss] shall be given for those who are not sinning as unto death. For there is a sin which is that of death; I do not say that anyone should make request respecting this. 17. For all wickedness is sin, and there is sin which is not that of death. 18. And we know that everyone who has been begotten by God, does not sin; for he who has been begotten by God, keeps himself, and the evil one does not come near him.

19. We know that we are of God, and that the whole world is placed in the evil one.

20. And we know that the Son of God has come, and has given us knowledge, that we might know the true [God], that we might be in him,—in the true [God], [and] in his Son, Jesus the Anointed. This is the true God, and life [-bliss] which is for ever.

21. My sons, keep yourselves from the worship of images. (a)

The Greek Text.

I JOHN V. 13—21.

of the Son of God. 14. And this is the confidence which we have in him,—that if we ask anything which is according to his will, he hears us. 15. And if we know that he hears us, respecting whatever we ask, we know that we are to have the very things which we have asked of him.

16. If anyone shall see that his brother is sinning a sin which is not unto death, he shall ask, and [God] will give him life for those who sin [a sin which is] not unto death. There is a sin unto death. I do not say that he should make request respecting it. 17. All unrighteousness is sin; and there is sin which is not unto death. 18. We know that everyone who has been begotten by God does not sin; but he who has been begotten by God keeps himself, and the evil one does not touch him.

19. We know that we are of God, and that the whole world lies in the evil one.

20. And we know that the Son of God has come, and has given us understanding, that we might know the true [God]; and we are in the true [God], [and in] his Son Jesus the Anointed. This is the true God and the life eternal.

21. Little children, keep yourselves from images. Amen. (b)

(a) Syriac, verse 21. This note is at the end of many copies,—"Is finished the first letter of John, the Chief Messenger.

(b) Ver. 21. Some good Greek copies, like the Syriac, have not "Amen."